US Politics &
Climate Change

US Politics & Climate Change

Science Confronts Policy

Glen Sussman
Byron W. Daynes

LYNNE
RIENNER
PUBLISHERS

BOULDER
LONDON

Published in the United States of America in 2013 by
Lynne Rienner Publishers, Inc.
1800 30th Street, Boulder, Colorado 80301
www.rienner.com

and in the United Kingdom by
Lynne Rienner Publishers, Inc.
3 Henrietta Street, Covent Garden, London WC2E 8LU

Library of Congress Cataloging-in-Publication Data
Sussman, Glen.
  US politics and climate change : science confronts policy /
Glen Sussman, Byron W. Daynes.
    pages ; cm
  Includes bibliographical references and index.
  ISBN 978-1-58826-899-0 (hc : alk. paper)
1. Environmental policy—United States. 2. Climatic changes—
Government policy—United States. I. Title.
  GE180.S88 2013
  363.738'745610973—dc23

                                                  2013006140

British Cataloguing in Publication Data
A Cataloguing in Publication record for this book
is available from the British Library.

Printed and bound in the United States of America

        The paper used in this publication meets the requirements
  ∞   of the American National Standard for Permanence of
        Paper for Printed Library Materials Z39.48-1992.

5 4 3 2 1

Contents

List of Tables and Figures   vii
Acknowledgments   ix

1   Policy Deadlock: Grappling with Climate Change   1
2   Science Meets Government Bureaucracy   21
3   Congress and the Legislative Process   51
4   Presidential Leadership from Truman to Obama   77
5   The Role of the Judiciary   109
6   Interest Groups and Public Opinion   131
7   The States Weigh In   163
8   Assessing the US Response to Climate Change   193

Bibliography   211
Index   237
About the Book   245

Tables and Figures

Tables

2.1 Emission Trend of Greenhouse Gases:
Comparing G8 Countries, 1990–2007   23

4.1 Carbon Dioxide Emissions by Top Emitters, 1990–2008   88

6.1 Americans' Views of the Scientific Consensus on Global
Warming, 1998–2010   145

6.2 Americans' Views of the Causes of Global Warming,
2003–2010   146

6.3 Partisanship and the Causes of Global Warming, 2011   147

6.4 Partisan Gap on the Causes of Global Warming, 2011   147

6.5 Partisanship and Actions to Reduce
Greenhouse Gases, 2011   148

6.6 Partisan Gap on Actions to Reduce
Greenhouse Gases, 2011   148

6.7 Comparing Americans' and Canadians' Views
on Climate Change, 2010   150

6.8 Is Climate Change a Serious Threat?
Comparing Citizen Concern in the Top Five
Greenhouse Gas–Emitting Countries, 2007–2008 and 2010   152

7.1 Carbon Dioxide Emissions by State, 1990 and 2008   171

7.2 State Renewable Electricity Generation Rankings, 2010 177

7.3 State Energy Efficiency Rankings, 2012 178

7.4 Transportation Policy and Performance on
Climate Change Goals Among the States, 2010 181

7.5 Green Employment Growth vs.
Overall Employment Growth, 1998–2007 183

8.1 Evaluation of Key Institutional Players' Actions on
Climate Change 200

Figures

2.1 The Keeling Curve:
Mauna Loa Fossil Fuel Trend, 1960–2015 28

3.1 Percentage of Pro-Environment Voting, by Party,
US House of Representatives, 1973–2010 68

3.2 Percentage of Pro-Environment Voting, by Party,
US Senate, 1973–2010 69

Acknowledgments

We have worked together for more than twenty years. For us, this is a true milestone that deserves recognition. We were introduced by our colleague and friend Nicolas P. Lovrich, emeritus professor of political science (Washington State University) at the 1989 American Political Science Association meeting. Two important projects resulted from that meeting. First, we were invited by Nick to join him and several others in a survey project that dealt with the issue of cameras in the courtroom. Second, we were invited by another friend and colleague, Dennis Soden, professor of political science (University of Texas, El Paso), to join him and several others in a book project that focused on "the environmental presidency." Our professional relationship has continued to be productive ever since.

Our ongoing interest in the environmental presidency, together with our interest in taking a behavioral and institutional perspective on US politics and narrowing our environmental focus to climate change, led us to examine the roles played by other institutional political actors involved with US environmental policy in general and climate change in particular. This interest eventually led to the publication of this book.

No undertaking occurs without assistance from others. We first want to acknowledge Lynne Rienner for recognizing the importance of exploring climate change policy in the United States. Second, we offer our deep appreciation to Jessica Gribble, acquisitions editor at Lynne Rienner Publishers, who saw the value of our work in the initial book proposal we showed her at an annual meeting of the American Political

Science Association. It has been a pleasure working with her. We found her to be a caring, friendly, and supportive partner in this endeavor and she always responded to our queries in a prompt and helpful manner. We also extend our appreciation to Karen Williams, project editor at Lynne Rienner Publishers, for her support throughout and to the copyeditor for the thorough editing that helped to improve the book.

We want to acknowledge the assistance provided by our research assistants: Todd Gee, Kristen Brown Meservy, Kyle Patterson, Tyson Prisbrey, and Tara Rountree. We also want to recognize Elizabeth Marie Burt for her compilation of a comprehensive bibliography and index for this book. We extend our sincere appreciation to the reviewers who volunteered their valuable time to read the manuscript and offer helpful advice for improving it. Finally, saving the best for last, we want to recognize our wives, Elizabeth and Kathy, for their support and sacrifice while we toiled on a manuscript about a complex and important issue that has domestic as well as international implications.

—*G. S. and*
B. W. D.

1

Policy Deadlock: Grappling with Climate Change

It is "unequivocal" that the climate is and will continue to change, and that human generation of greenhouse gases is responsible for most related changes since the 1950s. Climate change will affect national security in the broadest sense, potentially affecting everything from economic growth to social stability. More narrowly, global climate change may spur sudden onset (i.e., hurricanes and floods) and slow onset (i.e., droughts and famines) disasters around the world, provoking humanitarian crises that will require military and other government responses.
—*International Panel on Climate Change*[1]

Between 1990 and 2007, the Intergovernmental Panel on Climate Change (IPCC), a body composed of many of the world's leading scientists and established by the United Nations Environment Programme and the World Meteorological Organization, published several reports regarding global climate change. The latest report, published in 2007, made the case noted above regarding human-induced climate change.[2] The possibility that global climate change can have such serious social and political consequences in the United States and in the world at large is reason enough to look at this issue in greater context and detail. This is not to suggest that all policymakers and those interested in global climate change agree and fully subscribe to the IPCC's conclusions. In fact, those who feel most intensely about the seriousness of global climate change express concern that there is a general lack of public interest within the United States regarding the global conse-

1

quences of climate change.[3] We hope that our approach to climate change—which thoroughly appraises institutional decisionmaking, noting both support for and clashes with the scientific community's assessment of climate change—will add to the overall understanding of its significance.

Evolving Interest in Climate Change

Concern about climate change is certainly not a new problem. At the time of the Trojan War, Aristotle commented on climate change when he noted that "the Argive land was marshy and could only support a small population, whereas the land in Mycenae was in good condition (and for this reason Mycenae was the superior)." Later he observed that "now the opposite is the case. . . . The land of Mycenae has become completely dry and barren, while the Argive land that was formerly barren owing to the water has now become fruitful." Then he suggested the importance of this observation: "Now the same process that has taken place in this small district must be supposed to be going on over whole countries and on a large scale."[4]

In the United States, interest in climate change dates back to colonial America, when Cotton Mather observed in 1721 that "our cold is much moderated since the opening and clearing of our woods, and the winds do not blow roughly as in the days of our fathers, when water, cast up into the air, would . . . be turned into ice before it came to the ground."[5] And Benjamin Franklin made some of the more sophisticated observations of climate change beginning in 1766, when he stated: "Tho' we have had a very mild Winter, we have had the coldest and most backward Spring I think that ever I knew. There has not been but one warm Day properly speaking since the Month of February, and it is so cold now, that I am obliged to keep by the Fire: The Fruit I believe will be much affected by it."[6]

Although the physical and natural sciences have informed us that over the centuries Earth's climate has altered between warm periods and ice ages, in the nineteenth century human activities began to have an impact on the planet's climate as a result of the Industrial Revolution. During this period, several "greenhouse effect pioneers"—including French mathematician Joseph Fourier Jean Baptiste in 1827, British scientist John Tyndall in 1861, and Swedish chemist Svante Arrhenius in 1896—determined that the warming of the planet was associated with a buildup of greenhouse gases.[7]

Given these early studies and observations, we might ask at this point whether our focus should be on "global warming" or on "global climate change"? Although these terms are closely related, it is important to make a fundamental distinction between the two. According to the US National Academy of Science, *global warming* is characterized as "an average increase in the temperature of the Earth's surface and in the troposphere, which can contribute to changes in global climate patterns," while *climate change* is described as a "significant change in measures of climate (such as temperature, precipitation, or wind) lasting for an extended period."[8] Our focus here will be on *global climate change,* as it will allow us to assess the consequences of this environmental phenomenon in a broader context. In looking at global climate change, we will be able to assess the seriousness of the buildup of greenhouse gases in the atmosphere, as well as examine responses from policymakers and private and public institutions.

Carbon dioxide (CO_2), methane, nitrous oxide, hydrofluorocarbons, perfluorocarbons, and sulphur hexafluoride are the six main greenhouse gases focused on by the Kyoto Protocol and the Environmental Protection Agency (EPA). In providing a context for understanding the role played by greenhouse gases and climate change, Ronald Brunner and Amanda Lynch explained it as follows: "[Greenhouse] gases absorb and reradiate heat that would otherwise escape into space, warming the earth and making life as we know it possible. But increases in concentrations of greenhouse gases in the atmosphere force temperature increases and other climate changes. These in turn force changes on natural and human systems, mostly adverse changes because these systems evolved under different climate conditions."[9]

Political Approaches to the Study of Global Climate Change

Although the scientific community has written much about climate change, less has been written about the politics of climate change and climate policy. Throughout this book, we rely on the research that both supports and contradicts our own research. The purpose is to provide a framework in which the reader may become more familiar with climate change studies that have contributed a better understanding of the trends and patterns involved in global climate change.

The significant impact of human activities on climate change was most clearly stated in Glen Sussman's article "The Science and Politics

Problem: Policymaking, Climate Change, and Hurricanes," which references some of the primary recent studies.[10] We would add to this list Barry Rabe's books on climate change policy in the United States: *Statehouse and Greenhouse* and *Greenhouse Governance*.[11] In the former, Rabe discussed the important role of the states in addressing climate change, given inaction by the federal government. In the latter, Rabe offered a useful discussion of climate change within a "climate governance" framework. In doing so, he focused on international-, national-, and state-level politics and policy.

But the contrary belief that human activities do not affect the global climate makes resolution of the problem even more difficult. In a recent study, "Global Warming: Environmental Crisis or Scientific Hoax?" we focused attention on the damaging political debate between advocates who seek to take immediate action on global warming and climate change and those who undercut the importance of climate control findings.[12] This intense exchange has slowed any response to climate change.

Another factor that binds together many of the recent studies regarding global environmental policy is the difficulty of resolving concerns about climate change, particularly in the US political system. An example of this is found in Christopher Klyza and David Sousa's *American Environmental Policy, 1990–2006*.[13] Klyza and Sousa point out the difficulties in resolving environmental concerns in a complex governmental system, such as in the United States, where environmental measures are often delayed in legislative gridlock. The authors go on to say that, although resolution is not impossible, governments must seek alternative routes to secure agreement among the parties.

Though research on climate change is increasing, this effort can be fragmented by timing, focus, and perspective. The idea of global transformation in global climate change has also become a common theme in other recent works. One example is *Climate Change Justice,* by Eric Posner and David Weisbach. The authors make the case that, regardless of what the new policy of adjustment might be in climate control, most citizens will think it better than the status quo.[14] The authors themselves tend to favor the stricter protective measures that will be needed to respond to the consequences of climate change.

Differentiation in measures to address global climate change is the theme of *Beyond Smoke and Mirrors: Climate Change and Energy,* wherein Burton Richter argues that if reduction of greenhouse emissions is to remain our goal, there are several ways to achieve this:

managing the gases, reducing and more efficiently using polluting resources, seeking appropriate means for storing the emissions, and replacing fossil fuels with other sources of energy.[15] He supports the use of all of these options, but feels that major limits on emissions will never be achieved without relying also on alternative sources of energy.[16] The purpose of Henry Lee's *Shaping National Responses to Climate Change* was to bring a group of scholars together to begin the process of moving forward with resolutions, strategies, and programs to address climate change.[17] A number of recent books have focused on the Kyoto Protocol—the international environmental agreement to limit greenhouse gas emissions, signed in 1997, which served as an important first step in bringing some 191 nations (as of 2010) together to focus on the concerns of global climate change. The agreement expired in 2012, and other researchers have begun to look beyond Kyoto. Ernesto Zedillo, for example, brought together a group of individuals with varied international perspectives from science, politics, and academia to focus on the post-Kyoto era. In Zedillo's book *Global Warming: Looking Beyond Kyoto,* the contributors argue that we need to continue multilateral efforts to address climate change.[18] Dana Fisher, in her book *National Governance and the Global Climate Change Regime,* examines the responses to Kyoto of three nations: Japan, the Netherlands, and the United States. Fisher examines four independent variables—the state, civil society, the market, and science—in each of the countries. She concludes that the reluctance in the United States to support Kyoto can be blamed partially on the importance of the automobile and failure to control its emissions and partially on the supply of coal in the United States.[19] Henrik Selin and Stacy VanDeveer look at Canada, the United States, and Mexico and their responses to Kyoto in *Changing Climates in North American Politics, Institutions, Policymaking, and Multilevel Governance.*[20] For the United States, the authors find that while the federal government rejected Kyoto, many states responded differently, adopting and adapting many of the Kyoto standards in their climate change programs. Joseph Aldy and Robert Stavins's *Post-Kyoto International Climate Policy* points to the difficulty that the nations that agreed to the Kyoto Protocol will have in establishing another agreement with implementable objectives, goals, and timetables.[21] We have already seen some of these difficulties, as many of the same nations tried without success to come to an agreement in 2007 in Bali, in 2009 in Copenhagen, and in 2010 in Cancun. The 2011 Climate Change Summit was held in Durban, South Africa.

In none of these conferences and meetings were representatives able to secure binding agreements to limit greenhouse gas emissions. However, the Durban summit did result in some positive movement: the three primary polluter nations—the United States, China, and India—agreed with the other nations on the need to cut carbon emissions. The countries also agreed that the Kyoto Protocol would move to a "second commitment period" in 2013, in a transition from the end of the commitment period in 2012. There was an indication that some amendments would be added to the protocol, including one to reexamine the "range of greenhouse gases covered."[22] In 2012, the Climate Change Summit was held in Doha, Qatar, where governments agreed to complete a draft of a universal climate change agreement by 2015 that will cover all countries by 2020.[23] It is also anticipated that there will be a number of small meetings and workshops during 2013. The next scheduled large climate change summit will be in Warsaw, Poland, to be held the latter part of 2013.

One important aspect of the Kyoto Protocol that must be maintained is the form of its "mechanisms," which allow countries to continue to meet their commitments under the protocol. These mechanisms include clean development, joint implementation, and emissions trading.[24] In addition, they assist developing countries and the private sector in participating in emission reductions. The clean development mechanism, explained in Article 12 of the Kyoto Protocol, allows for investment in projects that reduce emissions in developing countries. Joint implementation, explained in Article 6, allows a country to conduct emission reduction projects with other countries. And emissions trading, the subject of Article 17, allows these countries to sell emission allowances to other countries that need this assistance. Thus these three instruments of the Kyoto Protocol were devised explicitly to facilitate the commitments made in the protocol and to provide a visible check on global climate change. These must be continued in the next commitment stage of the protocol.

Another of the major themes involved in the discussion of global climate change is the conflict between rich and poor countries. In their book, *A Climate of Injustice: Global Inequality, North-South Politics, and Climate Policy,* J. Timmons Roberts and Bradley Parks provide a good example of this approach.[25] They point out how one of the major challenges to resolution can be seen in the conflict of interest and suspicions between developed and developing nations regarding climate change. This comes down to the never-ending discord between the "haves" and the "have-nots," and how this has affected relations between them regarding global climate change. Roberts and Parks argue that some of the conflict in the Americas, for instance, can be explained by the historically "callous" relations between the North and South American countries.[26]

It is fair to ask why global climate change is so difficult to control. David Shearman and Joseph Smith suggest that the difficulty is due in part to a lack of confidence in the ability of democracy to respond to global climate change:

> If liberal democracy is to survive it will need to offer leadership, resolve, and sacrifice to address the problem. To date [2007] there is not a shred of evidence that these will be provided nor could they be delivered by those at the right hand of American power. Some liberal democracies that recognize that global warming is a dire problem are trying but nevertheless failing to have an impact on greenhouse emissions. To arrest climate change, greenhouse reductions of 60 to 80 percent are required during the next few decades. . . . The magnitude of the problem seems overwhelming, and indeed it is.[27]

Let us respond in the following way. First, the *transboundary nature* of global climate change makes it particularly challenging for policymakers. The very fact that climate change does not respect political boundaries—it is not limited to one geographic location but rather it has a cross-national effect—means that action taken on global problems in one country may be ineffectual if other countries do not also respond in kind.

During the mid-1990s, Lynton Caldwell and Michael Kraft examined environmental problems at the international level while also giving attention to political actors within the US political setting, and both were sensitive to a number of these difficult problems. In *International Environmental Policy,* Caldwell expressed his concern about how acute global environmental problems have recently become.[28] As he stated, "By early 1990, global climate change could be regarded as the single greatest international environmental policy issue."[29]

Kraft, in his research study *Environmental Policy and Politics,* assessed the dominant focus during three generations of environmental problems.[30] Air and water quality, he indicated, dominated the first generation, in the early 1970s, whereas the second generation, during the late 1970s, was concerned mostly with toxic chemicals and hazardous waste. The third generation of environmental problems, he suggested, are "global in origin and effects, are generally low in visibility and political saliency, and are characterized by significant scientific uncertainty—with experts often disagreeing about the magnitude, timing, and location of long-term impacts."[31] It is in this category that he placed global climate change and loss of biodiversity. Kraft described the third-generation problems as being "global in origin and effects," more "politically controversial," and more "difficult to address than the environmental issues of earlier eras."[32] In short, Kraft argued, it is this category of environmental concerns that have brought the greatest challenges to US policymakers, along with divergent agendas that have pressured government at both the national and state levels.

Global climate change can seem particularly difficult to address in that it *excites confrontation* as do other divisive social issues including abortion, the death penalty, or same-sex marriage. A specific example of confrontation focused on climate change took place in Copenhagen at the site where the Copenhagen Accord was signed. Here police and demonstration organizers estimated that on December 12, 2009, between 60,000 and 100,000 activists turned out, representing "environmental groups, human rights campaigners, climate activists, anti-capitalists and freelance protesters from dozens of countries."[33] Many of the demonstrators were representing groups of people whom they considered to be most vulnerable to global warming. Most of the demonstrations were peaceful, but police arrested between 600 and 700 persons who threw rocks through windows and set off small explosives. Juliet Eilperin noted that there were similar demonstrations in 3,000 other locations worldwide, including Papua New Guinea, Israel, Japan, and Saudi Arabia.[34]

Serious differences of opinion among elites as well as the general public make the problem of global climate change particularly difficult to resolve. Much of the confrontation has come in rhetorical exchanges among politicians, scientists, policymakers, and media spokespersons. Intense feelings on both sides of the issue have been expressed. In the United States, the debate over climate change and global warming falls into three major categories: policy supporters who have formulated their views based on scientific evidence; those who acknowledge that global warming is real but believe that it is due more to natural climate cycles than to human-made causes; and those who denounce the idea of global climate change altogether, arguing that it is nothing but a hoax.

In the first category are those who wish to respond immediately to the problem based on worldwide scientific discovery. One of the strongest claims made by these persons is the World Meteorological Organization's finding that the decade from 2000 until 2009 was "the warmest decade in the modern record, dating back 150 years."[35] In the United States, the National Climatic Data Center as well as the National Aeronautics and Space Administration (NASA) also demonstrated that the year 2009 was the "warmest on record" based on "new surface temperature figures."[36] NASA also found that 2009 was the "second warmest year since 1880, when modern temperature measurement began."[37]

Included in this category are those who assert that human-produced greenhouse gases are contributing to the warming of the planet. This warm-up does not seem to be caused by the sun's energy, according to research published by the Royal Academy.[38] Moreover, Piers Forster of Leeds University, who contributed to the 2009 Intergovernmental Panel on Climate Change, charges that "warming in the last 20 to 40 years can't have been caused by solar activity."[39] Yet in 2009 in the United States, despite the fact that "84 percent of U.S. scientists agree that 'the earth is getting warmer because of human activity such as burning fossil fuels'—only 49 percent of the public agreed."[40]

This is significant. Researchers Brent Steel, Richard Clinton, and Nicholas Lovrich, in their book *Environmental Politics and Policy,* argue that if any progress is to be made in resolving environmental difficulties, policymakers must reach out and persuade the general public and be willing to engage in political debate over policy options.[41] Two books by Ross Gelbspan, *The Heat Is On* and *Boiling Point,* offer a journalist's perspective on the issue of climate change.[42] Gelbspan shows how vested interests, especially the oil and coal industries, use their resources to influence energy policy but pay little attention to climate change and fail to inform the public.

In light of scientific findings, supporters can look to the 191 countries that have signed and ratified the Kyoto Protocol as evidence of world interest in resolving global climate change. With a multilateral treaty such as the Kyoto Protocol, both the signature of a country internationally and the subsequent ratification nationally are necessary. It is through national ratification that a country indicates sincere willingness to be bound by international responsibilities.[43]

Supporters can also look to the 193 countries that approved the Copenhagen Accord in 2009. Moreover, we find politicians and academics relying on this evidence. Former US vice president Al Gore made a convincing argument in support of the seriousness of global climate change by suggesting, in a 2009 interview, that "scientists have long held that the evidence in their considered word is 'unequivocal,' which has been endorsed by every national academy of science in every major country in the entire world."[44]

Academics who support these scientific findings include David Cromwell and Mark Levene, who advocate revolutionary change to mitigate the dangers of global warming;[45] Henry Diaz and Richard Murnane, who assert that climate change will have an extreme impact on society;[46] J. P. Bruce, Yi Hoe-song, and Erik Haites, who in 1996 argued that the social costs of climate change and its effects on the economies of the world have been serious;[47] and Robert Shackleton, who in 2009 in a research report for the US Congress reminded legislators of the worldwide consensus that something must be done about global climate change.[48]

In the second category are those who acknowledge that global warming is a problem but who believe that it is caused by natural climate cycles rather than human activities. They can be found in both academic circles as well as in the media, and are sincere in their belief that human beings have little to no control over climate change. For instance, Don Easterbrook of Western Washington University blames Earth's erratic patterns of warmth and coolness on ocean cycles. He maintains that global cooling from 1945 through 1977 coincided with a Pacific Ocean cycle.[49]

Other critics of human-induced global climate change base their opposition on conflicting scientific explanations. Tim Garrett of the University of Utah, for example, does not believe that global warming is caused by human activities. Garrett thinks that the efforts that have already been made to reduce global warming—such as increased energy efficiency and attempts to limit population growth—"are not meaningful." He believes that the only available option that might be effective would be to "switch to non-carbon-dioxide-emitting power sources." And he adds, "In my model, all you need to know is how fast energy consumption is rising."[50]

Among those scientists who prefer another explanation to human-caused warming is Geoffrey Duffy, a professor from the University of Auckland in New Zealand who indicated that "even doubling or tripling the amount of carbon dioxide will virtually have little impact, as water vapour and water condensed on particles as clouds dominate the worldwide scene and always will."[51] And meteorologist Hajo Smit from Holland indicated that "Gore prompted me to start delving into the science again and I quickly found myself solidly in the skeptic camp. . . . Climate models can at best be useful for explaining climate changes after the fact."[52]

Finally, in the third group are those who completely deny the existence of global climate change. In many ways, individuals in this group are the most extreme, rejecting all scientific findings and relying more on ideology. Persons in this category often seek support for their belief in the writings and broadcasts of such commentators as Rush Limbaugh, who in 1993 stated, in his own colorful language, that "you never hear the environmentalist wacko crowd acknowledge . . . that 96 percent of the so-called 'greenhouse' gases are not created by man, but by nature."[53] Sixteen years later Limbaugh had not changed his mind. On November 23, 2009, in denouncing global warming and the environmental movement, he contended:

> Now, the bottom line is, the whole man-made global warming movement is a fraud. It is a hoax. Its made-up lies. I have known this since the beginning of the movement. I'm the one who said that militant environmentalism is the home of displaced communists after the Berlin Wall came down. Now, scientists cannot rely on common sense. So the anti–global warmers have to go out there and get their own science to counter the science that the pro–global warming crowd is using, and they're making it up.[54]

Sean Hannity, on his *Fox News* show that same year, echoed much the same feeling when he stated: "Global warming is a crock . . . and a huge cover up. [The year 2009] is the ninth coldest year on record that we have chronicled."[55]

Among the prominent members of Congress in this category is US senator James Inhofe (R-OK), who in July 2003, as a member of the Senate Committee on Environment and Public Works, indicated much the same thing in similar language, stating that concern over global warming was the "greatest hoax ever perpetrated on the American people."[56] Inhofe claimed in 2009 that he could name some 700 international scientists who were in opposition to "man-made global warming claims."[57]

Other voices of denial come from such persons as novelist Michael Crichton, who in his novel *State of Fear* accused environmentalists of being radical and asserted that those supporting the notion of human-induced global warming and climate change were nothing but alarmists. As Crichton indicated, "The threat of global warming is essentially nonexistent. Even if it were a real phenomenon, it would probably result in a net benefit to most of the world."[58] This sentiment has appealed to such conservative ideologues and media outlets as Limbaugh,[59] George Will, Joseph Bast, the *National Review,* and the *Washington Times.*[60] In addition, former president George W. Bush met with Crichton in 2005 and, according to a report in the *New York Times,* the two "talked for an hour and were in near-total agreement. . . . The visit was not made public for fear of outraging environmentalists all the more."[61]

Another voice of opposition to human-made global climate change comes from Christopher Horner, who in his book *Red Hot Lies,* published in 2008, argued that the global warming campaign has used intimidation and has lied in making its case.[62] Joining Horner is atmospheric scientist Stanley Goldenberg of the Hurricane Research Division of the National Oceanic and Atmospheric Administration, who stated: "It is a blatant lie put forth in the media that makes it seem there is only a fringe of scientists who don't buy into anthropogenic global warming."[63] And environmental scientist Delgado Domingos, from Portugal, had this to say: "Creating an ideology pegged to carbon dioxide is a dangerous nonsense. . . . The present alarm on climate change is an instrument of social control, a pretext for major businesses and political battle. It became an ideology, which is concerning."[64]

Despite a consensus among members of the scientific community that human activities play a major role in global climate change, the arguments put forward by this small but vocal group of contrarians and deniers might encourage one to conclude that climate change problems at this point seem uncontrollable, and resolution difficult and all but unreachable. Miranda Schreurs thinks that the greatest problem in allowing this denial to continue is the negative effect it has on public opinion.[65] The situation in the United States today is perhaps best captured by Steven Brechin, of Syracuse University, who in 2011 contended:

> Climate change in the United States has become highly politicized among the warring political parties, a growing partisan media on what has become an ideological issue and not simply a material one. Public support for policies that address climate change is declining in many countries, including those whose publics have traditionally supported such policies. There is also mounting evidence that anti-climate-change-policy forces are organizing efforts globally. . . . So instead of growing legions of climate change voters, the opposite may become true. . . . [T]he world may be in for continued if not greater political stalemate.[66]

Understanding Global Climate Change
Through an Assessment of the US Political System

Since climate change is a global problem, how does understanding the US political system and its policymakers and institutions help us understand climate change decisionmaking? After all, as former vice president Al Gore recently put it, the US response will only be one contribution to remedying the problem, since global climate change "requires a global solution."[67] But there are good reasons why we need to understand how that "one contribution" has contributed to the global solution.

Let us offer several reasons why this is important. First, as Kathryn Harrison and Lisa Sundstrom point out in their book *Global Commons, Domestic Decisions,* even though most political scientists have approached climate change from the international relations perspective, it would best enhance our understanding of global climate change if they were to "reverse the lens of previous scholarship" by focusing on "domestic politics and decisions."[68] In short, great insights into the causes of climate change can be had through an examination of the US political system and the approach that the United States has taken toward understanding the concept of global climate change.

Second, the United States is an important world power and a leader in international affairs, so it is possible that US efforts in support of limiting global climate change may be persuasive in encouraging other nations to follow.[69] For instance, two months into his presidency, George W. Bush renounced the Kyoto Protocol, which 191 other countries had accepted. Instead, the United States acted virtually alone, adopting an approach based on voluntary goals and timetables and supportive of industry preferences regarding greenhouse gas emissions.[70] Few other countries subscribed to the US policy of refusing support to Kyoto. By contrast, Barack Obama has offered some support to climate change legislation domestically and has encouraged international allies to support a post-Kyoto global environmental agreement, making US leadership more visible.

A third reason to focus attention on the US political system is consistent with the situation that the United States found itself in until recently. The United States for years was the major emitter of the greenhouse gases that contribute to global warming and climate change. Consequently, the extent to which the United States—still a major producer of greenhouse gases—cooperates with other countries in an effort to reduce the production of greenhouse gases will have a profound impact on the future resolution of this global environmental problem. We agree with Steven Brechin that "domestic politics matter within an international context."[71]

In studying domestic politics in order to better understand the US response to global climate change, our approach must be both analytical and complete. The research questions we ask in our analysis will both guide us toward breaking through the global climate change stalemate in which we find ourselves, and assist us in our assessment of the major arguments that have been articulated about global climate change. We wish to carefully assess, in a systematic way, the role and actions of each major political actor in the United States who has responded and will respond to global climate change. Our hope is that this analysis of domestic politics in the United States will bring some semblance of order to the confusion over climate change policy. We will also pay attention to those constraints that the US federal system places on policymakers who seek to achieve a working consensus in order to reduce greenhouse gas emissions at home and abroad. Our research questions include the following:

1. Why should Americans be concerned about global climate change? What might be the consequences of climate change for Americans?

2. Why has there been difficulty within the United States in achieving cooperation among key players in order to craft a viable, consensual climate change agreement? Why has climate change been politicized?

3. How has the clash between science and politics affected climate change policymaking in the United States?

4. Have policy agendas been helpful in confronting climate change?

5. What are the prospects for a substantive resolution to global climate change within the US political setting?

Given the increasing importance of climate change internationally and within the US political setting, this book aims to attract a wide audience. As Steven Brechin recently stated: "It may be an understatement to say that global climate change is the collective action problem of our era. If not addressed effectively relatively soon, this mounting concern will likely dramatically affect every nation on earth—politically, economically and environmentally."[72]

Given the ever-increasing literature on climate change as examined from the US perspective, it is fair to ask what our research can add. First, our analysis is framed in a historical context as we assess the evolution of climate change policy over time. Second, this book sets forth the argument that the climate change policymaking process in the United States should be viewed within the context of the "science and politics" problem, where science and politics collide and ideology trumps the former. Third, we offer an institutional and behavioral perspective on US politics and climate change; here we address several distinct key players in US politics. Fourth, we assess the dynamics of US politics and policymaking in response to global climate change. The purpose is to provide a systematic examination of the roles governmental and nongovernmental actors have played with regard to shaping environmental policymaking related to climate change, pointing to those actors that have made a difference in terms of policymaking outcomes. Our study finds value in assessing the importance of institutions and environmental policymaking, similar to the approach taken by Oran Young, Leslie King, and Heike Schroeder in their book *Institutions and Environmental Change,* which was established on the "institutional dimensions of environmental change within a broader stream of research of interest to leading social scientists." It was their intent to bring their findings to the attention of "those who are interested in the role of institutions more generally." In discussing "new institutionalism," they argued that "an interest in institutions treated as clusters of rights, rules, and decision-making procedures constitutes the glue that holds those who work in this realm together and gives this movement a distinctive 'personality' that is well known not only to practitioners of the new institutionalism but also to the movement's critics."[73]

In short, we share the argument put forth by Elizabeth DeSombre in her book *Domestic Sources of International Environmental Policy,* where she asserted: "The way the United States pursues internationalization . . . is almost entirely a product of the interaction among domestic groups. Those who hope to influence international policy would be wise to pay attention to what happens within states as well as between them."[74]

This study focuses attention on specific actors and institutions in the United States that have in some way dealt with climate change. For example, in Chapter 2 we direct our attention to the scientific community and the bureaucracy. Science is an important and highly relevant factor in the policymaking process. The role played by the scientific community inside and outside federal government agencies is our focus, as well as how science and politics have interacted in response to efforts to address global climate change. In Chapter 3, we turn our attention to the Congress and the legislative process. We examine the impact of partisanship in the legislative institution and the role of key legislators in responding to global climate change, and we assess how the intellectual debate in the United States plays out legislatively. The presidency is also key to our understanding of climate change, and in Chapter 4 we assess the actions taken by individual presidents that have affected climate change policymaking, and we evaluate presidential leadership (or lack of leadership) in response to climate change. An institution that many do not take into account when thinking about climate change is the judiciary, which we treat in Chapter 5. Here we examine the significant federal court cases that have affected global climate change; for many social issues, the initial framing and agenda-setting takes place in the court, and we assess the extent to which the issue of global climate change follows this pattern. Interest groups and public opinion can determine in many ways the success or failure of climate policies. In Chapter 6 we note the role of interest groups and their impact on global climate change and provide a longitudinal appraisal of public opinion in order to gauge patterns and trends in the public's understanding of the issue. Chapter 7 addresses the role of the states. We assess the actions taken by the fifty states in response to climate change when federal leadership has been both weak and strong, and we also compare the states in their efforts to respond to global climate change. Finally, in Chapter 8 we remind the reader of the effect that our complex governmental system has on global climate change leadership. We note how most of the key players involved in possible decisionmaking often pose barriers to cooperative responses to the global crisis, and only the scientific community seems to have the most consensus of all possible decisionmakers. Yet even the scientific community needs to improve its communication with the people, given their ambivalence. The future remains problematic unless we find effective measures and determined policymakers to respond to the crisis.

Notes

1. Intergovernmental Panel on Climate Change, *Fourth Assessment Report*, 2007, quoted in Center for New American Security, "Climate Change," April 2010, www.cnas.org/naturalsecurity/consequences/climate-change.

2. The *Fifth Assessment Report* of the Intergovernmental Panel on Climate Change, assessing the scientific and socioeconomic aspects of climate change, will not be finalized until 2014.

3. Frank Newport, "Americans' Global Warming Concerns Continue to Drop," *Gallup World,* March 4, 2011, www.gallup.com/poll/126560/Americans -Global-Warming-Concerns-Continue-Drop.aspx.

4. Aristotle, *Meteorology,* translated by E. W. Webster, 1.14, http://classics .mit.edu/Aristotle/meteorology.1.i.html.

5. Ben Gelber, "Ben Franklin on Global Warming," *New York Times,* November 18, 2009, www.nytimes.com/2009/11/18/opinion.

6. Philip Ranlet, "What Does Weird Weather Really Tell Us?" History News Network, September 3, 2007, http://hnn.us/articles/42243.html.

7. Glen Sussman, Byron W. Daynes, and Jonathan West, *American Politics and the Environment* (New York: Longman, 2002), 291.

8. Environmental Protection Agency, "Climate Change: State of Knowledge," 2006, www.epa.gov/climatechange/stateofknowledge.html.

9. Ronald D. Brunner and Amanda H. Lynch, *Adaptive Governance and Climate Change* (Boston: American Meteorological Society, 2010), 7.

10. Glen Sussman, "The Science and Politics Problem: Policymaking, Climate Change, and Hurricanes," in *Hurricanes and Climate Change,* edited by James B. Elsner and Thomas H. Jagger (New York: Springer, 2009).

11. Barry G. Rabe, *Statehouse and Greenhouse: The Emerging Politics of American Climate Policy* (Washington, DC: Brookings Institution, 2004); Barry G. Rabe, *Greenhouse Governance: Addressing Climate Change in America* (Washington, DC: Brookings Institution, 2010).

12. Byron W. Daynes and Glen Sussman, "Global Warming: Environmental Crisis or Scientific Hoax?" in *Moral Controversies in American Politics,* 4th ed., edited by Raymond Tatalovich and Byron W. Daynes (Armonk, NY: Sharpe, 2011).

13. Christopher McGrory Klyza and David Sousa, *American Environmental Policy, 1990–2006: Beyond Gridlock* (Cambridge: Massachusetts Institute of Technology Press, 2008). See also Sussman, Daynes, and West, *American Politics and the Environment.*

14. Eric A. Posner and David Weisbach, *Climate Change Justice* (Princeton: Princeton University Press, 2010), 188.

15. Burton Richter, *Beyond Smoke and Mirrors: Climate Change and Energy in the 21st Century* (New York: Cambridge University Press, 2010), 184.

16. Ibid., 188.

17. Henry Lee, ed., *Shaping National Responses to Climate Change* (Washington, DC: Island, 1995).

18. Ernesto Zedillo, ed., *Global Warming: Looking Beyond Kyoto* (Washington, DC: Brookings Institution, 2008).

19. Dana Fisher, *National Governance and the Global Climate Change Regime* (Lanham: Rowman and Littlefield, 2004).

20. Henrik Selin and Stacy D. VanDeveer, eds., *Changing Climates in North American Politics, Institutions, Policymaking, and Multilevel Governance* (Cambridge: Massachusetts Institute of Technology Press, 2009).

21. Joseph E. Aldy and Robert N. Stavins, eds., *Post-Kyoto International Climate Policy: Summary for Policymakers* (New York: Cambridge University Press, 2009).

22. United Nations Framework Convention on Climate Change, "Looking Beyond 2012: The Durban Outcomes," http://unfccc.int/essential_background /items/6825.php, accessed August 27, 2012.

23. "Doha Climate Conference Opens Gateway to Greater Ambition and Action on Climate Change," December 9, 2012, www.unep.org/newscentre /default.aspx?DocumentID=2700&ArticleID=9353 (accessed April 5, 2013).

24. This discussion of the Kyoto mechanisms comes from United Nations Framework Convention on Climate Change, "The Mechanisms Under the Kyoto Protocol," http://unfccc.int/kyoto_protocol/mechanisms/items/1673.php, accessed September 21, 2012.

25. J. Timmons Roberts and Bradley C. Parks, *A Climate of Injustice: Global Inequality, North-South Politics, and Climate Policy* (Cambridge: Massachusetts Institute of Technology Press, 2007).

26. Ibid., 13.

27. David Shearman and Joseph Wayne Smith, *The Climate Change Challenge and the Failure of Democracy* (Westport: Praeger, 2007), 153–154.

28. Lynton Keith Caldwell, *International Environmental Policy: From the Twentieth Century to the Twenty-First Century,* 3rd ed. (Durham, NC: Duke University Press, 1996), 5–10.

29. Ibid., 212.

30. Michael Kraft, *Environmental Policy and Politics,* 2nd ed. (New York: Longman, 2001), 15.

31. Ibid.

32. Ibid.

33. Tom Zeller Jr., "Thousands March in Copenhagen, Calling for Action," *New York Times,* December 13, 2009, www.nytimes.com/2009/12/13/science /earth/13climate.html.

34. Juliet Eilperin, "Protesters Demand 'Climate Justice,'" *Washington Post,* December 13, 2009, www.washingtonpost.com/wp-dyn/content/article /2009/12/12/AR2009121200641.html.

35. Andrew C. Revkin and James Kanter, "Global Warming Is Not Slowing, New Analysis Says," *New York Times,* December 9, 2009, www.nytimes .com/2009/12/09/science/earth.

36. Tom M. L. Wigley et al., "Temperature Trends in the Lower Atmosphere: Understanding and Reconciling Differences," executive summary, National Climatic Data Center, http://climatescience.gov/Library/sap /sap1-1/finalreport/sap1-1-final-execsum.pdf, accessed March 26, 2010; Michael D. Mastrandrea and Stephen H. Schneider, "Global Warming," in *World Book Online,* 2005, www.worldbookonline.com/wb/Article?id =ar226310.

37. John M. Broder, "Past Decade Warmest on Record, NASA Data Shows," *New York Times,* January 22, 2010, www.nytimes.com/2010/01/22 /science/earth.

38. Richard Black, "'No Sun Link' to Climate Change," *BBC News,* July 10, 2007, http://news.bbc.co.uk/2/hi/6290228.stm.

39. Pew Research Center for the People and the Press, "Public Praises Science; Scientists Fault Public, Media," July 9, 2009, http://peoplepress.org/report/?pageid=1550.

40. Walter G. Moss, "Obama, Copenhagen, and the Global Warming Skeptics," History News Network, November 8, 2009, http://hnn.us/articles/121037.html.

41. Brent Steel, Richard Clinton, and Nicholas Lovrich Jr., *Environmental Politics and Policy* (Boston: McGraw Hill, 2003), 70.

42. Ross Gelbspan, *The Heat Is On* (Reading, MA: Addison-Wesley, 1997); Ross Gelbspan, *Boiling Point* (New York: Basic, 2004).

43. "Participating in Multilateral Treaties," http://untreaty.un.org/ola-internet/Assistance/handbook_eng/chapter3.htm, accessed September 18, 2012.

44. John Dickerson, "What in the Hell Do They Think Is Causing It?" *Slate,* December 8, 2009, www.slate.com.

45. David Cromwell and Mark Levene, eds., *Surviving Climate Change* (Ann Arbor: Pluto, 2007).

46. Henry F. Diaz and Richard J. Murnane, eds., *Climate Extremes and Society* (New York: Cambridge University Press, 2008).

47. J. P. Bruce, Yi Hoe-song, and Erik F. Haites, *Climate Change 1995* (New York: Cambridge University Press, 1996).

48. Robert Shackleton, *Potential Impacts of Climate Change in the United States* (Washington, DC: Congressional Budget Office, May 2009).

49. Paul Hudson, "What Happened to Global Warming?" *BBC News,* October 9, 2009, http://newsvote.bbc.co.uk.

50. Wendy Leonard, "University of Utah Professor Tim Garrett Says Conservation Is Futile," *Deseret News,* November 23, 2009, www.deseretnews.com/article/print/705346695/University–of-Utah-professor-Tim.

51. Marc Morano, "UN Blowback: More Than 650 International Scientists Dissent over Man-Made Global Warming Claims," *Inhofe EPW Press Blog,* December 10, 2008, http://epw.senate.gov.

52. Ibid.

53. Rush Limbaugh, *See, I Told You So* (New York: Pocket, 1993), 179–180.

54. Rush Limbaugh, "From the Climate Hoax to Health Care to 'Hope,' Liberalism Is Lies," *Rush Limbaugh Show,* November 23, 2009, www.rushlimbaugh.com.

55. Sean Hannity, *The Sean Hannity Show,* December 1, 2009, quoted in Union of Concerned Scientists, "Global Warming Deniers Are Full of Hot Air," n.d., www.ucsusa.org/cation/GotScience.

56. Moss, "Obama, Copenhagen, and the Global Warming Skeptics."

57. US Senate Environment and Public Works Committee (Minority), "U.S. Senate Minority Report," 110th Congress, 2nd session, Washington, DC, December 22, 2008, January 27, 2009, and March 16, 2009.

58. Michael Crichton, *State of Fear* (New York: HarperCollins, 2004), 407.

59. Limbaugh, "From the Climate Hoax to Health Care to 'Hope.'"

60. Joseph L. Best, "Michael Crichton Is Right!" Heartland Institute, January 11, 2005, www.heartland.org/policybot/results/16260/Michael_Crichton.

61. Michael Janofsky, "Bush's Chat with Novelist Alarms Environmentalists," *New York Times,* February 19, 2006, www.nytimes.com/2006/02/19/national.

62. Christopher C. Horner, *Red Hot Lies* (Washington, DC: Regnery, 2008).

63. Morano, "UN Blowback."

64. Ibid.

65. Miranda Schreurs, "Climate Change Politics in the United States: Melting of the Ice," *Analyse & Kritik* 32, no. 1 (2010): 177–189.

66. Steven R. Brechin, "Review of *Global Commons, Domestic Decisions: The Comparative Politics of Climate Change,* by Kathryn Harrison and Lisa McIntosh Sundstrom," *Perspectives on Politics* (March 2011): 132.

67. James Hansen, "Power Failure: Politicians Are Fiddling While the Planet Burns—What's a Voter to Do?" *Newsweek,* December 14, 2009.

68. Kathryn Harrison and Lisa McIntosh Sundstrom, eds., *Global Commons, Domestic Decisions: The Comparative Politics of Climate Change* (Cambridge: Massachusetts Institute of Technology Press, 2010), 2.

69. Glen Sussman, "The USA and Global Environmental Policy: Domestic Constraints on Effective Leadership," *International Political Science Review* 25 (October 2004): 349–369.

70. See Byron W. Daynes and Glen Sussman, "The 'Greenless' Response to Global Warming," *Current History* 104 (December 2005): 438–443.

71. Brechin, "Review of *Global Commons, Domestic Decisions,*" 133.

72. Ibid., 132.

73. Oran R. Young, Leslie A. King, and Heike Schroeder, *Institutions and Environmental Change: Principal Findings, Applications, and Research Frontiers* (Cambridge: Massachusetts Institute of Technology Press, 2008), 6–7.

74. Elizabeth R. DeSombre, *Domestic Sources of International Environmental Policy* (Cambridge: Massachusetts Institute of Technology Press, 2000), 17.

2

Science Meets
Government Bureaucracy

In this chapter we examine the role of the scientific community in addressing the problem of global climate change, including the work of scientists in federal agencies in the US government as well as of those in nongovernmental institutions. We begin with a brief discussion of the scientific basis for a warming planet.

As noted in Chapter 1, several "greenhouse pioneers" during the nineteenth century determined that there was a relationship between the buildup of greenhouse gases in Earth's atmosphere and the warming of the planet. Scientific knowledge about this atmospheric phenomenon expanded as new research findings were provided by British engineer G. S. Callendar in 1938, Roger Revelle and Hans Suess of the Scripps Institution of Oceanography in the late 1950s, and Stephen Schneider of the National Center for Atmospheric Research and James Hansen of the Goddard Institute of Space Studies (part of the National Aeronautics and Space Administration [NASA]) in the late 1980s.[1] In 2007, the Intergovernmental Panel on Climate Change (IPCC), in its fourth report on climate change, made the case for human activities being a fundamental cause of a global problem.

Carbon dioxide (CO_2), produced primarily from the burning of fossil fuels (oil, coal, natural gas) has been identified as a major greenhouse gas. And carbon dioxide emissions have in most instances been increasing on a global basis. On the one hand, in 2004, the Energy Information Administration of the US Department of Energy described how the greenhouse process *should* work, in equilibrium:

Many chemical compounds found in the Earth's atmosphere act as "greenhouse gases." These gases allow sunlight to enter the atmosphere freely. When sunlight strikes the earth's surface, some of it is reflected back towards space as infrared radiation (heat). Greenhouse gases absorb this infrared radiation and trap the heat in the atmosphere. Over time, the amount of energy sent from the sun to the Earth's surface should be about the same as the amount of energy radiated back into space, leaving the temperature of the Earth's surface roughly constant.[2]

On the other hand, a few years earlier, in 2001, the US National Research Council had reported: "Greenhouse gases are accumulating in the Earth's atmosphere as a result of human activities, causing surface air temperatures and sub-surface ocean temperatures to rise. Temperatures are, in fact, rising. The changes observed over the last several decades are most likely due to human activities, but we cannot rule out that some significant part of these changes is also a reflection of natural variability."[3]

In 2006 the US Environmental Protection Agency (EPA) reported that "scientists know with virtual certainty" that the buildup of greenhouse gases in the atmosphere, including from the burning of fossil fuels, is largely the result of human activities. Yet as we see in Table 2.1, the effort to reduce greenhouse gases remains problematic. For the Group of Eight (G8) countries, for instance, only half of them (France, Germany, Russia, and the United Kingdom) have moved in a positive direction in reducing greenhouse gases. At the same time, Canada, Italy, Japan, and the United States continue to struggle. Although Russia and Germany, in particular, show significant progress, the same cannot be said for Canada and the United States, two countries that fail to show leadership on this issue.

While Germany and Russia have made progress, it has been for different reasons. To ascertain the reasons underlying the success of both countries one must look to domestic factors, which is a theme that runs throughout this book. As Raymond Vernon has argued, "one must understand the internal policymaking processes of the negotiating states themselves that differ markedly among countries in response to their distinctive histories, values, and institutions."[4] It has been Germany that has played a leadership role in proposing significant reductions of greenhouse gas emissions for itself and for other member states of the European Union. Among the factors that have played an influential part in Germany's progressive actions regarding climate change are political parties, public opinion, and political leadership.[5] The major parties in Germany, along with the smaller Green Party, have worked together in support of policies to address climate change. Moreover, in contrast to the United States, for instance, public opinion in Germany has been much more supportive of the government taking action on climate change. Furthermore, Angela Merkel assumed an important place in climate change policy. During the mid-1990s she served as minister of environment and a decade later, in 2005, she was elected chancellor of Germany. In both instances, she was able to push a green agenda as it related to climate change policymaking. While greenhouse gas emissions have also declined in Russia, it has been for different reasons compared to Germany. In the early 1990s, following the collapse of the former Soviet Union, Russia was dealing with industrial decline when it made the important move to ratify the Kyoto Protocol and put that international environmental agreement into effect. As Laura Henry and Lisa Sundstrom aptly capture the role being played by Russian leaders, ratification of the Kyoto Protocol "was not primarily driven by a sense of urgency about climate change prevention . . . but by its ability to achieve other desirable benefits from international partners and concern for its international image."[6] Moreover, Russia "received such a generous target in the Kyoto Protocol that it does not have to undertake mitigation measures in order to comply."[7]

Table 2.1 Emission Trend of Greenhouse Gases: Comparing G8 Countries, 1990–2007

	Emission Trend (percentage change, 1990–2007)	Direction Regarding Kyoto Target (2007)
Canada	+26.2	Negative
France	−5.3	Positive
Germany	−21.3	Positive
Italy	+7.1	Negative
Japan	+8.2	Negative
Russia	−33.9	Positive
United Kingdom	−17.3	Positive
United States	+16.8	Negative

Source: Adapted from Allianz and World Wildlife Fund, "G8 Climate Scorecards 2009," July 2009, www.worldwildlife.org/climate/Publications/WWFBinaryitem /2911/pdf.

Note: "Negative" indicates that the country is moving away from the Kyoto Protocol target and "positive" indicates moving toward the target.

In short, this has allowed the country to continue to produce greenhouse emissions while remaining below its Kyoto target.

The Science and Politics Problem

While the science informs us that global warming and climate change demand increasingly urgent attention, an additional factor that plays a role in climate change policymaking is the "science and politics" problem. The scientist and the public official function in two entirely different worlds with different cultures and different languages. The problem is, as Dennis Soden put it, "how to overcome the mission of science and the self-interests which drive politics."[8] Or, as Lynton Caldwell described the problem:

> Science alone cannot save the environment. Political choice is required to translate the findings of the environmental sciences into viable policies. Scientific information, even in its limited present state, is far from being fully utilized in contemporary society. Unless political will and ecological rationality can bring about the transformations necessary to achieve a sustainable future of high environmental quality, science can do little more than to slow the pace of environmental decline and to project the consequences for a world in which all things are not possible.[9]

Moreover, as Andrew Dessler and Edward Parson have suggested: "In addition to the challenges that policy debates pose to science, science also poses hard challenges to policy debates, because citizens and politicians are not generally able to make independent judgments of the merits of scientific claims."[10]

In 2000, in an attempt to determine the influence of science in the policy process, Arild Underdal argued that political actors' confidence in the scientific community is based upon two key factors—competence and integrity.[11] One might expect, therefore, that when there is a "consensus" on an issue among members of the scientific community and there is a feasible "cure" for the problem, science will be more likely to be integrated into the policy process. As Underdal put it, "faced with broad consensus among competent experts on the description and diagnosis of a (severe) environmental problem, governments do in fact most often take some kind of collection action. . . . [T]hinking about the role of science in international environmental regimes we probably see science as a supplier of warnings serving as spurs for protection measures."[12] However, as has been seen in the United States, politics has trumped science on the climate change issue. We believe that this is due, in part, to what Underdal identified as the relevance of the issue to decisionmakers, which he considered just as important as confidence in the work of the scientific community.

Several additional factors remain central to any discussion of the connection between science and policy. In the words of Sheila Jasanoff, the purpose of policymakers is to "harness the collective expertise of the scientific community so as to advance the public interest."[13] In short, improving the relationship between those who produce a body of scientific knowledge and those who are responsible for policy-making is imperative. Yet problems remain. For instance, those stakeholders who are concerned about the negative impact of the findings of scientific research on their interests will focus on the complexity of the issue and suggest that more research is needed, and will use any degree of uncertainty on the part of the scientific community to oppose political action on the part of lawmakers.[14] Moreover, the issue of climate change, like the issue of tobacco before it, has become politicized in public discourse and in the halls of government. Rather than engaging in rational debate, those concerned about collective action in response to scientific research about climate change engage in strategies to obfuscate, delay, and oppose. As Chris Mooney put it, "science politicization threatens not just our public health and the environment, but the very integrity of American democracy, which relies heavily on scientific and technical expertise to function."[15] The debate continues as other observers make the case that effective communication and interaction are needed sooner rather than later. As Brent Steel, Richard Clinton, and Nicholas Lovrich have argued:

> Human cloning, global warming, biodiversity protection, and yet unknown issues affecting the biosphere we share with the rest of nature are all going to involve the active interaction of science, scientists and major political institutions. . . . It seems clear that public education, scientific outreach to policy makers, active debate, and political engagement over policy options all need to occupy a high priority on the public agenda for the development of effective environmental policies in our country and elsewhere across the world.[16]

Given this background, the challenge is quite profound as effective policy hangs in the balance. As Glen Sussman pointed out elsewhere:

An increasing number of governmental and non-governmental organizations as well as work conducted by members of the scientific community have provided research findings that point to the increasing likelihood that human activities have had an increasing impact on climate change. . . . From the World Meteorological Organization to the Pew Center on Global Climate Change to the US National Center for Atmospheric Research, studies show that human beings are increasingly responsible for global warming and global warming is having a direct impact on weather patterns.[17]

Two compelling examples of the science and politics problem show the disconnect that is evident between scientists and public officials. First, in 1988, James Hansen, head of NASA's Goddard Institute of Space Studies, argued before a US Senate subcommittee that it was "time to stop waffling so much and say that the evidence is pretty strong that the greenhouse effect is here," while at the same time, Joseph Mullan, speaking on behalf of the National Coal Association, stated to a *New York Times* reporter that the American people had no reason to worry about global warming because, as he put it "the earth faces another ice age within a thousand years [and so] one calamity might cancel out the other."[18] Second, where Oklahoma Republican senator James Inhofe, along with media celebrities Rush Limbaugh and Glenn Beck, among others, push the notion that global warming is an "environmental hoax," the vast majority of climatologists agree that human activities have a significant impact on global climate change.

Furthermore, we are confronted with a two-level political problem. Domestically, scientific knowledge can be used for policymaking but can also be delayed, revised, or ignored altogether. The research findings of the scientific community also face problems at the global level. As Neil Harrison and Gary Bryner lament, "Uncertain problems . . . are especially difficult to handle in the anarchic international system, because the nature of the problem must be negotiated through contending national preferences and interpretations."[19] Climate change fits quite neatly into this two-level problem. At home, ideology and partisanship have confronted science. Abroad, the failure of US international leadership has subjected efforts to substantively address this problem to continued debate and delay. In the case of the United States, we see how domestic constraints have had a major influence on international environmental policy in general and on climate change policy in particular. As Sussman argued in addressing this problem, "When the USA provides leadership, it bolsters multilateral efforts to address global environmental problems. When it fails to offer leadership it weakens that effort. Either way, domestic political factors . . . play a central role in shaping US global environmental policy."[20]

Before turning to the next section, it is important to frame the importance of this issue in the words of two climate change researchers. Stephen Schneider of the National Center for Atmospheric Research argued in 1988 that the "greenhouse effect is one of climatology's most accepted notions" and that the "actual result of the pollutant gas buildup in the atmosphere can't be proved to everyone's satisfaction except by performing the experiment on the real climatic system—with us and other living things on earth along for the ride."[21] Two decades later, while remaining optimistic about the important role played by the scientific community in understanding Planet Earth, James McCarthy, a professor of biological oceanography at Harvard University who also served as president of the American Association for the Advancement of Science, spoke with a sense of urgency about global climate change while addressing the association:

> The combustion of coal, oil, and natural gas worldwide fueled the industrial era, and today global use of these fossil fuels provides about 80% of the energy that we consume to heat buildings, power industries, propel vehicles, and generate electricity. Physical and biological systems in the ocean and on land that remove CO_2 from the atmosphere are unable to absorb or assimilate additional CO_2 at the rate at which it is being produced by the combustion of fossil fuels. More than half of the fossil fuel carbon released by human activities today will remain in the atmosphere for up to a century.[22]

The thread that runs through the climate policy process concerns the difficulty in establishing appropriate climate change policymaking, which has resulted, in part, from the "science and politics" problem. In this case, as Sam Earman has argued, "although there may be such a thing as 'science policy,' science and policy are two entirely different things, and they are practiced by groups that are, for the most part, mutually exclusive."[23]

The Evolution of Scientific Opinion on Global Climate Change in the United States

During the 1950s, two scientists at the Scripps Institute of Oceanography played an instrumental role in helping to establish the research agenda for global climate change. Scientists Roger Revelle and Hans Suess framed the issue in an intriguing way: "Human beings are now carrying out a large scale experiment of a kind that could not have happened in the past nor [be] reproduced in the future. Within a few centuries we are returning to the atmosphere and oceans the concentrated organic carbon stored in sedimentary rocks over hundreds of millions of years."[24] These researchers reported that, based on their research on CO_2 production, the atmosphere and the oceans would eventually become unable to absorb the increasing amount of greenhouse pollutants resulting from industrialization in general and from the burning of fossil fuels in particular. Revelle recruited a young marine chemist, Charles Keeling of the Scripps Institute, to begin the first detailed measurements of carbon dioxide concentrations in the atmosphere while working at Mauna Loa, Hawaii. Keeling's research findings demonstrated a noticeable increase in atmospheric CO_2 during his research period, 1958–1986. The important finding of Keeling's research was profound: as reported by the *New York Times*, although CO_2 levels "rise and fall over the course of a day, . . . [Keeling's] measurements also showed that carbon dioxide measurements were rising year after year. That upward trend of carbon dioxide [became] known as the Keeling Curve" (see Figure 2.1).[25]

2.1 The Keeling Curve: Mauna Loa Fossil Fuel Trend, 1960–2015

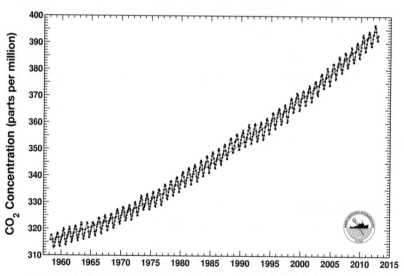

Source: Scripps Institution of Oceanography, Scripps CO_2 Program, January 2012, http://scrippsco2.ucsd.edu/graphics_gallery.html, reprinted here with permission.

In 1987, based on his research on the greenhouse effect, Gordon MacDonald testified to members of the US Senate in a joint hearing before the Subcommittee on Environmental Protection and the Subcommittee on Hazardous Wastes and Toxic Substances, both of the Committee on Environment and Public Works. He stated that "Keeling's observations have been duplicated in various parts of the world over shorter periods of time. In all sets of observations, the exponential increase is clear. . . . The exponential growth in atmospheric CO_2 concentration correlates with the release of CO_2 by the burning of oil, coal, gas, and wood."[26] Moreover, the findings of Keeling have been confirmed as atmospheric CO_2 has increased with each passing year.[27] Keeling's findings have been displayed graphically as an upward curve that shows a sharp increase in atmospheric CO_2. The Keeling Curve shows a continuation of the upward trend through 2015.

Despite the concerns raised at that time, it took two decades before the US federal government provided the legal authority to support further climate research and Congress passed the National Climate Act in 1978. In short, during the period from the late 1950s to the late 1970s, no institutionalized foundation existed to support climate research. But with this new legislation, federal agencies were directed to begin a formal research agenda on climate studies. For instance, in 1983, as reported in the *New York Times,* the EPA indicated that global warming was "not a theoretical problem but a threat whose effects will be felt within a few years."[28] Two years later, in 1985, while NASA and the National Oceanic and Atmospheric Administration (NOAA) were engaged in research on the hole in Earth's ozone layer as well as on the climate of other planets, NASA also began pushing for a similar study whereby a new generation of satellites would provide the capability for a "fully integrated understanding of how the Earth's atmosphere regulates climate through its role in transmitting and distributing energy."[29]

In 1988, James Hansen, the head of NASA's Goddard Institute for Space Studies, argued forcefully at a congressional committee hearing that global warming had reached a level such that a cause-and-effect relationship between the greenhouse gas emissions and the observed warming of the planet could be ascribed, with a high degree of confidence. However, at the same time, differences in policy orientation were evident among various agencies. For instance, where the EPA, NASA, and NOAA were viewed as "pro-environment," other agencies, including the Department of Energy, the Department of Commerce, and the Office of Management and Budget, were more likely to be viewed as "business-friendly" as they "catered to domestic economic and industrial interests."[30]

During the late 1990s, scientific research continued to confirm the problems associated with global warming and climate change. For instance, during a brutal heat wave that claimed numerous lives in Europe in 1997, scientists at NOAA's National Climate Data Center discovered that, due to heat-trapping carbon dioxide, in addition to an increase in Earth's temperature during the daytime, "nighttime low temperatures [were] rising nearly twice as fast as the daytime high temperatures."[31] Three years later, in 2000, research provided by both NOAA and the Scripps Institution of Oceanography on the increasing warming of the oceans, led Sydney Levitus, NOAA's lead scientist, to remark: "I believe our results represent the strongest evidence to date that the Earth's climate system is responding to human-induced forcing."[32] In other words, human activities were having a profound impact on the planet's climate. In 2003, another oppressive heat wave resulted in the deaths of tens of thousands in Europe.

In early summer 2002, the EPA's *US Climate Action Report* acknowledged that the United States would be profoundly affected by global warming and climate change. However, as reported by the *New York Times,* the EPA report "strongly concludes that no matter what is done to cut emissions in the future, nothing can be done about the environmental consequences of several decades worth of carbon dioxide and other heat-trapping gases already in the atmosphere."[33] In short, despite acknowledging the problem, the George W. Bush administration was not offering any substantive or fundamental solutions or policy changes in response to the threats posed by global climate change.

The following summer, in 2003, the *New York Times* reported that the EPA had produced the first comprehensive examination of global warming and climate change, commissioned by EPA administrator Christine Whitman. However, the final draft was edited by the White House. For example, an introductory sentence stating that "climate change has global consequences for human health and the environment" was changed to "the complexity of the Earth system and the interconnections among its components make it a scientific challenge to document change, diagnose its causes, and develop useful projections of how natural variability and human actions may affect the global environment in the future."[34] At the same time, scientists at NASA discovered that the "ice cover on the Arctic Ocean [was] vanishing at an astonishing rate . . . about three times faster than scientists had predicted."[35] Moreover, while Donald Kennedy, editor of the prestigious journal *Science,* maintained that "the scientific evidence on global warming is now beyond doubt," science fiction writer Michael Crichton gave a lecture at the California Institute of Technology "in which he argued that belief in global warming derived from belief of space aliens" and then published his novel *State of Fear* in 2004, wherein he "explored environmentalists' global warming hoax in detail."[36] Around the same time, British prime minister Tony Blair argued in an article in *The Economist* that "the overwhelming view of experts is that climate change, to a greater or lesser extent, is man-made, and without action, will get worse."[37]

During the next few years, several important factors emerged that impacted the global climate change issue. Scientific findings produced by NASA indicated that the year 2005 was the "warmest year on record," that 2009 was the "second warmest year on record,"[38] and that "eleven [years] of the twelve-year span 1995–2006 rank among the warmest years in the instrumental record of global surface temperature."[39] Moreover, in 2007, despite the recommendation by EPA staff urging the agency to link greenhouse gas emissions to human health problems, EPA administrator Stephen Johnson rejected his "scientific and technical staff's recommendation" and instead took a go-slow approach.

In April 2009, Johnson's successor, newly appointed EPA administrator Lisa Jackson, announced that under the Clean Air Act, the EPA had determined that greenhouse gases endangered the health of the American people. As she stated, "The finding confirms that greenhouse-gas pollution is a serious problem now and for future generations." In contrast to the positive approach initiated by EPA administrator Jackson were the negative actions taken by her predecessors in the EPA, as reported by Jim Tankersley and Alexander Hart of the *Los Angeles Times* in October 2009. The two journalists indicated that the EPA had "released a long-suppressed [2007] report by Bush administration officials who had concluded—based on science—that the government should begin regulating greenhouse gas emissions because global warming posed serious risks to the country," but that the administration refused to make it public because "the Bush White House . . . opposed new government efforts to regulate the gases most scientists see as the major cause of global warming."[40] Moreover, Tankersley and Hart emphasized that the 2007 EPA report offered "an unequivocal endorsement of the prevailing views among climate scientists. It includes a declaration that the U.S. and the rest of the world are experiencing the effects of climate change now and warns that in the U.S., those effects could lead to a variety of environmental and public health problems."[41]

While deniers of human-induced global climate change tend to focus instead on natural variability, toward the end of 2009 some deniers of human-induced climate change argued that solar radiation, instead, was the real culprit. This view directly challenged the growing consensus among climate scientists that human activities were a major factor contributing to global warming and climate change. In January 2012, NOAA responded to the critics and, in a stinging refutation of this allegation, made clear the role played by human-produced greenhouse gases:

> Since our entire climate system is fundamentally driven by energy from the sun, it stands to reason that if the sun's energy output were to change, then so would the climate. Since the advent of space-borne measurements in the late 1970s, solar output has indeed been shown to vary. . . . There is . . . a great deal of uncertainty in estimates of solar irradiance beyond what can be measured by satellites, and still the contribution of direct solar irradiance forcing is small compared to the greenhouse gas component. . . . In addition to changes in energy from the sun itself, the Earth's position and orientation relative to the sun (our orbit) also varies slightly, thereby bringing us closer and further away from the sun in predictable cycles. . . . Over several centuries, it may be possible to observe the effect of these orbital parameters; however, for the prediction of climate change in the 21st century, these changes will be far less important than radiative forcing from greenhouse gases.[42]

Summary of Selected Issues

Climatologist Kerry Emanuel explains in his discussion of global climate change that "although the notion that fossil-fuel combustion might increase CO_2 and alter climate originated in the 19th century, general awareness of the issue dates to a National Academy of Sciences Report in 1979 that warned that doubling CO_2 content might lead to an . . . increase in global average temperature."[43] A decade later, in 1988, the Intergovernmental Panel on Climate Change was created by the United Nations Environment Programme and the World Meteorological Organization. The IPCC was to serve as a formal and authoritative voice for researchers studying global warming and climate change. Beginning in 1990, the IPCC issued four reports that provided a foundation upon which to assess this most important global environmental problem. The fourth report, issued in 2007, was noteworthy because it stressed that scientists were, at the time of the publication of the document, 90 percent certain that human activities play a major role in the warming of the planet, due in part to the excessive burning of fossil fuels. Moreover, NOAA, the EPA, and NASA have added their voices in support of the IPCC's focus on the role of human activities in inducing climate change. Nevertheless, a small but vocal group of deniers continue to dispute this research finding.

Building on this background, we turn now to a brief discussion of several important implications of global climate change—decrease of sea ice and rise in sea level, extinction of a variety of terrestrial and marine species and dangers to coral reefs, the impact of planetary warming patterns on hurricane activity, and national security. We then offer a brief timeline of scientific findings.

Sea Ice and Sea Level

In 2004 the Arctic Council, composed of eight member countries including the United States, issued a major "Arctic Climate Impact Assessment" policy document based on research conducted by 300 scientists that outlined ten "critical issues" resulting from climate change in the Arctic region and the need for governments to implement mitigation and adaptation strategies to address the problem.[44] Among the findings were the following: rapid warming of the Arctic climate, Arctic warming with worldwide implications, and significant impacts on flora and fauna, people, and ecosystems. Two years later, in 2006, NOAA updated the 2004 Arctic Council report. According to NOAA: "Taken together, the observations presented in the report show convincing evidence of a sustained period of warm temperature anomalies in the Arctic, supported by continued reduction in sea ice extent, observed at both the winter maximum and summer minimum, and widespread changes in Arctic vegetation."[45] The following year, in 2007, NOAA's head of oceanography, Eric Lindstrom, reported that data gathered from satellites indicated that "sea level rise" and "polar ice–melting" were serious threats.[46] The use of satellite technology has provided scientists with an important instrument to measure the polar caps, and they are finding a "steady melting of its ice zones, from disappearing sea ice in the Arctic to shrinking glaciers worldwide."[47] In 2008 the *Washington Post* reported that scientists had become increasingly concerned about the loss of sea ice in the Arctic region, that Arctic summer ice might disappear altogether by the year 2100, and that the region had already lost sea ice of an "immense magnitude and unprecedented nature."[48] In the 2009 report "State of Polar Research," the International Council for Science and the World Meteorological Organization provided more evidence about the impacts of global warming, including the loss of ice sheets in Antarctica and Greenland, which is more widespread than anticipated. Moreover, this is occurring in unanticipated ways, along with larger concentrations of CO_2 in permafrost that will add to the existing concentrations in the atmosphere as warming continues.[49] The same year, Orrin Pilkey and Rob Young, in their book *The Rising Sea,* reported:

> If climate is getting warmer, the glaciers will begin to melt and return water to the sea. So, fluctuations in global temperature will change the balance between water stored on land and water stored in the oceans. Currently, nearly all of the world's glacial ice is retreating and thinning, adding water to the oceans. The feared collapse of the Atlantic ice sheets and melting of the Greenland ice sheet could create a catastrophic rise in sea level. . . . The health of the world's glaciers will be closely watched by scientists monitoring the future of rising sea levels.[50]

In late 2010, NOAA reported in its "Arctic Report Card" the continuing decline of ice melt and sea ice and a decrease in glaciers. In the words of Jane Lubchenco, NOAA administrator and undersecretary of commerce for oceans and atmosphere:

> Beyond affecting the humans and wildlife that call the area home, the Arctic's warmer temperatures and decreases in permafrost, snow cover, glaciers and sea ice also have wide-ranging consequences for the physical and biological systems in other parts of the world. The Arctic is an important driver of climate and weather around the world and serves as a crucial feeding and breeding ground that supports globally significant populations of birds, mammals, and fish.[51]

The latest NOAA "Arctic Report Card," produced in 2011, indicates continuing problems in the Arctic region. The report card states that "record setting changes are occurring throughout the Arctic environmental system. Given the projection of continued global warming, it is very likely that major Arctic changes will continue in years to come, with increasing climatic, biological and social impacts."[52] Moreover, sea ice continues to decline, in both thickness and summer extent.

An important element involved in the evaluation of environmental conditions is the assessment process. For example, while the Arctic Council's "Arctic Climate Impact Assessment" is concerned with climate change in the Arctic and its consequences, its "Arctic Resilience Study," scheduled for the period 2012–2015, is a "science-based assessment that aims to better understand the integrated impacts of change in the Arctic."[53] The goal is to develop and improve methodologies for "assessing interactions among social and ecological processes" in order to provide options for policymakers involved in mitigation and adaptation efforts along with strengthening the ability to confront a changing environment.[54]

Annika Nilsson, a senior research fellow at the Stockholm Environment Institute who has studied Arctic climate conditions, describes scientific assessments as "formal efforts to assemble and evaluate knowledge in a form that makes it useful for decision making."[55] As a result of their research on the assessment process, Robert Mitchell and his colleagues determined that three factors—salience, credibility, and legitimacy—helped explain the extent to which scientific assessments were influential in the policymaking process.[56] More recently, Dessler and Parson have argued that "successful scientific assessments must skillfully navigate a path between the requirements of the domains of science and policy" and that one way to do this is to disaggregate the larger issue (e.g., climate change) into smaller, manageable questions.[57] For instance, where "global warming" and "climate change" as concepts can generate dissension among political actors, one could instead pose clear, cogent questions about the rise in sea level. In this case, stakeholders could discuss what is happening and what can be done to resolve this specific problem. The point is that it is increasingly important that the assessment process be revised and refined in order to improve the influence science has on decisionmakers.

More than a decade ago, scientists informed us that the rise in sea level is a serious problem, as "extra water comes from melting glaciers and ice sheets, and swelling of the oceans as they heat," while at the same time not all coastal areas will be affected equally—for example, the "coast of California, which sits higher off the water than most Atlantic coastlines . . . could easily weather a sea-level rise of several inches. Coastlines along the Gulf of Mexico and Florida, on the other hand, would be devastated."[58] Today, scientists at the University of Arizona inform us that "rising sea levels could cover up to nine percent of the land area in 180 cities by 2100" and that the areas that will suffer most are the "southern Atlantic coast and the Gulf coast," while cities including "Miami, New Orleans, Tampa, and Virginia Beach could lose over 10 percent of their land area by the turn of the century."[59]

Threats to Marine Species

An increasing body of research is presenting policymakers with a better portrait of the impact of increasing warming trends on the oceans and marine life and on terrestrial biodiversity as well. For instance, a 2010 study published in the journal *Conservation Biology* reported that US federal agencies have yet to implement viable strategies to deal with loss of marine and wildlife despite the fact that global warming is the greatest threat to endangered species.[60] Moreover, while the oceans absorb large amounts of carbon dioxide, there is a price to be paid. One example concerns the already fragile coral reefs. In 2004, Christopher Sabine of NOAA warned that "with no end in sight to the greenhouse gases spewed out when humans burn fossil fuels, . . . the oceans could become acidic enough to slash the growth of corals and plankton in half. Such a catastrophe would throw entire food chains out of whack, severely disrupting marine ecosystems."[61] Furthermore, some research has focused specifically on coral reefs. According to the World Resources Institute, the threat to coral reefs in the Caribbean, which act as a "coastal defense against the ravages of storms and hurricanes," has been increasing as a result of warming oceans, among other threats.[62] Meanwhile, on the other side of the planet, concerns have been raised about the "longest chain of living coral" in the world—Australia's Great Barrier Reef. According to Ove Hoegh-Guldberg, director of the Center for Marine Studies at the University of Queensland: "We are likely to see corals rapidly disappear from great parts of the Barrier Reef, as it has already from large parts of the Caribbean."[63]

Hurricane Activity

There was a time when a hurricane like Katrina might be considered an anomaly. However, after the 2005 hurricane slammed into New Orleans, scientists became more concerned about "ferocious" rather than "frequent" hurricanes. "Better science," argues Sharan Majumdar of the Rosenstiel School of Marine and Atmospheric Sciences, "is the only way to get people to trust the warnings."[64] Research findings resulting from the first International Summit on Climate Change and Hurricanes, in 2007, indicated that we are moving inexorably toward "stronger tropical cyclones in a warmer future"; according to Sussman, "the cumulative impact of rising seas, a warmer planet, and increased residential and commercial development in coastal zones along with the increasing likelihood of severe hurricanes" suggests a sufficiently dire future that citizens in coastal areas should heed Majumdar's concern.[65] What does science tell us about hurricanes and future threats? Climate scientist Benjamin Santer, lead author of a 2007 study about hurricanes published in the *Proceedings of the National Academy of Sciences,* was clear when he stated that "it's human-induced burning of fossil fuels that have altered the levels of greenhouse gases in the atmosphere [which in turn] have led to this warming in regions where Atlantic and Pacific hurricanes form."[66] With considerable certainty, human-induced climate change has been identified by the scientific community as the cause of the increasing threat of hurricane activity to coastal areas around the world. This suggests that governments, especially in countries with low-lying coastal areas, should begin to plan sooner rather than later. In short, as indicated by the National Center for Atmospheric Research, the Pew Center on Global Climate Change, and a recent study by Morris Bender and colleagues published in the journal *Science,* although we are still uncertain about how climate change will affect the frequency of hurricanes, we can expect more intense hurricanes in the future.[67]

National Security

Just as American citizens expect their president and Congress to ensure a healthy economy and job creation at home, one of the defining values of the federal government is protecting the United States from threats arising from abroad. National security has usually been framed within the context of dangers posed by other nation-states as well as nonstate actors. However, in the twenty-first century, concern about the global environment has become part and parcel of national security policy, and environmental security has been increasingly viewed as a primary issue. For instance, during her tenure as secretary of state during the Bill Clinton administration, Madeleine Albright stated unequivocally that the environment is a central element of US foreign policy.[68] In 2007, Ban Ki-moon, Secretary-General of the United Nations, asserted that "climate change is the defining issue of our time."[69] The following year, Thomas Fingar, deputy director of national intelligence analysis and chairman of the National Intelligence Council, confirmed the positions put forward by Albright and Ban when he indicated that "climate change will have wide-ranging implications for US national security interests over the next twenty years."[70]

How have the armed forces of the United States responded to global climate change? One example is found in an April 2010 report, "U.S. Navy Climate Change Roadmap," produced by Task Force Climate Change and the Oceanographer of the Navy. In the report, while the Navy does not take a position on the causal aspects of climate change, it does focus on the implications of climate change for its mission. The report states:

> Climate change is a national security challenge with strategic implications for the Navy. Climate change will lead to increased tensions in nations with weak economies and political institutions. While climate change alone is not likely to lead to future conflict, it may be a contributing factor. Climate change is affecting, and will continue to affect, US military installations and access to natural resources worldwide. It will affect the type, scope, and location of future Navy missions.[71]

While the US Navy acknowledges "criticism on the details of the methods and results found in reports published by the IPCC and other entities," it makes clear its concerns about environmental problems associated with a warming planet. For instance, the Navy reports that "melting permafrost is degrading roads, foundations, and structures on [military] installations in Alaska. Droughts in the southeast and southwest U.S. are challenging water resource management. Sea level rise and storm surge will lead to an increased likelihood of inundation of coastal infrastructure, and may limit the availability of overseas bases."[72] In short, global climate change is playing a profound role in the decisionmaking process of the US Navy.

Targeting Non-CO_2 Greenhouse Gases

While a variety of greenhouse gases are relevant to climate change, carbon dioxide lies center stage in discussions both within the United

States and abroad. However, a recent report by NOAA indicated that "scientists know that stabilizing the warming effect of CO_2 in the atmosphere would require a decrease of about 80 percent in human-caused CO_2 emissions—in part because some of the carbon dioxide emitted today will remain in the atmosphere for thousands of years."[73] Such a decrease would be difficult at best, given the tenor of the discussion about greenhouse gas emissions and climate change.

A recent study by three NOAA scientists published in the journal *Nature* in August 2011 presented an alternative approach to the policy debate. The authors of the study repeat what we already know about climate change, but narrow their focus to non–carbon dioxide greenhouse gases that contribute to the warming of the planet:

> Earth's climate is warming as a result of anthropomorphic emissions of greenhouse gases, particularly carbon dioxide (CO_2) from fossil fuel combustion. Anthropomorphic emissions of non-CO_2 greenhouse gases, such as methane, nitrous oxide and ozone-depleting substances (largely from sources other than fossil fuels), also contribute significantly to warming. . . . Some non-CO_2 greenhouse gases have much shorter lifetimes than CO_2, so reducing their emissions offers an additional opportunity to lessen future climate change.[74]

Of course, given the vitriolic conversation surrounding climate change due to divisive relations among the various stakeholders, viable alternatives (such as a focus on non-CO_2 emissions) should be sought, along with continued efforts to implement significant steps toward a substantive and consistent reduction of carbon dioxide emissions. The authors of the *Nature* article have pointed out both the problems and the prospects of targeting non-CO_2 greenhouse gases. In setting forth their conclusions, they offer an enthusiastic and hopeful view about future climate change policy:

• "First, because non-CO_2 GHGs [greenhouse gases] at present account for about one-third of total CO_2-*eq* emissions . . . cuts in their emissions could substantially lessen future climate forcing."

• "Second, cuts in emissions of the shorter-lived, non-CO_2 GHGs . . . could cause a rapid decrease in the radiating forcing attributable to these gases."

• "Third, the potential benefits of cuts in non-CO_2 GHG emissions have limits" and such cuts "would not be sufficient to completely offset continued CO_2 increases at present rates."

• "Fourth, the stabilization of climate forcing will be managed more effectively with scientific advances that enhance our understanding of the sensitivities of natural GHG fluxes to climate change and that improve our ability to quantify both natural and anthropomorphic GHG fluxes."[75]

In short, if there are global environmental benefits to be had from pursuing a diversity of efforts to reduce human-forced climate change, they should be studied and, when found to be effective, they should be implemented.

Conclusion

Stefen Rahmstorf, professor of ocean physics at Potsdam University and a scientist at the Potsdam Institute for Climate Impact Research, has framed the issue of global climate change succinctly in response to the question of whether and to what extent the recent rise in CO_2 is the result of human activities. He responds in three ways. First, "this is . . . undisputed. We have tracked and we know how much fossil fuel has been burned and therefore how much CO_2 we have injected directly into the atmosphere." Second, "there is no viable alternative explanation. . . . Other possible causes, such as solar activity, volcanic activity, cosmic rays, or orbital cycles, are well observed, but they do not show trends capable of explaining the observed warming." And finally, as Rahmstorf argues, "taken together, the very strong evidence, accumulated from thousands of independent studies, has over the past decades convinced virtually every climatologist around the world (many of whom were initially quite skeptical, including myself) that anthropogenic global warming is a reality with which we need to deal."[76]

The study of climate change dates back over a century to several important researchers whose work involved a closer examination of the greenhouse effect—of a warming planet—and the factors that were associated with this global phenomenon. From Svante Arrhenius in the 1890s to the work of G. S. Callendar in the 1930s, from the research of Charles Keeling to the work of Roger Revelle and Hans Suess in the 1950s, and the scientific advocacy of James Hansen of NASA's Goddard Institute for Space Studies beginning in the 1980s into the early twenty-first century, individual researchers were providing a body of climate research that indicated not only that the planet was getting warmer, but also and more importantly that the warming was resulting in global climatic changes. Moreover, the seriousness of this problem assumed increasing attention as it became increasingly clear that human activities rather than natural factors and cycles were responsible for global warming and the associated atmospheric, oceanic, and terrestrial changes. Consequently, a foundation upon which further research could be pursued was set in place due to the work of numerous climate change scientists.

What has more recently given increased salience to the related issues of global warming and climate change has been the eventual consensus among climate researchers that can be found in governmental and nongovernmental scientific publications, where it is argued that human-forced climate change is a serious, contemporary global problem. Key among global research centers are the Intergovernmental Panel on Climate Change and the World Meteorological Organization, which have provided research findings for the larger scientific community and political and governmental leaders. Examples of research centers and agencies within the United States include the Environmental Protection Agency, the National Oceanic and Atmospheric Administration, the National Center for Atmospheric Research, the National Aeronautics and Space Administration, the National Research Council, the National Academy of Sciences, and the Scripps Institution of Oceanography. What is central to the climate change issue is the consensus among these agencies that human activities, especially the burning of fossil fuels, are a major contributor to a warming planet.

The essential dangers posed by climate change are the multiple, simultaneous effects of human activities and their consequences. The most severe of these problems include melting sea ice and the rise in sea level, threats to marine species, increasingly severe hurricane activity, health threats as waters warm, changes in agricultural and precipitation patterns, and potential threats to national security. Moreover, each one of these problems has associated issues that increases the threat. For instance, some low-lying areas that are already being affected by the rising sea level are also experiencing the sinking of coastal land; an increasing threat from mosquito and airborne health risks; storm surges and their threat to coastal residential and commercial property; socioeconomic problems associated with increasingly severe hurricanes and tsunamis; and security issues that require new defense strategies.

The science undergirding the notion of human-forced climate change has increased over the years. Moreover, the consequences of climate change have become increasingly evident as demonstrated by ongoing scientific studies. We present here a few examples of the evolution of authoritative scientific findings about concentrations of greenhouse gases in the atmosphere and global climate change.

In 1977, President Jimmy Carter asked the Council on Environmental Quality and the Department of State to prepare a study of the global environment through the end of the century. In 1982, the *Global 2000 Report to the President* was published and global climate change was among the many issues addressed. Included in the study was consideration of the impact of human activities and natural factors along with a warning: "While no major worldwide climatic changes are expected by 2000, anthropomorphic forces affecting the world's climate will be accelerating, and unless these forces and their effects are soon studied, monitored, and analyzed much more carefully, human institutions will be ill prepared to make some of the difficult choices that may be required in the 1980s or at least the 1990s."[77]

In 1979, a report issued by the National Academy of Sciences "warned that doubling CO_2 content might lead to an . . . increase in global average temperature."[78] In 1985, as reported by the *Washington Post:* "At a greenhouse hearing in December, . . . scientists testified to a virtually empty chamber." But just three years later, in 1988, "[James] Hansen, head of NASA's Goddard Institute for Space Studies, filled a room with senators, lobbyists and reporters to proclaim with 99 percent certainty that the greenhouse effect 'is changing our climate now.'"[79] And in 1989, as mandated by the 1987 Global Change Research Act, the US Global Change Research Program began issuing an annual report to Congress about scientific observations and implications of climate change. According to the program's website, it envisions "a nation, globally engaged and guided by science, meeting the challenges of climate and global change." The program's mission is "to build a knowledge base that informs human responses to climate and global change through coordinated and integrated federal programs of research, education, communication, and decision support."[80]

In 1992, President George H. W. Bush attended the Earth Summit in Rio and used his influence to ensure voluntary rather than mandatory measures before he agreed to sign the Convention on Global Climate Change. This international environmental agreement, ratified by the US Senate, required signatories to "improve [climate] science and cooperate internationally on it, as well as . . . communicate about climate change to the public."[81] The fact that Bush signed the agreement gave legitimacy to climate concerns.

In 1997, in an effort to strengthen the 1992 Convention on Global Climate Change, the Kyoto Protocol issued mandatory rather than voluntary guidelines to ensure that signatories would implement measures to reduce greenhouse gas emissions. However, although the Clinton administration supported the measure, the US Senate made it clear that the international environmental agreement would not be ratified.

In 2006, the Environmental Protection Agency reported the following:

• "Scientists are certain that human activities are changing the composition of Earth's atmosphere, and that increasing the concentration of greenhouse gases will change the planet's climate."
• "The atmospheric buildup of CO_2 and other greenhouse gases is largely the result of human activities such as the burning of fossil fuels."
• "Most of the warming in recent decades is likely the result of human activities. Other aspects of the climate are also changing, such as rainfall patterns, snow and ice cover, and sea level."[82]

Also in 2006, the National Academy of Sciences reported that a re-analysis of global average surface temperatures showed "additional supporting evidence . . . that human activities are responsible for much of the recent warming."[83] And Kevin Trenberth and Dennis Shea of the National Center for Atmospheric Research reported that same year on new research showing that "global warming produced about half of the extra hurricane-fueled warmth in the North Atlantic in 2005, and natural cycles were a minor factor."[84]

The Intergovernmental Panel on Climate Change published four reports about global climate change between 1990 to 2007. While the first three reports established a basis for understanding the problem, the 2007 report stressed that scientists are 90 percent certain that human activities are the cause of the increase in the warming of Earth's atmosphere. In the words of IPCC chair R. K. Pachauri, the "warming of the climate system is unequivocal, as is now evident from observations in increases in global average air and ocean temperatures, widespread melting of snow and ice, and rising mean global sea level."[85]

In 2007, according to a Congressional Research Service report for Congress: "Human activities, such as the use of fossil fuels, production of crops and livestock, manufacture of various products, now emit certain gases in sufficient quantities to have raised concentrations higher than they have been for hundreds of thousands of years; the elevated concentrations are changing the balance of solar radiation in and out of the Earth's atmosphere and, consequently, altering the Earth's climate."[86] Also in 2007, the World Meteorological Organization announced the following:

• "Levels of carbon dioxide, the main greenhouse gas emitted by burning fossil fuels, hit a record high in the atmosphere in 2006, accelerating global warming."
• "Rising levels of [greenhouse gases] could disrupt the climate, producing more heat waves, floods, droughts, and rising ocean levels."[87]

In 2009, the EPA, acting in response to a Supreme Court decision in 2007, announced that greenhouse gases are pollutants that are harmful to human health and therefore called upon Congress to take action while reserving the option of EPA regulation of these gases.[88] In 2010, NASA reported that "the decade ending in 2009 was the warmest on record. . . . The agency also found that 2009 was the second warmest year since 1880" and that "the warmest year was 2005."[89] And despite a decline in CO_2 emissions in 2009 due to the global financial crisis, the International Energy Agency reported that energy sector CO_2 emissions in 2010 were the highest in history, with 44 percent of CO_2 emissions coming from coal, 36 percent from oil, and 20 percent from natural gas.[90]

Following the International Energy Agency report, an article by three NOAA scientists was published in *Nature* in August 2011 to promote the idea that while conflict continues to plague national and international discussions about limiting carbon dioxide emissions, non-CO_2 greenhouse gases could still be reduced as a means to slow climate change.[91] And last of note here, in March 2012 the European Union was recognized for its success in leading the way in terms of meeting or exceeding carbon dioxide reduction targets despite suffering from financial turmoil. Several countries, excluding the United States, have followed the European Union's "cap and trade" approach to reduce greenhouse gases, including Australia, China, Japan, New Zealand, and South Korea.[92]

* * *

As we have attempted to demonstrate in this chapter, the scientific community and public officials are, whether they like it or not, intrinsically connected when it comes to global climate change. Although they function in different cultures, speak different languages, and are guided by different criteria (scientists follow the scientific method, whereas public officials are influenced by party, ideology, interest groups, and elections), both need to work together in order to secure an appropriate response to a changing climate. However, as seems to be the trend, we will likely face more conflict than cooperation in the foreseeable future. The task is essentially simple: to reduce the production of greenhouse gas emissions. Yet "simple" does not mean easy in the political arena. Michael Glantz, a senior scientist at the National Center for Atmospheric Research in Boulder, Colorado, put the problem quite succinctly: "Climate politics refers to the varied processes pursued by different actors to achieve a policy objective desired by one group or nation, often at the expense of the objectives of other groups or nations. . . . [W]hen it comes to making policy and law, there are many special interests locked in heavy competition to have their views prevail in a final policy document or process. People come to the negotiating table on climate-related issues with a wide range of backgrounds, allegiances, interests, and beliefs."[93] For the scientific community, in contrast, John Dutton set forth the challenge in the following way almost two decades ago: on the one hand, the "task of understanding a complex and fascinating system"; and on the other hand, the "responsibility of providing a reliable basis for policy decisions concerning possible modification of human activities in order to mitigate or adapt to global change."[94]

Consequently, despite the fact that the vast majority of the scientific community embrace the proposition that human-forced climate change is a major element in the policy debate, a small but vocal group of deniers (including some scientists as well as public officials and media celebrities) continue to offer opposition to the prevailing position held among the larger body of scientists. Moreover, domestic factors in the United States, including the structure of the US political system, partisanship, ideology, constituency interests, and pressure from business and industry, among others, will likely result in continued dissension and delay of government action on climate change. Let us conclude this chapter with an image of a warming planet provided by Rahmstorf in 2008:

The "canaries in the coal mine" of climate change (as glaciologist Lonnie Thompson puts it) are mountain glaciers. We know, both from old photographs and from the position of the terminal moraines heaped up by the flowing ice, that mountain glaciers have been in retreat all over the world during the past century. . . . Another powerful sign of warming, visible clearly from satellites, is the shrinking Arctic sea ice cover, which has declined 20 percent since satellite observations began in 1979.[95]

Notes

1. Sussman, Daynes, and West, *American Politics and the Environment,* 291.

2. US Department of Energy, Energy Information Administration, "Greenhouse Gases, Climate Change, and Energy," 2004, www.eia.doe.gov /oiaf/1605/ggccebrfo/chapter.html.

3. Ibid.

4. Raymond Vernon, "The Triad as Policymakers," in *Shaping National Responses to Climate Change,* edited by Henry Lee (Washington, DC: Island, 1995), 147.

5. Miranda Schreurs and Yves Tiberghin, "European Leadership in Climate Change: Mitigation Through Multilevel Reinforcement," in Harrison and Sundstrom, *Global Commons, Domestic Decisions,* 46–49.

6. Laura A. Henry and Lisa McIntosh Sundstrom, "Russia and the Protocol: From Hot Air to Implementation?" in Harrison and Sundstrom, *Global Commons, Domestic Decisions,* 127.

7. Kathryn Harrison and Lisa McIntosh Sundstrom, "Conclusion: The Comparative Politics of Climate Change," in Harrison and Sundstrom, *Global Commons, Domestic Decisions,* 281.

8. Dennis L. Soden, "At the Nexus: Science Policy," in *At the Nexus: Science Policy,* edited by Dennis L. Soden (Commack, NY: Nova Science, 1996), 2.

9. Lynton Keith Caldwell, *Between Two Worlds: Science, the Environmental Movement, and Policy Choice* (New York: Cambridge University Press, 1990), 19–20.

10. Andrew L. Dessler and Edward A. Parson, *The Science and Politics of Global Climate Change* (Cambridge: Cambridge University Press, 2006), 39.

11. Arild Underdal, "Science and Politics: The Anatomy of an Uneasy Partnership," in *Science in International Environmental Regimes,* edited by S. Andresen et al. (New York: Manchester University Press, 2000).

12. Ibid., 184–185.

13. Sheila Jasanoff, *The Fifth Branch: Science Advisors as Policymakers* (Cambridge: Harvard University Press, 1990), 250.

14. Lawrence Susskind, *Environmental Diplomacy: Negotiating More Effective Global Agreements* (Oxford: Oxford University Press, 1994), 201.

15. Chris Mooney, *The Republican War on Science* (New York: Basic, 2005), 11.

16. Steel, Clinton, and Lovrich, *Environmental Politics and Policy*, 70.

17. Sussman, "The Science and Politics Problem," 393.

18. Zachary Smith, *The Environmental Policy Paradox*, 5th ed. (Upper Saddle River, NJ: Prentice Hall, 2009), 116.

19. Neil Harrison and Gary Bryner, "Toward Theory," in *Science and Politics in the International Environment*, edited by Neil Harrison and Gary Bryner (Lanham: Rowman and Littlefield, 2004), 329.

20. Sussman, "The USA and Global Environmental Policy," 349.

21. Richard Wolkomir, "The Greenhouse Revolution," *Oceans* (April 1988): 19.

22. James J. McCarthy, "Presidential Address: Reflections on Our Planet and Its Life, Origins, and Futures," *Science* 326 (December 2009): 1647.

23. Sam Earman, "The Intersection of Science and the Law: Who Has the Right-of-Way?" in Soden, *At the Nexus*, 13.

24. McCarthy, "Presidential Address," 1647.

25. Kenneth Chang, "Charles D. Keeling, 77, Who Raised Global Warming Issue, Dies," *New York Times*, June 23, 2005, www.nytimes.com/2005/06/23/science. See also Scripps Institution of Oceanography, "Research Overview: Global Change and the Greenhouse Effect," 2000, www.sio.ucsd.edu/about_scripps/research_overview/global_change.htm.

26. Gordon MacDonald, "Scientific Basis for the Greenhouse Effect," in *The Challenge of Global Warming*, edited by Dean Edwin Abrahamson (Washington, DC: Island, 1989), 129.

27. Mark Maslin, *Global Warming* (Oxford: Oxford University Press, 2009), 26.

28. Philip Shabecoff, "E.P.A. Report Says Earth Will Heat Up Beginning in 1990s," *New York Times*, October 18, 1983.

29. Erik Conway, *Atmospheric Science at NASA* (Baltimore: Johns Hopkins University Press, 2008), 5–6.

30. Shardul Agrawala and Steinar Andresen, "Indispensability and Indefensibility? The United States in the Climate Treaty Negotiation," *Global Governance* 5 (1999): 471–472.

31. Gelbspan, *Boiling Point*, 8.

32. Ibid., 29–30.

33. Andrew C. Revkin, "Climate Changing, US Says in Report," *New York Times*, June 3, 2002.

34. Andrew C. Revkin and Katherine Q. Seelye, "Report by the E.P.A. Leaves Out Data on Climate Change," *New York Times*, June 19, 2003; Jarrett Murphy, "White House Guts Warming Study: Strong Language on Climate Change Deleted from EPA Report," *CBS News*, June 19, 2003.

35. Gelbspan, *Boiling Point*, 21, 26.

36. Conway, *Atmospheric Science at NASA*, 307.

37. Tony Blair, "A Year of Huge Challenges," *The Economist*, December 24, 2004, www.economist.com/node/3518491/print.

38. Deborah Zabarenko, "NASA Says That 2005 Was Warmest Year on Record," Environmental News Network, January 25, 2006, www.enn.com; Jeremy Hance, "NASA: 2009 Second Warmest Year on Record," Environmental News Network, January 25, 2010, www.enn.com; Broder, "Past Decade Warmest on Record."

39. R. K. Pachauri, "The IPCC: Establishing the Evidence," in Zedillo, *Global Warming,* 15.

40. Jim Tankersley and Alexander C. Hart, "Bush-Era EPA Document on Climate Change Released," *Los Angeles Times,* October 14, 2009.

41. Ibid.

42. National Oceanic and Atmospheric Administration, "Global Warming: Frequently Asked Questions," National Climate Data Center, August 20, 2012, www.ncdc.noaa.gov/oa/climate/globalwarming.html.

43. Kerry Emanuel, *What We Know About Climate Change* (Cambridge: Massachusetts Institute of Technology Press, 2007), 56.

44. Arctic Council, "Arctic Climate Impact Assessment: Policy Document," November 24, 2004, www.acia.uaf.edu/PDFs/ACIA_Policy_Document.pdf.

45. National Oceanic and Atmospheric Administration, "State of the Arctic Report 2006," www.arctic.noaa.gov/soa2006.

46. Michael Byrnes, "Scientist Says Sea Level Rise Could Accelerate," Environmental News Network, March 13, 2007, www.enn.com.

47. Michael D. Lemonick, "High Above the Earth, Satellites Track Melting Ice," Environmental News Network, July 8, 2010, www.enn.com.

48. Juliet Eilperin, "Scientists Report Further Shrinking of Arctic Ice," *Washington Post,* August 27, 2008, www.washingtonpost.com/wp-dyn/content /article/2008/08/26.

49. International Council for Science and World Meteorological Organization, "The State of Polar Research," 2009, www.wmo.int.

50. Orrin H. Pilkey and Rob Young, *The Rising Sea* (Washington, DC: Island, 2009), 34–35.

51. National Oceanic and Atmospheric Administration, "Arctic Report Card: Region Continues to Warm at Unprecedented Rate," October 21, 2010, www.noaanews.noaa.gov/stories2010/20101021_arcticreportcard.html.

52. National Oceanic and Atmospheric Administration, "Arctic Report Card: Update for 2011," www.arctic.noaa.gov/reportcard/exec_summary.html.

53. Arctic Council, "Arctic Resilience Report," 2012, www.arctic-council .org/arr.

54. Ibid.

55. Annika E. Nilsson, "Arctic Climate Change: North American Actors in Circumpolar Knowledge in Production and Policymaking," in Selin and VanDeveer, *Changing Climates in North American Politics,* 200.

56. Robert B. Mitchell et al., eds., *Global Environmental Assessments* (Cambridge: Massachusetts Institute of Technology Press, 2006).

57. Andrew L. Dessler and Edward A. Parson, *The Science and Politics of Global Climate Change,* 2nd ed. (Cambridge: Cambridge University Press, 2010), 5, 57.

58. Claude Morgan, "Sea-Level Rise: Does a Rising Tide Lift All Boats?" Environmental News Network, September 21, 2000, www.enn.com.

59. David A. Gabel, "How Rising Sea Levels Will Affect the US Coastline," Environmental News Network, February 18, 2011, www.enn.com.

60. Tony Povilitis and Kieran Suckling, "Addressing Climate Change Threats to Endangered Species in U.S. Recovery Plans," *Conservation Biology* 24 (April 2010): 372–379.

61. Christopher L. Sabine et al., "The Ocean Sink for Anthropogenic CO_2," *Science* 305 (July 2004): 367.

62. World Resources Institute, "WRI Report Says Human Activities Threaten Bulk of Caribbean Coral Reefs," Environmental News Network, September 30, 2004, www.enn.com.

63. "Report Warns Great Barrier Reef Could Die in 20 Years," Environmental News Network, February 14, 2005, www.enn.com.

64. Thomas Hayden, "Super Storms: No End in Sight," *National Geographic,* August 2006.

65. Elsner and Jagger, *Hurricanes and Climate Change,* vii; Sussman, "The Science and Politics Problem," 393.

66. "Humans Affect Sea Warming in Hurricane Zones," Environmental News Network, 2007, www.enn.com.

67. "Study: Warming Tied to Hurricanes," June 22, 2006, www.msnbc .msn.com; Center for Climate and Energy Solutions, "Hurricanes and Global Warming: Q&A," 2007, www.pewclimate.org/hurricanes.cfm; Morris A. Bender et al., "Modeled Impact of Anthropogenic Warming on the Frequency of Intense Atlantic Hurricanes," *Science* 327 (January 2010): 454–458.

68. US Department of State, "Environmental Diplomacy: The Environment and U.S. Foreign Policy," www.state.gov/www/global/oes/earth.html.

69. Stacy D. VanDeveer and Henrik Selin, "Re-engaging International Climate Governance: Challenges and Opportunities for the United States," in Rabe, *Greenhouse Governance,* 313.

70. Ibid., 313.

71. US Department of the Navy, Task Force Climate Change and Oceanographer of the Navy, "U.S. Navy Climate Change Roadmap," April 2010, 3.

72. Ibid., 5.

73. National Oceanic and Atmospheric Administration, "NOAA Study: Slowing Climate Change by Targeting Gases Other Than Carbon Dioxide," August 3, 2011, www.noaanews.noaa.gov/stories2011/20110803_nonco2.html.

74. S. A. Montzka, E. J. Dlugokencky, and J. H. Butler, "Non-CO_2 Greenhouse Gases and Climate Change," *Nature* 476 (August 2011): 43–50.

75. Ibid., 49–50. *Eq* is a "metric used to compare the emissions from various greenhouse gases on the basis of their global-warming potential . . . by converting amounts of other gases to the equivalent amount of carbon dioxide with the same global warming potential"; "Glossary: Carbon Dioxide Equivalent," European Environment Agency, 2001, http://epp.eurostat.ec.europa.eu /statistics_explained/index.php/Glossary:CO2_equivalent.

76. Stefen Rahmstorf, "Anthropogenic Climate Change: Revisiting the Facts," in Zedillo, *Global Warming,* 36, 47, 49.

77. Council on Environmental Quality and US State Department, *The Global 2000 Report to the President* (New York: Penguin, 1982), 269.

78. Emanuel, *What We Know About Climate Change,* 56; "Carbon Dioxide and Climate: A Scientific Assessment," Report of an Ad Hoc Study Group on Carbon Dioxide and Climate (Washington, DC: National Academy of Sciences, 1979).

79. Michael Weisskopf, "The Evidence on the Greenhouse Effect," *Washington Post National Weekly,* August 29–September 4, 1988.

80. US Global Change Research Program, www.globalchange.gov.

81. Jane A. Leggett, "Climate Change: Science and Policy Implications," Report for Congress (Washington, DC: Congressional Research Service, 2007), 3.

82. Environmental Protection Agency, "State of Knowledge: Climate Change Science," October 19, 2006, www.epa.gov/climatechange/science /stateofknowledge.html; Environmental Protection Agency, "Basic Information: Climate Change," December 14, 2006, www.epa.gov/climatechange /basicinfo.html.

83. John Heilprin, "Earth Hottest It's Been in 2000 Years," Environmental News Network, June 23, 2006, www.enn.com.

84. Ibid.

85. Pachauri, "The IPCC: Establishing the Evidence," 14.

86. Leggett, "Climate Change," 20.

87. Alister Doyle, "Carbon Dioxide at Record High, Stoking Warming: WMO," Environmental News Network, November 23, 2007, www.enn.com.

88. Bryan Walsh, "EPA's CO_2 Finding: Putting a Gun to Congress's Head," *Time,* April 18, 2009, www.time.com.

89. Broder, "Past Decade Warmest on Record."

90. International Energy Agency, "Prospect of Limiting the Global Increase in Temperature to 2° Is Getting Bleaker," May 30, 2011, www.iea.org.

91. National Oceanic and Atmospheric Administration, "NOAA Study: Slowing Climate Change."

92. Akhila Vijayaraghavan, "Climate Leadership Continues in the European Union," Environmental News Network, March 21, 2012, www.enn.com /wildlife/article/44160/print.

93. Michael H. Glantz, *Climate Affairs* (Washington, DC: Island, 2003), 123, 141.

94. John Dutton, "The Challenges of Global Change," in *Science, Technology, and the Environment,* edited by James Roger Fleming and Henry A. Gemery (Akron, OH: University of Akron Press, 1994), 78–79.

95. Rahmstorf, "Anthropogenic Climate Change," 43–44.

3

Congress and
the Legislative Process

The reaction of the US Congress to global climate change can best be explained by noting the structure of this institution and in considering its relationship to the president. This chapter attempts to capture the complexity of this institution as it responds to global climate change. We look at Congress's party composition, review the similarities and differences between the House and Senate, examine individual committee systems in Congress, and consider its role in funding such projects as climate change. Since Congress is the primary institution sharing interests with the president, we also look at its effectiveness in checking and balancing legislative and executive powers. Finally, we note Congress's representative function as it attempts to mirror the primary interests of this very divisive American society and its reliance on incremental policymaking.

The Structure of Congress

Party Composition

Congress accommodates two major parties in its committee system, in its seating of members, in its governing and seniority, and in its voting procedures. Any elected minority-party member or Independent must determine which majority-party caucus he or she will join. Conflict can often be intense when the parties differ over a social issue such as climate change, where there is little consensus and minimal compromise, with gridlock always a possibility. Charles Jones, in his book *Separate but Equal Branches: Congress and the Presidency,* points out how complex these party relationships can be.[1] He indicates that we can think of partisan variation along a continuum ranging from "partisanship to bipartisanship, with differences in the numbers of those defecting marking the points along the continuum." He then identifies the four classic types:

- *Partisan:* where the strength of one party makes it unnecessary to attract support from the other party.
- *Cross-partisan:* where support from the other party is essential because of either defections or divided government.
- *Bipartisan:* where a national issue may be important enough to allow party differences to be overcome.
- *Co-partisan:* where both parties have strong policy interests.

As a result, the complexity of party division can make decision-making difficult. An example of this happened in June 2009 when the 111th Congress (2009–2010) was considering specific climate change legislation, the Clean Energy Jobs and American Power Act.[2] During the debate over this legislation, House Republicans staged a major boycott, with all but seven Republican members choosing not to participate, in protest against how the Democrats had managed the "process" of the bill in committee.[3]

The intensity of party opposition often depends on which party controls the Congress and the party of the president. In 1995, for example, Republicans gained control of both the House and the Senate, for the first time since the 1950s. Accompanying this, House Republicans selected a strong Republican Speaker in Newt Gingrich (R-GA), who bound House Republicans together through his "Contract with America," a document that each House Republican was expected to support in order to ensure voting unity. The contract supported the following measures: upholding fiscal responsibility, developing stronger criminal sentencing procedures, as well as favoring stronger death penalty provisions. In addition, the contract was designed to grant more support for childcare, encourage middle-class tax relief, create small-business incentives, and encourage term limits for all congresspersons.[4] Republicans wanted to fully dominate the congressional agenda, and they did this through the contract, leaving Democrats little room to act on their priority issues. The parties have been at odds with each other over environmental matters for years. And Republicans today certainly do not need such a "contract" to take a position opposed to Democrats' support for climate change regulation.

These same partisan battles have continued into the twenty-first century as Congress has considered global climate change. Aaron McCright and Riley Dunlap, based a study on Gallup Polls from 2001 to 2010, maintain that liberals and Democrats have consistently been more supportive of science findings and are more concerned about global warming than are conservatives and Republicans.[5] What these authors suggest is that both partisanship and ideology may divide congresspersons in their voting. Dana Fisher, Philip Leifeld, and Yoko Iwaki also found evidence in the 109th and 110th Congresses (2005–2006 and 2007–2008) that ideological cliques crossed "beyond partisan or other commonly understood coalitions" on the question of climate change.[6]

This divide between parties can be seen not only in their consideration of climate change as being caused by human activity, but also in their support for or opposition to the role of the Environmental Protection Agency (EPA) regarding climate regulation; for it is this agency that has acted for President Barack Obama as the fallback agency in lieu of Congress's inability to pass climate change legislation. Alaska senator Lisa Murkowski (R-AK), to name but one opponent of climate change legislation, offered an amendment on January 20, 2010, to bring to a halt any EPA regulations on climate change. As Emily Figdor, the federal director of global warming at Environment America, stated: "It's incredibly disappointing that Alaska is seeing such profound effects from global warming already and yet the senior senator from Alaska is spearheading the effort to block federal action on global warming by striking at the heart of the Clean Air Act. It's really hard to make sense of that."[7]

Where congressional leaders have seen that bipartisan cooperation is necessary to effectively pass legislation on climate change, too often polarization has been the outcome, as occurred in the 111th Congress. In this Congress, Senate Majority Leader Harry Reid (D-NV) was set to bring a climate and energy proposal to the Senate floor. Once he sensed a lack of the bipartisan support he needed, he announced in July 2010 that there would be no legislation capping the limits on greenhouse gas emissions, and this decision "effectively ended action on climate legislation for the 111th Congress."[8]

Party controversy over climate change, and conflict over environmental issues in general, have been seen to be particularly intense during or near a presidential election year, especially with a Democrat as president being opposed on an issue by a Republican-controlled House that is heavily influenced by members of the Tea Party. It has been suggested that the 112th Congress (2011–2012) was the most anti-environment Congress since the mid-1990s. The House averaged more than one anti-environmental vote for every day the House was in session in 2011. More than one in five of the legislative roll-call votes taken in 2011, or 22 percent, were votes on measures thought to undercut environmental protections. About 228 Republican members of the House, or 94 percent of the House Republican membership, voted an anti-environmental position on these roll-call votes, while 86 percent of the Democrats, or 164 members, voted a pro-environmental position. Of those anti-environmental positions, some 27 votes were cast to block action on climate change, while 77 votes were cast to undercut Clean Air Act protections.[9]

Not since the 104th Congress (1995–1996) of Speaker Newt Gingrich has there been such polarization. Critics like Michelle Bachmann indicate that proposing climate change legislation is just President Obama's way of establishing his own political agenda.[10] House Speaker John Boehner (R-OH) has also been skeptical of the president's efforts related to global climate change, as he has accused the administration of implanting too many regulations through the EPA. The Speaker sees this as harming employment for Americans.[11]

Thus the social issue of climate change continues to generate party opposition, as both Democrats and Republicans seem committed to resisting each other's propositions on the issue. Signing climate change legislation into law will require both chambers of Congress and the president to agree to settle their differences and work toward agreement. Such agreement over social issues happens most quickly when both parties recognize that a crisis exists and must be resolved. So far, the scientific evidence has not convinced the parties that climate change is a crisis, and so conflict and gridlock continue.

Bicameralism

The excessive polarization in the 112th Congress over climate change was not an unusual situation when considering the differences between the House and Senate. Given the makeup of the two houses and the way that their members relate to each other, it is often difficult for the House and Senate to reach agreement on a piece of legislation. House members are largely concerned with representing the interests of their own congressional districts, while senators must make an effort to represent the concerns of entire states. Moreover, while senators enjoy the breathing room afforded by six-year terms, members of the House are continually running for reelection to two-year terms and so are always looking to the interests of their districts in order to retain their seats. This leads to what Dana Fisher and her colleagues discovered: that Congresses themselves differ, not just the two chambers, as evident in the markedly different voting on climate change between the 109th and 110th Congresses. There was much polarization in the 109th Congress as Republicans and business interests separated from Democrats and environmental interests. This was not the case in the 110th Congress, where polarization was much less severe.[12]

Committee System

When several congressional committees and subcommittees are considering different aspects of a complex bill, this makes it difficult to consider the bill as a whole. Barry Rabe suggested something similar when he stated: "A further impediment to Congressional deliberations on climate change remains the myriad House and Senate Committees that can lay claim to at least some semblance of jurisdiction over this issue. This is reflected in the numerous committee sponsors of legislative hearings, suggesting rival entities competing for input."[13]

A climate change example will illustrate this problem. The 112th Congress was quite willing to cease funding of certain aspects of climate change legislation, as was seen when the House passed the Full-Year Continuing Appropriations Act resolution in 2011,[14] which prohibited the use of appropriated funds to implement various EPA regulatory activities regarding greenhouse gas emissions.[15] The League of Conservation Voters claimed that the resolution was, at the time it passed the House, "the greatest legislative assault ever on the environment and public health."[16] At the same time, the House also passed a resolution that would have repealed the EPA's endangerment finding, redefined "air pollutants" to exclude greenhouse gases, and prohibited the EPA from promulgating any regulation to address climate change.[17] The Senate was able to defeat both of these resolutions, with the latter failing on a vote of 50 to 50.[18]

Following the House's introduction of the Full-Year Continuing Appropriations Act resolution, it was referred to the House Committee on Appropriations. While in committee, it was considered by members from twelve subcommittees, including Agriculture, Rural Development, Food and Drug Administration, and Related Agencies; State Foreign Operations and Related Agencies; and Commerce, Justice, Science, and Related Agencies. A total of 167 amendments were offered on the bill, of which 52 were agreed to. The bill passed the House by a vote of 235 to 189, with 9 abstentions.[19] In July 2011 the House introduced another resolution involving similar appropriations provisions;[20] consideration of the bill was halted on July 28, but there were still 150 amendments pending.

Since 2009, the Senate has been less successful in passing climate change legislation than has the House, but some bills and regulations that have passed the House have of course been anti-environmental in nature. When climate change legislation has been introduced in the Senate, it has been distributed to four or five committees to consider different aspects of climate change, and few of these bills have made their way out of committee. For example, in June 2009 the Senate Energy and Natural Resources Committee passed the American Clean Energy Leadership Act, which was then placed on the Senate's legislative calendar, where it remained until early 2013, when it died after being reported by committee.[21] This bill would require 15 percent of the country's electricity to come from renewable resources—either wind or solar power—by 2021.

Other climate change bills that have been introduced and referred to committee have included the Clean Energy Partnerships Act of 2009, which was referred to the Senate Environment and Public Works Committee;[22] the Clean Energy Act of 2009,[23] introduced by Senators Lamar Alexander (R-TN) and Jim Webb (D-VA) on November 1, 2009; and the Carbon Limits and Energy for America's Renewal Act of 2009,[24] introduced by Senators Maria Cantwell (D-WA) and Susan Collins (R-ME) on December 1, 2009. As of early 2013, none of the climate bills introduced in the House in 2009 have made their way to the Senate floor for discussion.

The Politics of Funding

Funding climate change efforts has been a major issue of contention in Congress. Of primary concern has been how the United States will be able to afford implementation of climate legislation once it has been passed. We can presume that any major alteration in climate change policy will be expensive and that arguments concerning priorities will arise, as they should.

This environmental conflict between the parties over funding was seen in July 2011 as House Republicans added some thirty-nine riders to the 2012 appropriations bill, seeking to limit environmental regulation. The Senate, controlled by the Democrats, preserved the bill from being significantly changed by the Republicans. Democratic congressman Henry Waxman (D-CA) said that the attitude of the new Republican majority reminded him of another era, suggesting that the Republicans were "intent on restoring the robber-baron era where there were no controls on pollution from power plants, oil refineries and factories."[25]

Environmental matters are a priority for only a very few congresspersons, particularly when one considers crisis priorities to which Congress and the president are expected to respond: the economy, employment, and national security. In President Obama's first couple of months in office, he had to deal with two wars, in Iraq and Afghanistan, as well as a faltering economy. During his first hundred days in office, the president witnessed the loss of 2 million American jobs and the foreclosure of 908,000 homes. When considering these figures, one can understand how the president's attention to other issues such as climate change would be quickly shifted to getting Americans back to work.[26]

One of the few climate change priorities on the president's agenda, however, has been raising contributions for the $30 billion "Green Fund," which was agreed to at the Copenhagen Conference of December 7–18, 2009. This fund is to grow to $100 billion by 2020 to assist developing countries in their fight against global climate change. While this fund was proposed during the Copenhagen meetings, it was not until the Durban summit in South Africa, held from November 28 to December 11, 2011, that it was formally accepted by the nations in attendance at both conferences. The Obama administration claims to have contributed over $5 billion to the fund.[27]

However, many House members in the 112th Congress backed away from long-term financial commitments to climate change. Dana Rohrabacher (R-CA), chair of the House Foreign Affairs Oversight and Investigations Subcommittee of the House Foreign Affairs Committee, in reference to the Senate spending bill responsible for funding international assistance that was to make available "1.2 billion for climate change programs funded by the State Department, the US Agency for International Development and the Treasury Department," said that it was "pure fantasy" that the United States would contribute so much to the Green Fund. Senator Jim DeMint (R-SC) called for halting US efforts to send aid overseas to fight global warming.[28]

Congress has made it known that it is unwilling to take steps toward limiting greenhouse gas emissions unless all major emitting countries participate. Many members of Congress are particularly concerned about China, a major greenhouse gas emitter that has been reluctant to limit its own emissions.[29] Congress fears that passing legislation that curbs greenhouse gas emissions without securing a similar commitment from China will create an economic disadvantage for the United States.[30] Given these attitudes of members from the House, the administration hopes that much of the money for the Green Fund will come from the private sector.[31]

Economic Interests

Differences in voting on climate change legislation can also result from congresspersons representing different economic interests in the United States. Dana Fisher found that the importance of the automobile in the United States, "one of the best predictors of carbon dioxide emissions in the developed world," and Americans' reliance on coal, which is in abundant supply in the United States, have "exerted a profound impact on policy."[32] The presence of such resources in a congressional district can be persuasive in determining whether the congressperson will vote to support climate change legislation or oppose it.

Relations Between Congress and the President

Policymaking Responsibility

In addition to resolutions regarding the funding or nonfunding of climate change legislation, opponents in both parties have introduced legislation focused on the Environmental Protection Agency—to either delay the EPA's ability to regulate gas emissions, or, as many Republicans would prefer, to strip the EPA completely of its means to regulate emissions at all. The Energy Tax Prevention Act,[33] introduced March 3, 2011, was one of the more notable bills directed at the EPA; it sought to immobilize the EPA's authority to regulate greenhouse gases under the Clean Air Act.

Although most Democrats would reject such an effort to immobilize the EPA's authority, not all Democrats are supportive of the administration's position on the EPA. For example, Senator Jay Rockefeller, a Democrat representing West Virginia, a state that is rich in coal, introduced on January 31, 2011, a bill seeking to impose a two-year delay on the EPA's regulation of greenhouse gases.[34] Senator Rockefeller did exempt light-, medium-, and heavy-duty vehicle standards from the delay, which provided some regulation protection.

The attempt to immobilize the EPA was not the only example of anti-environmental legislation that came out of the 112th Congress. Henry Waxman (D-CA), ranking member of the Energy and Commerce Committee, unveiled a new, searchable database of the 317 anti-environment votes by members of the 112th Congress who opposed legislation to protect the environment. As Waxman indicated: "This is the most anti-environment House in history. The House has voted to block action to address climate change, to stop actions to prevent air and water pollution, to undermine protections for public lands and coastal areas, and to weaken the protection of the environment in dozens of other ways."[35]

Also in the 112th Congress, John Sullivan (R-OK) introduced the Transparency in Regulatory Analysis of Impacts on the Nation Act (TRAIN Act).[36] This bill, according to the League of Conservation Voters, "grew into the single biggest assault on the Clean Air Act in its more than 49-year history." The league explained that the bill "would allow for the indefinite delay of two life-saving clean air safeguards (the Cross-State Air Pollution Rule and the Mercury and Air Toxics Standards for power plants). . . . The bill would also require any future standards to be based on the most polluting power plants and incorporate the Latta amendment . . . to eliminate the health-based underpinning of the Clean Air Act."[37] The House passed the TRAIN Act in September 2011 by a vote of 249 to 169. However, the Senate has yet to act on it as of early 2013.

President Obama, when he first came to office in 2009, favored a "cap and trade" approach to climate change, which he originally hoped would be a mechanism to attract support for climate change legislation from both sides of the aisle to reduce pollution from carbon dioxide. This system was intended to limit emissions and gradually reduce pollution over time. Permits under this system would be sold to emitters and the total allowances would be equal to the "cap." The less a company polluted, the less it would have to pay. Companies would also be able to trade allowances, providing them with more flexibility. But as David Fahrenthold, writing in the *Washington Post,* suggested, "the Senate will be a much harder sell since the Senate wishes to broaden its bill beyond the committed environmentalists, to the skeptical, the agnostic and the distracted."[38] And Senator Lindsey Graham (R-SC) added, in more definitive terms: "Realistically, the cap-and-trade bills in the House and Senate are going nowhere. . . . They're not business-friendly enough, and they don't lead to meaningful energy independence."[39]

Once it became clear that the Obama administration did not have the votes needed to pass the "cap and trade" system, a new option was introduced, known as the "fee and dividend" system, which has been encouraged by the Citizens Climate Lobby. This system proposes returning some money back to the consumer from carbon pollution allowances.[40] The key to this approach is that a "carbon fee would be collected at the mine or port of entry for each fossil fuel (coal, oil and gas). The fee would be uniform, a certain number of dollars per ton of carbon dioxide in the fuel. The public would not directly pay any fee, but the price of goods would rise in proportion to how much carbon-emitting fuel is used in their production."[41]

There has been a great deal of climate change activity in Congress since the 1990s, involving debate, committee actions, and hearings, and this continued through the 112th Congress. But little legislation has come out of Congress since 1990. Roger Pielke Jr. and Daniel Sarewitz reminded us that during these years the politics of climate change became increasingly "intractable, and the path toward scientific certainty much more challenging."[42] One reason for this was the election in 1992 of Democratic president Bill Clinton and his vice president Al Gore. Both were committed to adding the United States to the international coalition of more than 170 nations supporting the Kyoto Protocol—an international environmental agreement designed to reduce the dangers of climate change. At the same time, Republicans secured majorities in the House and the Senate in the 1994 congressional elections, thereby assuming control of both chambers of Congress for the first time since the 1950s.

Of the two chambers, the House in 2006 found itself slightly more supportive of the Obama administration's views on climate change than did the Senate. But even in the House, there was only one bill of importance that passed that chamber. Henry Waxman (D-CA) had first introduced the Safe Climate Act of 2006 in the previous year.[43] The intent of this bill was to freeze emissions in 2010 at their 2009 level, and beginning in 2011 it was to reduce emissions by 2 percent per year to eventually reach their 1990 level. The bill also provided that by 2020 the United States would cut its emissions by 5 percent per year, and that by 2050 its emissions would be 80 percent lower than they were in 1990.[44] The Waxman bill never became law; the last action taken was on July 17, 2006.

The 2009 Waxman-Markey House bill—the American Clean Energy and Security Act[45]—the one bill that did pass the House, is interesting in that it does not even use the phrase "climate change" in its title; nor does the Senate's 2009 companion bill—the Clean Energy Jobs and American Power Act[46]—incorporate "climate change" language in its title.[47] The House bill was written to "set a price on carbon, and would put progressively tighter limits on greenhouse gas emissions with a 17 percent cut from 2005 levels by 2020, and 80 percent by 2050."[48] The House bill was passed by a close margin of 219 to 212. It was described by the Environmental Defense Action Fund as "the most important environmental measure of the past 20 years."[49] The action fund also considered it an important jobs bill, since limiting climate pollution would create green jobs. That argument was not one that the American Petroleum Institute supported. As Lou Hayden of the institute argued, the climate bill would destroy more jobs than it would create.[50] The Senate Environmental Committee was supportive of the House bill, but the Senate as a whole objected to it. The Senate Environmental Committee passed a measure that was even stronger than the House bill, supporting a 20 percent reduction by 2019 and an 83 percent reduction by 2050.[51] It had yet to be voted on by the full Senate as of early 2013.

Certainly most policymakers in and out of Congress think it would be far better for climate change legislation controlling greenhouse gas emissions to come from Congress rather than in the form of regulations coming from the Environmental Protection Agency, an agency made up of "unelected bureaucrats," as its opponents argue.[52] That threat of the EPA taking control of climate change is always present, since it was given this authority by the Supreme Court in the case of *Massachusetts v. Environmental Protection Agency* in 2007.[53] It is also the president's desire that legislation come from Congress, if at all possible, but he wishes to retain the EPA's potential to regulate climate change in case legislation stalls—which has recently been the case.

As legislative activities in earlier sessions of Congress demonstrate, one can see trends in support of and opposition to climate change initiatives, as well as a change in tactics used by the two major parties in responding to climate change. One thing that has remained constant, however, is the opposition by Republicans to the EPA's efforts to enforce the president's will on Congress. This proved to be so in the 104th Congress, characterized by the clash of leadership styles and priorities between President Bill Clinton and Speaker Newt Gingrich. An example of this policy clash occurred on September 27, 1995, when the Senate passed an appropriations bill[54] that would have cut the EPA's funding by $1.5 billion, and would have eliminated the EPA's ability to enforce clean-air regulations. The bill passed by a vote of 55 to 45, but President Clinton vetoed it on December 18, 1995.

In the 105th and 106th Congresses (1997–1998 and 1999–2000), different tactics and strategies were used by opponents of efforts to reduce greenhouse gases. Rather than directly attack environmental legislation, opponents in the Senate, in a "Trojan horse" tactic, attached anti-environment riders to important appropriation bills and other essential legislation. For example, in the first session of the 106th Congress, lawmakers included more than fifty anti-environment riders.[55]

On June 21, 2000, the House approved the Linder-Collins amendment, 225 to 199, which was a rider that prohibited the EPA from identifying areas that fail to meet new ozone standards. This, in essence, delayed the EPA from informing communities regarding their air quality (in violation of federal health standards), and delayed state and federal clean air planning. A year before, on July 13, 1999, the House had passed the Sanders amendment, which decreased the funding for fossil fuel research by $50 million. Fossil fuel research is aimed at finding less polluting ways to burn fossil fuels, but environmentalists prefer to reduce or even eliminate this research money and seek alternative fuel methods.[56]

It is interesting that even though little climate change legislation has been forthcoming from Congress, this has not stopped lawmakers on both sides of the aisle from introducing legislation. As increasing evidence has mounted regarding the dangers of climate change, more and more legislation has been introduced in Congress. Noting this in the 110th Congress, Barry Rabe indicated that "the recent uptick in the saliency of climate change and a feeding frenzy of new legislative proposals introduced in the opening weeks of the new Congress suggest the possibility of intensified legislative attention in the coming months and years."[57]

In the 105th Congress (1997–1998), only 7 climate change legislative proposals were introduced. The number of such proposals grew to 25 in the 106th Congress (1999–2000), to more than 80 in the 107th (2001–2002), to 96 in the 108th Congress (2003–2004), and to 106 bills, amendments, and resolutions dealing with global climate change in the 109th (2005–2006).[58] It would appear that members of Congress were catering to their representation role, allowing them to take credit for proposing climate change laws without actually working to pass those laws.

By the 109th Congress, both parties were also introducing measures in the Senate. Debate on the Energy Policy Act of 2005, for example, attracted two climate change amendments that passed, including a nonbinding resolution that indicated acknowledgment by the Senate of the warming effects of greenhouse gas emissions; as stated in the resolution: "Congress should enact a national mandatory, market-based program to slow, stop, and reverse the growth of these emissions."[59] One would presume that in the 109th Congress, both parties wanted to do something about greenhouse gas emissions and that this was as near to a bipartisan agreement that any legislation from the Senate would come. By the middle of July 2008, the 110th Congress, through both chambers, had introduced more than 235 bills, amendments, and resolutions on climate change; though none successfully made their way from House to Senate, or vice versa, this did show that the interest in climate change had heightened in both chambers.[60]

In the 111th Congress, President Obama wanted Waxman-Markey's American Clean Energy and Security Act of 2009 enacted into law.[61] However, only the House passed the bill, which would have established a cap on greenhouse gases throughout the economy. Once the House passed the Waxman-Markey bill, it went to the Senate, but failed, despite passing in the Senate Energy and Natural Resources Committee in June 2009. In November 2009 the Senate Environmental and Public Works Committee passed the Clean Energy Jobs and American Power Act, but as mentioned previously, all but seven Republican members boycotted the final vote.[62] The bill has been placed on the Senate's legislative calendar.

In the 112th Congress, the parties remained at loggerheads with each other for reasons suggested by Charles Jones, as previously mentioned. A possible breakthrough came when a small group of senators from both parties along with one Independent decided to see if there was a proposal they could submit that both parties could, and would, accept. After the Senate rejected the "cap and trade" proposal that the president had favored, Senators John Kerry (D-MA), Joseph Lieberman (I-CT), and, for a time, Lindsey Graham (R-SC) began working on an alternative. The three senators worked on a proposal that would cut the country's greenhouse gas output by focusing their attention on emissions from transportation, electric utilities, and industry.[63] Transportation would undergo a carbon tax on fuel; power plants would undergo a tax that would become increasingly stringent over time; while industries would not have to cap emissions immediately, but following a delay. In addition, the senators recommended increased offshore gas and oil drilling, funding for the construction of nuclear power plants, and "carbon sequestration and storage projects at coal-fired utilities."[64] Although this plan was eventually rejected, these efforts did show that there is potential in a small group of policymakers to develop creative approaches that may someday pay off for party members on both sides of the aisle.

The same pattern of introducing multiple bills into Congress, but passing few of them, was noted by Barry Rabe in how frequently congresspersons talked about the topic:

> Although Congress has proven generally incapable of reaching any policy agreement on climate change, it has certainly demonstrated an ability to talk about the subject. Between September 1975 and December 2006, at least 175 Congressional hearings were conducted that gave substantial attention to climate change. . . . Seventeen standing House or Senate Committees sponsored at least one of these hearings, with particularly heavy concentrations in the years 1989 (20), 1998 (15), 1993 (12), and 1992 (11).[65]

Separation of Powers and Checks and Balances

Separation of powers and the system of checks and balances define the relationship between Congress and the president. As a result of this structure, Congress is a major check on the president. This has been a major roadblock in passing climate change legislation. For instance, President Obama was very much aware of this, as he learned on his way to the Copenhagen climate change conference. It was his intent to become a world leader and spokesperson for global efforts to halt climate change. This did not happen, however, and one reason for this was articulated by a primary opponent to climate change legislation, Senator James Inhofe (R-OK), who indicated that the president was "handcuffed by Senate fractiousness on the issue and new doubts among some about the basic science underpinning the talks."[66]

On other occasions, it has not been necessary for Congress to exert its constitutional check on the president. Instead, the president has been a check on himself, failing to offer strong and effective leadership to effectively sell climate change legislation to Congress. Because of this, Obama has found that his own party has not always been behind his efforts to do something regarding climate change. Midwest Democratic congresspeople, for example, have been slow to join with the president, given that their constituents are so tied to coal-fired power plants. Jason Grumet, president of the Bipartisan Policy Center and an energy adviser during the presidential campaign in 2008, put it this way: "This is definitely a Goldilocks problem. . . . The trick is finding something just right in balancing the importance of demonstrating international leadership while not undermining the legislative dynamics here at home."[67] *New York Times* journalist John Broder adds that any international cooperation on climate change is in jeopardy unless the Senate is willing to support the president. Before the Copenhagen climate change conference took place, Broder put it this way: "The lack of consensus in Congress puts Mr. Obama in a tricky domestic and diplomatic bind. He cannot promise more than Congress may eventually deliver when it takes up climate change legislation next year. But if he does not offer some concrete pledge, the United States will bear the brunt of the blame for the lack of an international agreement."[68] As he further stated with regard to Copenhagen, without the Senate "the entire international project is in jeopardy because without the participation of the United States—which emits 20 percent of all greenhouse gases—any international regime is bound to fall short."[69]

Allies of the president in the Senate did allow Obama to take a plan to Copenhagen in 2009. It was Kerry, Lieberman, and Graham who developed a working plan for Obama that would cut greenhouse gas emissions by 17 percent below the 2005 levels by the year 2020, a level that had been approved previously by the House. This gave the president a bargaining position for the Copenhagen talks.[70]

Congress's primary check on the president was also manifested during the Clinton years. The Senate's opposition to the Kyoto Protocol came in 1997. This protocol was designed to respond to the negative aspects of global climate change, and was supported by more than

170 nations. Vice President Al Gore exerted a great deal of effort to convince the nations to support and ratify the protocol. The one nation he failed to convince was his own, the United States itself, which at the time was the greatest emitter of greenhouse gases. Clinton signed the protocol, but did not anticipate the opposition he received from the Senate. The Senate, in the Byrd-Hagel Resolution, voted to oppose Kyoto by a vote of 95 to 0. The Senate's major objection was that the United States should not sign the protocol until the document restrained the emissions of developing countries.[71]

This brought an inglorious halt to the efforts of the United States to join with other nations in subscribing to the Kyoto Protocol. Some in the administration thought that had Clinton worked harder with individual senators, he might have worked out a compromise or guarantee of future negotiations with India and China to make it possible for the United States to move forward on climate change, and to make it less of an embarrassment for the president.

Legislative Incrementalism

Members of Congress think more in terms of incremental steps rather than sweeping changes. President Obama wants what is called a "broad approach to climate and energy. . . . They [White House officials] are also pressing forward with Environmental Protection Agency regulation of emissions of heat-trapping gases over the virtual unanimous opposition of Republicans in the House and Senate."[72] Could this be a suggestion as to why there is a problem between Congress and the president?

The presumption was made in January 2010 that if the president was unwilling to scale back his sweeping approach to climate change, chances were good that no agreement would come out of the partisan confrontation or, alternatively, that only partial agreement on a portion of a climate change bill would be reached, which would not be satisfactory to the president.

Where Bill Clinton was constrained by a House and Senate controlled by Republicans, President Obama has been restricted by Republican control of the House. In both instances, Republicans have opposed the president's broad policy efforts and have thought more in incremental terms with regard to policy—limiting the broad reach that climate change legislation might otherwise have in attracting support and/or opposition. House Republicans sought to eliminate the salary of his top climate change envoy, Todd Stern, the president's chief treaty negotiator at the United Nations global warming talks, in order to force his resignation. Their effort was joined by thirteen Democrats who opposed the administration's position on climate change. They also attempted to eliminate the position of the president's climate adviser, formerly occupied by Carol Browner, as well as several other positions that Republicans thought were unaccountable to Congress.[73] In response, President Obama refused to give up his claim on those positions, indicating that it would be a violation of separation of powers and, as he stated, of the provision that the Republicans had put forth: "The provision undermines 'the President's ability to exercise his constitutional responsibilities and take care that the laws be faithfully executed.'"[74]

Regarding the one climate change bill that passed the House in the 111th Congress, Robert Neubecker reported that given that this took place during an election year, "some senators have talked about breaking up the House bill and passing only the most popular portions, such as the mandate for electric utilities and renewable power, or loans for green technology." But he added that "splitting off the easy items now could make it more difficult to attract votes for emission limits down the road."[75] Although this did not happen, it does illustrate again how incrementally the Congress thinks about policy compared to the president.

Charles Jones makes the point even more clearly, suggesting how difficult it can be for Congress and the president to agree on anything during an election year. As he noted, even if Congress could endorse the president's ideas, to support them would be to "accept his leadership, thus enhancing his party for the next election."[76] This means that any climate change proposals put forth by the White House during an election year will surely be rejected, given that neither party wants to give the opposition party an advantage to take control over the White House.

Part of the problem with climate change legislation might not even be entirely blamable on increased conflict during an election period, but rather on weak leadership and disinterest on the part of the president in not wanting to bring legislation forward because he senses it might not pass. Obama admitted as much in his 2012 State of the Union address when he stated: "The differences in this Chamber may be too deep right now to pass a comprehensive plan to fight climate change."[77]

The Role of Congress in Representing the Interests of American Society

While conventional wisdom would suggest that Congress is a forum for society's basic concerns, this has not always been the case regarding climate change. Since the 104th Congress, there have been blocks of support for and opposition to climate change in Congress. As Figures 3.1 and 3.2 indicate, the gap between the two parties on climate change has increased since the 1970s, as measured by environmental voting records. This pattern contrasts, however, with public opinion polls that reveal that Americans on the whole have maintained a more consistent stance in support of environmental protection.

It is clear that neither party, as shown in recent opinion polls, mirror the public's impressions of climate change. In fact, the public's views seem more reflected in the sentiments of Independents. Democrats, by and large, believe that global climate change is a severe prob-

Figure 3.1   Percentage of Pro-Environment Voting, by Party, US House of Representatives, 1973–2010

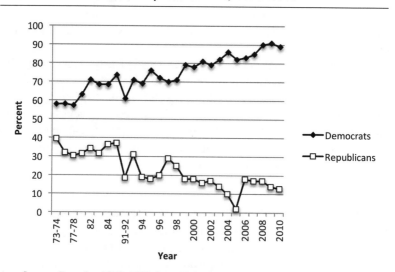

Source: Data for 1973–2000 from R. E. Dunlap, C. Xiao, and A. M. McCright, "Politics and Environment in America: Partisan and Ideological Cleavages in Public Support for Environmentalism," *Environmental Politics* 10, no. 4 (2001): 23–48. Data for 2001–2010 from League of Conservation Voters, "Scorecard Archives," www.lcv.org /scorecard/scorecard-archives.

lem in need of an immediate response, while Republicans tend to think of climate change as a nonissue. Looking at this pattern in 2012, there is no reason to presume that the parties have come closer together than they were in 2000, given the rhetorical exchanges between them. It leads one to wonder whether the growing gap between Democrats and Republicans can best be explained by the fact that neither side wishes to give in to the other side's views, particularly in an election year, fearing that to do otherwise would show a sign of weakness while giving the other party an advantage. Certainly, at least on the issue of climate change, Congress does not seem to be very reflective of American society.

One persistent societal interest that has influenced the voting on climate change legislation in the United States is activity at the subnational level. As Henrik Selin and Stacy VanDeveer remind us: "The United States is often identified as a global laggard on climate change policymaking and implementation. Although this reputation may be

Figure 3.2 Percentage of Pro-Environment Voting, by Party, US Senate, 1973–2010

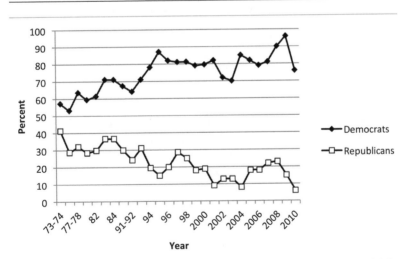

Source: Data for 1973–2000 from R. E. Dunlap, C. Xiao, and A. M. McCright, "Politics and Environment in America: Partisan and Ideological Cleavages in Public Support for Environmentalism," *Environmental Politics* 10, no. 4 (2001): 23–48. Data for 2001–2010 from League of Conservation Voters, "Scorecard Archives," www.lcv.org /scorecard/scorecard-archives.

deserved by the US federal government, a look across all levels of the US federal system and a multitude of political actors demonstrates the existence of a significant number of climate change and energy-related activities."[78] Most of these activities have occurred at the state and municipal levels.

A number of other researchers have seen progress on climate change at the subnational level. As Barry Rabe, for example, suggests: "Climate change has routinely been framed as an issue to be addressed through an intergovernmental regime guided by a set of large nations. The evolving reality of climate change policy development in the United States and abroad, relies heavily on sub-national initiative."[79] Rabe also suggests that

> American legislatures are not inherently incapable of enacting climate change legislation or providing oversight and resources to guide implementation. However, such legislatures operate in state capitals rather than Washington, D.C. More than half of the American state legislatures have enacted one or more policies designed to reduce greenhouse gas emissions, representing clusters of states in every region of the nation except the Southeast. Multiple states are now implementing policies that are essentially replicas of ideas that have been floating about Congress for many years and are confronting the challenges of operating renewable portfolio standards, cap-and-trade systems, and a wide range of related initiatives.[80]

Conclusion

The record shows that Congress has been quite active in its focus on its climate change agenda, but much of that activity has led to negative results. There have been many debates, many committee hearings, numerous speeches from the floor, and countless bills and resolutions introduced, but little legislation to show for all the activity, and little support for the initiatives of the president. And this could be one reason for President Obama's more passive leadership on climate change during his second term. The president admitted as much in his 2012 State of the Union address, when he indicated that Congress was not ripe for receiving a comprehensive climate change proposal.

To best understand Congress's response to climate change, one must understand how Congress operates, its role in the political system, and its relationship to the president. In particular, understanding how the parties operate in Congress and how chamber division and committee proliferation influence potential legislation will help us better understand how Congress responds to climate change. Party conflict can often be intense when the two major parties differ over climate change, an issue that engenders little consensus and minimal compromise. The ensuing result is gridlock. This, of course, makes decisionmaking difficult, with Republicans and Democrats opposing each other on the issue of global climate change in general and on regulations to reduce greenhouse gases in particular.

We also need to recall that Congress has the powers it does, as given by the Framers, in order to be an effective check on presidential power and the issues on the president's agenda. Yet it is not always the case that Congress so checks the president in negotiations and on policy issues. In foreign policy matters, for example, Congress is always at a disadvantage in checking the president, given the powers granted to him as commander in chief and chief diplomat. Moreover, where the president and Congress are of the same party, the president feels free to propose measures he is confident will be supported by Congress, as happened during George W. Bush's first years in office. When a president enjoys such support from Congress, he is unlikely to consider vetoing congressional decisions, since such decisions are unlikely to challenge his own priorities. Instead, Congress will be dutiful and loyal; thus, as Charles Jones contends, "what the Founding Fathers separated" are often not separate.[81]

Not to be lost in importance are the differences in perspective and approach to change between these two institutions—the broad and comprehensive approach of the president as opposed to the more gradual approach of Congress. This can help us understand why some policies are accepted, while others are revised or dismissed as unworkable. Finally, it is helpful to assess how representative Congress is of society's concerns and what motivations and elements are necessary to make the institution more reflective of society.

In some ways, Congress, compared to the other federal institutions, is not only the largest but also the most complex and divisive of them. Its members act together only occasionally, most often during a major crisis that is recognized by all. For most policymakers, global climate change is not the sort of crisis that unites, despite the preponderance of evidence provided by the scientific community. Thus, as we have seen, Congress's behavior regarding climate change can be explained by several factors. The more we know about this institution, the easier it is to make sense of its diverse opinions and its ability, or inability, to collectively act on those opinions.

Notes

1. Charles O. Jones, *Separate but Equal Branches: Congress and the Presidency,* 2nd ed. (New York: Chatham, 1999), 30–31.

2. Clean Energy Jobs and American Power Act, S. 1733, 111th Congress, 1st session (2009).

3. Center for Climate and Energy Solutions, "111th Congress Climate Change Legislation," www.c2es.org/federal/congress/111.

4. "Republican Contract with America," www.c2es.org/federal/congress/111.

5. Aaron M. McCright and Riley E. Dunlap, "The Politicalization of Climate Change and Polarization in the American Public's Views of Global Warming, 2001–2010," *Sociological Quarterly* 52, no. 2 (Spring 2011): 155.

6. Dana Fisher, Philip Leifeld, and Yoko Iwaki, "Mapping the Ideological Networks of American Climate Politics," White Paper No. 2 (College Park: Center for Society and Environment, University of Maryland, 2012), http://cse.umd.edu/pdf/csewhitepaper2_MappingIdeologicalNetworks.pdf, 19.

7. Darren Samuelsohn, "Both Sides Gird for Bruising Senate Debate over EPA Amendment," *New York Times,* January 8, 2010, www.nytimes.com.

8. Center for Climate and Energy Solutions, "111th Congress Climate Change Legislation."

9. Senate Committee on Energy and Commerce, "Anti-Environmental Votes in the 112th Congress, 1st Session," http://democrats.energycommerce .house.gov/sites/default/files/image_uploads/Anti-EnvironmentVotes.pdf.

10. Evan Lehmann, "Huntsman Warns That GOP Can't Win the White House by Denying Climate Science," *New York Times,* September 8, 2011, www.nytimes.com/cwire/2011/09/08.

11. Brian Darling, "Want Stimulus? Reduce Regulations," Heritage Network, August 26, 2011, http://blog.heritage.org/2011/08/26/want-stimulus -reduce-regulation.

12. Fisher, Leifeld, and Iwaki, "Mapping the Ideological Networks of American Climate Politics," 18, 20.

13. Barry Rabe, "Can Congress Govern the Climate?" Research Brief no. 1 (New York: John Brademas Center for the Study of Congress, New York University, April 2007), 4–5.

14. Full-Year Continuing Appropriations Act, H.R. 1, 112th Congress, 1st session (2011).

15. Ibid.

16. League of Conservation Voters, "Scorecard: 2011 National Environmental Scorecard, 112th Congress, First Session," www.lcv.org/scorecard.

17. Energy Tax Prevention Act, H.R. 910, 112th Congress, 1st session (2011).

18. McConnell Amendment to SBIR/STTR Reauthorization Act of 2011, S.Amdt. 183 to S. 493, 112th Congress, 1st session (2011).

19. Civic Impulse, "Bill Overview of H.R. 1: Full-Year Continuing Appropriations Act, 2011," www.govtrack.us/congress.

20. Department of the Interior, Environment, and Related Agencies Appropriations Act, H.R. 2584, 112th Congress, 1st session (2012).

21. American Clean Energy Leadership Act, S. 1733, 111th Congress, 1st session (2009); see also Govtrack.us, "S. 1462 (111th): American Clean Energy Leadership Act," www.govtrack.us/congress/bills/111/s1733#overview (accessed April 16, 2013).

22. Clean Energy Partnership Act, S. 2729, 111th Congress, 1st session (2009).

23. Clean Energy Act, S. 2776, 111th Congress, 1st session (2009).

24. Carbon Limits and Energy for America's Renewal Act, S. 2877, 111th Congress, 1st session (2009).

25. Leslie Kaufman, "Republicans Seek Big Cuts in Environmental Rules," *New York Times,* July 27, 2011, www.nytimes.com/2011/07/28/science/earth.

26. Jennifer Loven, "Obama's First 100 Days in Office Putting Up the Numbers," *Virginian-Pilot,* April 30, 2009.

27. Geof Koss, "'Green' Funds Withering in Current Climate," *CQWeekly,* December 10, 2011, http://public.cq.com/docs/weeklyreport/weeklyreport-000003997655.html (accessed April 19, 2013).

28. Ibid.

29. Jane A. Leggett, "A U.S.-Centric Chronology of the International Climate Change Negotiations," Report for Congress (Washington, DC: Congressional Research Service, 2012).

30. Ibid.

31. Koss, "'Green' Funds Withering in Current Climate."

32. Fisher, *National Governance and the Global Climate Change Regime,* 114.

33. Energy Tax Prevention Act, H.R. 910, 112th Congress, 1st session (2011).

34. EPA Stationary Source Regulations Suspension Act, S. 231, 112th Congress, 1st session (2011).

35. Committee on Energy and Commerce Democrats, "The Anti-Environment Record of the 112th House of Representatives," November 14, 2012, http://democrats.energycommerce.house.gov/index.php?q=legislative-database-anti-environment&legislation=All&topic=All&statute=All&agency=All (accessed April 16, 2013).

36. Transparency in Regulatory Analysis of Impacts on the Nation Act, H.R. 2401, 111th Congress, 1st session (2011).

37. League of Conservation Voters, "Scorecard: 2011."

38. David A. Fahrenthold, "Environmental Groups at Odds over New Tack in Climate Fight," *Washington Post,* November 6, 2009, www.washingtonpost.com.

39. John M. Broder and Clifford Krauss, "Advocates of Climate Bill Scale Down Their Goals," *New York Times,* January 27, 2010, www.nytimes.com/2010/01/27/science/earth.

40. Juliet Eilperin and Steven Mufson, "Senators to Propose Abandoning Cap-and-Trade," *Washington Post,* February 27, 2010, www.washingtonpost.com.

41. James Hansen, "Cap and Fade," *New York Times,* December 7, 2009, www.nytimes.com/2009/12/07/opinion.

42. Roger Pielke Jr. and Daniel Sarewitz, "Wanted: Scientific Leadership on Climate," *Issues in Science and Technology* (Winter 2002–2003), www.issues .org/19.2/p_pielke.htm.

43. Safe Climate Act of 2006, H.R. 5642, 109th Congress, 2nd session (2006).

44. BeSpacific, "Waxman Introduces the Safe Climate Act of 2007," *GAO Report on Fiscal Year 2006,* March 20, 2007, www.bespacific.com/mt /archives/014322.html.

45. American Clean Energy and Security Act, H.R. 2454, 111th Congress, 1st session (2009).

46. Clean Energy Jobs and American Power Act (2009).

47. Ruth Walker, "Will Words Fail Us in Copenhagen?" *Christian Science Monitor,* November 29, 2009.

48. Susan Goldenberg, "US Climate Change Legislation Q&A: What Will Happen in 2010?" *The Guardian,* January 7, 2010, www.guardian.co.uk/environment /2010/jan/07.

49. David Yarnold, "Why Do Climate Deniers Hate America?" Environmental Defense Action Fund e-mail, February 12, 2010, as cited in Byron W. Daynes and Glen Sussman, "Global Warming: Environmental Crisis or Scientific Hoax?" in *Moral Controversies in American Politics,* 4th ed., edited by Raymond Tatalovich and Byron W. Daynes (Armonk, NY: M. E. Sharpe, 2011), 200.

50. Fahrenthold, "Environmental Groups at Odds."

51. "Beyond Copenhagen," *New York Times,* December 7, 2009, www.ny times.com/2009/12/07/opinion.

52. Charles Abbott, "House Bill Would Prevent EPA Regulating Carbon," Reuters, February 3, 2010, www.reuters.com.

53. *Massachusetts v. Environmental Protection Agency,* 549 US 497 (2007).

54. Fiscal 1996 Veterans Administration–Housing and Urban Development–Independent Agencies Appropriations Bill, H.R. 2099, 104th Congress, 1st session (1995).

55. League of Conservation Voters, "Scorecard: 1999 National Environment Scorecard," www.lcv.org/scorecard.

56. Ibid.

57. Rabe, "Can Congress Govern the Climate?" 3.

58. Center for Climate and Energy Solutions, "Legislation in the 109th Congress Related to Global Climate Change," www.c2es.org/federal/congress/109.

59. Ibid.

60. Center for Climate and Energy Solutions, "Legislation in the 110th Congress Related to Global Climate Change," www.c2es.org/federal/congress/110.

61. American Clean Energy and Security Act (2009).

62. Clean Energy Jobs and American Power Act (2009).

63. Eilperin and Mufson, "Senators to Propose Abandoning Cap-and-Trade."

64. Ibid.

65. Rabe, "Can Congress Govern the Climate?" 4.

66. John M. Broder, "Senate Poses Obstacles to Obama's Climate Pledge," *New York Times,* December 12, 2009, www.nytimes.com/2009/12/13/weekin review.

67. Ibid.

68. John M. Broder, "US to Set Emissions Target Before Climate Talks," *New York Times,* November 24, 2009, www.nytimes.com/2009/11/24/science/earth.

69. Broder, "Senate Poses Obstacles to Obama Pledge."

70. John M. Broder, "Senators Offer New Climate Proposals," *New York Times,* December 10, 2009, http://green.blogs.nytimes.com/2009/12/10.

71. Resolution Expressing the Sense of the Senate Regarding the Conditions for the United States Becoming a Signatory to Any International Agreement on Greenhouse Gas Emissions Under the United Nations Framework Convention on Climate Change, S.R. 98, 105th Congress, 1st session (1997).

72. Broder and Krauss, "Advocates of Climate Bill Scale Down Their Goals."

73. Evan Lehmann et al., "House Republicans Fire White House Advisers As Frenzied Budget Debate Continues," *New York Times,* February 18, 2011, www.nytimes.com/cwire.

74. Emily Vehle, "Congress Can't Kill Advisory Posts, Obama Declares in Signing Statement," *New York Times,* April 18, 2011, www.nytimes.com/gwire /2011/04/18.

75. Robert Neubecker, "Hot Seat," *New Republic,* February 4, 2010.

76. Jones, *Separate but Equal Branches,* 60–61.

77. Barack Obama, "Address Before a Joint Session of Congress on the State of the Union," January 24, 2012, online by John Woolley and Gerhard Peters, *The American Presidency Project,* www.presidency.ucsb.edu/ws/index .php?pid=99000.

78. Henrik Selin and Stacy D. VanDeveer. "US Climate Change Politics and Policymaking," *Wiley Interdisciplinary Reviews: Climate Change* 2, no. 1 (2011), http://people.bu.edu/selin/publications/SelinVanDeveerWileyReview2011.pdf.

79. Barry Rabe, "Contested Federalism and American Climate Policy," *The Journal of Federalism* 41, no. 3 (2011): 494.

80. Rabe, "Can Congress Govern the Climate?" 8–9. For additional detail, see also Rabe's book *Statehouse and Greenhouse* as well as his chapter "Second Generation Climate Policies in the American States: Proliferation, Diffusion, and Regionalization" in Selin and VanDeveer, *Changing Climates in North American Politics.*

81. Jones, *Separate but Equal Branches,* 59.

4

Presidential Leadership from Truman to Obama

Since the mid–twentieth century, the US presidency, from Harry Truman to Barack Obama, has exhibited three major responses to environmentalism—protection of the environment, cautious behavior, and an anti-environmental agenda. During this time, threats to the environment have become increasingly prominent, including air and water pollution, stratospheric ozone depletion, loss of biodiversity, and climate change.

Although climate change was not so much an issue of concern to early modern presidents, air pollution has long been of interest to the public health sector as the United States has become more urbanized, industrialized, and sensitive to national and global health conditions. For instance, in 1930, sixty-three persons died in Belgium as a result of a thermal inversion,[1] whereas in 1948 in Donora, Pennsylvania, twenty persons died because of polluted air.[2] In 1952 Britain saw an even worse disaster as 1,600 persons succumbed to the London fog.[3]

Although members of the scientific community responded first to the air pollution situation, publishing their research about the warming impact of burning fossil fuels, the political response has lagged well behind. This chapter discusses the role of the US presidency in addressing climate change, but first it is important to explore how presidents addressed air pollution.

From Air Pollution to Climate Change:
Truman to Carter

As a result of domestic and international concern regarding air pollution, Harry Truman, in 1950, became the first modern president to address the problem. He organized the US Technical Conference on Air Pollution and invited those in the United States who were working in areas related to air pollution to share ideas about how to reduce air pollution.[4]

Truman's successor, Dwight Eisenhower, also paid some attention to air pollution. In a special message to Congress as well as in his State of the Union address in January 1955, he made a point of increasing funding for research on the public health consequences of air pollution.[5] Congress responded in 1955 by passing the Air Pollution Control Act—the first federal legislation dealing with this issue. Though Eisenhower did sign this bill, it was limited in a number of important ways, in that it put the responsibility for enforcing the law not on the federal government but on individual states and municipalities.

Next in the presidency, John Kennedy made seven references to air pollution in major speeches from 1961 to 1963. Six of these references were made to Congress, including one in his 1962 State of the Union address.[6] That same year, in a special message to Congress on "protecting the consumer interest," Kennedy laid out his plan to have the Department of Commerce and the Department of Health, Education, and Welfare consult with the automobile industry regarding changes that could be made to reduce car accidents and lessen the "pollution of the air we breathe."[7] In an address to Congress in February 1963, Kennedy stated: "In the light of the known damage caused by polluted air, both to our health and to our economy, it is imperative that greater emphasis be given to the control of air pollution by communities, States and the Federal Government."[8] In the same speech, he referred to the need to control air pollution and preserve environmental health as well.

In an important legislative response to Kennedy's concerns about polluted air, the Clean Air Act of 1963, which incorporated federal governmental powers to control air pollution, was passed by Congress and signed into law by Lyndon Johnson, forty-seven days after Kennedy's assassination. This legislation set emission standards for industry and other stationary sources, but did not include standards for controlling pollution from automobiles and trucks. However, a foundation was laid that would result in later amendments to the Clean Air Act in 1965, 1966, 1967, and 1969.

Air pollution was a particular concern for Lyndon Johnson. As he pointed out in 1965:

> Pollution now is one of the most pervasive problems of our society. With our numbers increasing and with our increasing urbanization and industrialization, the flow of pollutants to our air, soil, and waters is increasing. This increase is so rapid that our present efforts in managing pollution are barely enough to stay even, surely not enough to make the improvements that are needed. . . . I intend to give high priority to increasing the numbers and quality of the scientists and engineers working on problems related to the control and management of pollution.[9]

Air pollution was so important to Johnson, in fact, that he addressed it again in his January 1967 State of the Union address, putting forth an idea of establishing "regional air sheds" to monitor the degree of pollution throughout the nation.[10] He followed this up later in the month with a special message to Congress indicating he was intent on doing something about polluted air, since it "corrodes machinery. It defaces buildings. It may shorten the life of whatever it touches—and it touches everything."[11]

Johnson's successor, Richard Nixon, saw clean air as one of three points of focus on his conservation agenda. In his 1970 State of the Union address, for instance, he indicated that "clean air, clean water, open spaces—these should once again be the birthright of every American. If we act now, they can be."[12] And it was on the last day of 1970 that Richard Nixon signed a new Clean Air Act to amend its previous incarnation.[13] Nixon stated on signing the bill that it was "the most important piece of legislation, in my opinion, dealing with the problem of clean air that we have this year and the most important in our history." He later added: "I think that 1970 will be known as the year of the beginning, in which we really began to move on the problems of clean air and clean water and open spaces for the future generations of America."[14]

As a result of the Watergate scandal, Nixon resigned and Gerald Ford assumed the presidency. During Ford's presidency, there was somewhat of a setback in advancing interest in reducing air pollution, although he did address a special session of Congress in 1976 to urge the passage of Clean Air Act amendments that would permit further use of coal, without sacrificing clean air standards. In addition, Ford supported the amendments that would allow for increased vehicle efficiency, without increasing the cost to consumers. His purpose in proposing these amendments, however, was primarily to reduce energy costs rather than to protect the environment.[15] His concern with the 1976 Clean Air Act amendments, as they stood, was that many of them, he feared, might lead to a "no growth policy" in the United States. And since his primary concern was to ensure industrial growth rather than clean air, he threatened to veto any legislation that might interfere with such growth. As he stated: "This country got where it is today with all the material benefits, all the moral and spiritual benefits, by having a progressive, forward-looking growth policy, and that's the kind of a country I want in the future."[16]

Following prior presidents' concerns regarding clean air, it was Jimmy Carter who first laid the groundwork for Americans' awareness of global warming and climate change. His concern with the global environment led him to become the first president to think in terms of interconnected climate systems. When Carter assumed the presidency, he was ready to initiate measures to protect both the domestic and the global environment. During his first year in office, Carter announced to Congress in an environmental message that he intended to organize the first comprehensive study of the global environment. As he stated: "Environmental problems do not stop at national boundaries. In the past decade, we and other nations have to recognize the urgency of international efforts to protect our common environment."[17] He then asked the Council on Environmental Quality, the Department of State, the Environmental Protection Agency (EPA), the National Science Foundation, and the National Oceanic and Atmospheric Administration to undertake a one-year study (to extend through the year 2000) that would take account of changes in the world's population, in its natural resources, and in the environment.[18]

The result of this study was the *Global 2000 Report to the President,* in which an entire chapter was devoted to climate change.[19] The report warned that "some human activities, especially those resulting in releases of carbon dioxide into the atmosphere, are known to have the potential to affect the world's climate." Further, the report concluded that "many experts . . . feel that changes on a scale likely to affect the environment and the economy of large regions of the world are not only possible but probable in the next 25 to 50 years."[20] President Carter also was the first president to mention climate change in any presidential speech. In his message to Congress on science and technology, for example, he indicated that "advances that can be made in understanding climate change, in predicting it—and perhaps in influencing it beneficially—will be of enormous help to us and the rest of the world."[21]

Yet in his efforts to resolve the energy crisis, Carter also advocated increased coal production, which may have compromised his efforts to reduce greenhouse gases. In April 1977, in presenting his national energy plan to a joint session of Congress, Carter indicated that he wished to increase US coal production by more than two-thirds, to more than 1 billion tons a year, along with reducing energy consumption by more than 2 percent and reducing gasoline consumption by 10 percent. He also wanted to use solar energy in more than 2.5 million US homes.[22] Despite encouraging the use of coal, by far the most important contribution Carter made regarding global climate change was the production of the *Global 2000 Report,* which became the founding document for climate change action in the United States for the years following his presidency.

The Dynamics of US Climate Change Policy: Reagan to Obama

Though Jimmy Carter's *Global 2000 Report* set the foundation for further research on climate change, his successor, Ronald Reagan, made few contributions to promote continued support for climate research. Although Reagan signed the 1988 Global Climate Protection Act, his administration failed in its responsibility to make a substantive effort to stabilize the "concentration of greenhouse gases in the atmosphere."[23] His priorities tended more toward economic development rather than environmental protection.

President Reagan's most significant action regarding climate change was his signing of the Montreal Protocol on Substances That Deplete the Ozone Layer in 1989, but that protocol had little to do with climate change, since its focus was exclusively on depletion of the ozone layer. Moreover, some of the personnel whom Reagan recruited for his administration were anti-environmental, such as Interior Secretary James Watt and EPA director Anne Burford. When Reagan's ideology conflicted with climate change science, it was his ideology that took precedence. Unlike Carter, who responded to the findings of climate change science by expanding research, Reagan "attempted to reduce the climate research effort," paying little attention to the science.[24]

After Reagan's two terms as president, the Republican Party was successful in retaining the White House as a result of the 1988 presidential election. In the 1988 campaign, George H. W. Bush announced that he would be an environmentalist in the tradition of Theodore Roosevelt.[25] Environmental protection was given a much higher priority in his administration than in the two terms of Reagan. During Bush's campaign for the presidency, he stated that clean air was an important item on his agenda. Consequently, in 1990 he "built a coalition of environmentalists, business and industry, and government officials that eventually resulted in the passage of the clean air act amendments."[26] During the first half of his term in office, he used the resources of the White House to ensure passage of the 1990 Clean Air Act amendments— amendments that had been debated for more than a decade. As he indicated: "I have worked actively to break the legislative stalemate which has precluded early action on clean air."[27] This was an important accomplishment, because the 1970 Clean Air Act, which was renewed in 1977, had languished during the presidency of Reagan, who refused to take action and support its renewal.

In the area of environmental diplomacy, however, Bush had difficulty building an environmental legacy. In the summer of his first year in office, for example, it appears that the president was well aware of the dangers to the global climate posed by human activities. As he stated at the 1989 Paris Economic Summit, there were "serious threats to the atmosphere, which could lead to future climate changes."[28] Yet when he had the opportunity to offer leadership to combat global warming in 1990, and again in 1992, he failed to do so. At the 1990 World Climate Conference, Bush refused to sign a carbon dioxide emission reduction agreement, making the United States the only industrialized country to fail to do so.[29] Instead, he submitted to pressure from political and business interests that were encouraging him to reject inclusion of the United States in the agreement.

Two years later, at the United Nations Conference on Environment and Development in Rio de Janeiro, known as the Earth Summit, Bush was in attendance for three days and once again had the opportunity to demonstrate climate leadership. But again he submitted to pressure at home, making the United States, as the *New York Times* described it, a "spoiler" to the conference's climate change treaty.[30] And although

Bush did sign it, making the United States the "world's first industrialized nation to ratify a treaty on climate change," he did so only after its goals and timetables were made voluntary rather than mandatory.[31] Bush justified his firm stance on the treaty by stating that "the ultimate objective of the Convention is to stabilize greenhouse gas concentrations (not emissions) in the atmosphere at a level that would prevent dangerous human interference with the climate system."[32] He further stressed the need not to hamper economic growth with extra mandates. In an address delivered to the Intergovernmental Panel on Climate Change, the president indicated that the world needed to move "beyond the practice of command, control, and compliance toward a new kind of environmental cooperation and toward an emphasis on pollution prevention rather than mere mitigation and litigation."[33]

As far as his environmental legacy is concerned, Bush understood the importance of making an effort to join with others in combating climate change. In his first year in office, in 1989 during a speech in the Netherlands, he asserted: "Concerns like the environment—global warming, acid rain and pollution of the world's oceans: these are problems that know no borders, that no line on a map has the power to stop. And pollution crosses continents and oceans, and it's time for nations to join forces in common defense of our environment. The United States will do its part." He indicated further that these were changes that would ensure that "every American, in the space of one generation, will breathe clean air." And he announced that he would make an effort to work with both Poland and Hungary to "combat their pollution problems." He concluded his speech by suggesting that the next step was clear: "We must work together, take concerted action to combat this common problem—clean up our environment for ourselves and for our children."[34]

Bush's primary shortcomings regarding climate change came in the area of foreign affairs, which is somewhat surprising given that he had spent much of his career dealing with international affairs. More important, however, his stance on foreign affairs made the United States, then the number one emitter of greenhouse gases, resistant to consent to binding emission restrictions, which seriously impeded the effort to resolve the problem of global climate change.

After twelve years of Republican dominance of the White House, Democrats in general, and environmentalists in particular, were elated with the election of Bill Clinton to the presidency in 1992. Although Clinton lacked environmental credentials, he did select Tennessee Democratic senator Al Gore, who had a proven pro-environment record, as his vice president. Clinton also appointed Carol Browner to head the EPA and Arizona senator Bruce Babbitt to serve as secretary of interior, both of whom had a positive record of environmental accomplishments. Clinton's environmental agenda was slowed during his first term as Republicans captured both chambers of Congress in the 1994 midterm election, making it difficult for him to forcefully encourage measures through Congress and succeed in international environmental affairs.

Clinton's effort to address global warming and climate change also faced setbacks as Republicans, some Democrats, and the fossil fuel industry opposed his efforts to address greenhouse gas emissions. The Clean Air Act was one of the critical acts under attack from the Republican Congress. Clinton found it necessary to "lead by veto" in order to protect critical environmental laws. Many of his thirty-seven regular vetoes during his two terms in office were used to protect the environment from the Republican Congress, which sought to undercut the advances that he and the Democrats had made.[35]

Whereas George H. W. Bush had supported the global warming accords (with revisions) that resulted from the Earth Summit in 1992, Bill Clinton did not capitalize on this progress. As Elizabeth Kolbert asserted, "Under Bill Clinton . . . the U.S. took no meaningful action to reduce its emissions."[36] Against the backdrop of the Earth Summit, Clinton stated in September 1997 that "when the nations of the world gather again in December [1997] in Kyoto for the UN Climate Change Conference, all of us, developed and developing countries, must seize the opportunity to turn back the clock on greenhouse gas emissions so that we can leave a healthy planet to our children."[37]

Clinton, Gore, and others in the administration put a lot of effort into recruiting and encouraging nations to support the Kyoto Protocol. US leadership was important in soliciting this support. Clinton sent Gore to the negotiations with the primary mission to encourage European countries and energy producers and coal users to accept a "workable middle ground."[38]

The Kyoto Protocol was intended to bring stability to greenhouse gases in the atmosphere by setting firm emission limits. It was the first effort to bind nations together to reduce greenhouse gases globally. It divided nations into groups based on their emission levels. Those that presumably emitted the most greenhouse gases were obligated to reduce their emissions by 2012. Nations that emitted smaller quantities of greenhouse gases were not restricted. The primary target for reduction was carbon dioxide, the largest component of greenhouse gas emissions. Five other gases were also included: methane, nitrous oxide, hydrofluorocarbons, perfluorocarbons, and sulphur hexafluoride. Major developed nations were to reduce their combined emissions by 5.2 percent by 2012 compared to their 1990 levels.

These negotiations were not easy. Under the Clinton administration, the United States showed flexibility, allowing for developing countries to be excluded from some of the emission cuts. Because of this approach, the *Washington Times* reported that "Mr. Clinton's Kyoto proposal was immediately attacked as too harsh by skeptics and too modest by believers."[39] As Clinton would later say in 2005: "I like the Kyoto agreement; I helped write it, and I signed it." But he admitted that "it was not a perfect agreement, and there were criticisms of it at the time," two in particular:

> First, that Kyoto would hurt the economies of the developed nations by chaining them to greenhouse gas reductions that were not achievable, and certain to lead to top down bureaucratic solutions that would wreck economic growth. The second was that Kyoto did not include developing nations, which were already large greenhouse gas emitters [and] which, given present rates of growth, would become larger than even the United States, the worst offender, in the next decades.[40]

In responding to the two criticisms, Clinton indicated: "The second criticism was fair; the first one was just flat wrong. It was factually wrong. And we know from every passing year, we get more and more objective data that if we had a serious disciplined effort to apply on a large scale [to] existing clean energy and energy-conservation technologies, we could meet and surpass the Kyoto targets easily in a way that would strengthen, not weaken our economies."[41] Despite dissatisfaction from European countries, however, flexibility by the United States arguably allowed for the Kyoto Protocol to be accepted.[42]

Despite his support for the protocol, Clinton faced opposition from the Republican-controlled Senate, as well as from Democrats representing fossil fuel states and from the automobile industry. In 1997 the Senate voted 95 to 0 in favor of the Byrd-Hagel Resolution, which opposed adherence to the Kyoto Protocol unless developing countries like China and India were included. As Cass Sunstein noted, this Senate resolution "asked President Clinton not to agree to limits on green-

house gas emissions if the agreement would injure the economic interests of the United States." The Senate also added that "any exemption
for Developing Country Parties is inconsistent with the need for global
action on climate change and is environmentally flawed."[43] As a result,
the president never sent the protocol to the full Senate for ratification.

Despite President Clinton's difficulty with Congress, he continued
to express his support for the Kyoto Protocol, which he saw as an important step in addressing the increasing levels of greenhouse gas
emissions. Though he worked with Russian president Vladimir Putin
in producing a joint statement on the issue of global warming and climate change, it was not Clinton's involvement that convinced Putin to
sign the Kyoto Protocol; it was Putin's desire to join the World Trade
Organization (WTO).[44] Putin indicated that he would sign the protocol
if he could be guaranteed European support for WTO membership. As
Putin stated: "We are for the Kyoto process. . . . We support it, although we do have some concerns over the obligations that we will
have to assume. The European Union has met us halfway in negotiations on the WTO, and it could not help but have a positive effect on
our attitude toward ratification of the Kyoto protocol."[45]

As a result, the Russian Federation eventually ratified the Kyoto
Protocol, on February 16, 2005, making it the fifty-fifth country to do
so. While 191 countries, in addition to the European Union, eventually
signed the protocol, numbers say little about how many of those countries have complied with their obligations under Kyoto. Moreover,
some of the nations that emit large quantities of greenhouse gases, like
China and India, have no obligations at all under the protocol.[46]

This raises the question as to how successful the Kyoto Protocol
has been in responding to global climate change. Supporters would
say, as noted by Miranda Schreurs, that "the Protocol did set into place
new institutions for addressing greenhouse gas emissions both nationally and internationally (e.g., the Clean Development Mechanism,
Joint Implementation, emissions trading) and helped to raise awareness
in many parts of the world about climate change."[47] As mentioned, nations were divided into groups based on emission levels and were collectively bound to different reduction targets. The fifteen states that
were European Union members at the time that the Kyoto Protocol
was adopted agreed to an 8 percent reduction of greenhouse gases by
2012 compared to 1990 levels, based on the provision in the protocol
that allows nations to buy emission credits from those that can surpass
their reduction targets. The overall goal of the protocol was that all

participants collectively reduce their greenhouse gas emissions by 5.2 percent by 2012 compared to 1990 levels.[48]

Yet if we look at government reports on the effectiveness of Kyoto, there are clearly some problems with the protocol. The Carbon Dioxide Information Analysis Center reported that from 1751 until 2010, "approximately 227 billion tons of carbon have been released to the atmosphere from consumption of fossil fuels and cement production. Half of these emissions have occurred since the mid-1970s. The 2007 global fossil-fuel carbon emission estimate, 8,365 million metric tons of carbon, represents an all-time high and a 1.7% increase from 2006."[49] For the period from 1990 to 2008, as shown in Table 4.1, clearly China and the United States are by far the largest producers of carbon dioxide (CO_2) emissions.

Based on data for 2009 and 2010 regarding global and national preliminary estimates of CO_2 emissions from fossil fuel combustion and cement manufacturing, Tom Boden and T. J. Blasing concluded that "2010 was by far a record year for CO_2 emissions. Globally 9,139 Teragrams of oxidized carbon (Tg-C) were emitted from these sources. A teragram is a million metric tons. . . . Converted to carbon dioxide, so as to include the mass of the oxygen molecules, this amounts to over 33.5 billion metric tons of carbon dioxide. . . . Much of the 5.9% global increase from 2009 to 2010 is due to increased emissions from the world's largest fossil-fuel emitter, the People's Republic of China, where emissions rose 10%."[50] Boden and Blasing also indicated that CO_2 emissions for 2010 within the United States had risen 4 percent over the emissions estimate for 2009. They added that "the record year for the United States was 2007 with an estimated emissions of 1,589 Tg-C. The 2010 total is about 94% of that value, reflecting economic conditions."[51]

Kyoto's failures did not discourage President Clinton from maintaining his focus on resolving the climate change problem; in fact, he became even more assertive. This was not surprising given Clinton's tendency to advocate for social change in a variety of different areas. He made references to climate change in every State of the Union address from 1997 to 2000, with each message directing more attention to climate change than the previous one. In his last State of the Union address, for 2000, he stated: "The greatest environmental challenge of the new century is global warming. The scientists tell us the 1990's were the hottest decade of the entire millennium. If we fail to reduce the emission of greenhouse gases, deadly heat waves and droughts will

Table 4.1 Carbon Dioxide Emissions by Top Emitters, 1990–2008 (thousand kilotons)

	1990	1992	1994	1996	1998	2000	2002	2004	2006	2008
China	246.07	269.60	305.82	346.31	332.43	340.52	369.42	528.82	641.45	703.19
United States	487.94	487.60	522.72	534.35	544.91	551.24	543.78	556.38	551.48	546.10
India	69.06	78.36	86.49	100.22	107.19	118.67	122.68	134.66	150.44	174.27
Russia	222.07	175.30	166.90	151.13	155.35	153.72	160.30	166.96	170.87	n/a
Japan	109.47	112.37	117.42	120.58	115.92	121.96	121.68	125.97	123.18	120.82
Germany	92.83	90.36	92.40	89.55	83.21	83.09	82.85	81.19	78.67	n/a
Canada	45.01	46.76	45.45	46.79	47.89	53.74	52.18	55.59	54.87	54.41
Iran	22.72	24.75	29.67	28.66	31.62	33.92	37.52	44.25	49.23	53.84
United Kingdom	57.02	58.75	56.38	58.07	55.41	54.37	53.19	54.57	54.33	52.29
South Korea	24.38	28.66	34.04	40.10	36.38	43.25	46.56	48.23	47.08	50.92
European Union	413.43	412.52	398.63	417.74	406.95	388.88	394.52	405.07	403.71	390.68

Source: World Bank, "CO$_2$ Emissions Data," http://data.worldbank.org/indicator/EN.ATM.CO2E.KT/countries?display=default.
Notes: Carbon dioxide emissions from consumption of fossil fuels in gas, liquid, and solid form. Data for Russia and Germany for 2008 are not available.

become more frequent, coastal areas will flood, and economies will be disrupted. That is going to happen, unless we act."[52]

Bill Clinton's presidency was important for the development of climate change as a legitimate environmental issue. Still, similar to most people during the 1990s, he used the terms "climate change" and "global warming" interchangeably throughout his presidency. He referred to "global warming" 240 times from 1993 until the end of his second term in 2001.[53] During the same period he referred to "climate change" 284 times.[54]

Finally, Clinton's influence on the Democratic Party is evident when comparing the party's 1992 and 1996 platforms. The former merely stated: "The United States must become a leader, not an impediment, in the fight against global warming. We should join our European allies in agreeing to limit carbon dioxide emissions to 1990 levels by the year 2000."[55] In contrast, the latter platform was more detailed and focused on the accomplishments of the Clinton-Gore administration in its efforts to address global climate change: "After years in which Republicans neglected the global environment, the Clinton Administration has made America a leader in the fight to meet environmental challenges that transcend national borders and require global cooperation. . . . We will seek a strong international agreement to further reduce greenhouse gas emissions worldwide and protect our global climate."[56]

In the disputed election of 2000, George W. Bush won the presidency, a political result that would eventually have profound implications for environmental policy in general, and for global warming and climate change policy in particular.[57] Two months into his presidency, Bush renounced the Kyoto Protocol, arguing that it would have a negative impact on the US economy and jobs and that the agreement neglected to include developing countries, especially China and India—two countries that appeared to be major polluters.

The decision by the president to refuse to cooperate with international partners in reducing greenhouse gas emissions alienated much of the world against the United States. Bush preferred a unilateral approach, to go it alone, with only one major industrialized democracy, Australia, supporting his approach. Bush's approach not only rejected the Kyoto Protocol, but also rejected the legitimacy of the Clean Air Act. Bush sought to replace the act, which had been in existence since the Nixon administration, with his Clear Skies Initiative.[58] Clear Skies would set limits on nitrogen oxide (which creates smog) and sulfur dioxide (the primary cause of acid rain), and would limit mercury by 70 percent by 2018. But importantly, it would not set uniform national standards for clean air, unlike the Clean Air Act, which forced polluting industries to comply with the law.[59] Instead, Clear Skies would allow those polluting industries to buy and sell pollution credits, essentially allowing them to pollute freely among themselves.[60] Critics of Clear Skies, like former vice president Al Gore, argued that it "actually allows more toxic mercury, nitrogen oxide and sulfur pollution than if we enforced the laws on the books today. It ought to be called the dirty skies initiative."[61]

With the United States, a major producer of greenhouse gases, isolated from its global allies, Bush's options were limited. With Britain, he tried to persuade the prime minister to accept an alternative, market-based voluntary approach to addressing greenhouse gas emissions. With Japan, he was willing to share "clean energy technology" to power automobiles, homes, and businesses.[62] With Germany, he sought to advance "climate science" and develop "effective national tools for policy action" as well as take joint action to "raise the efficiency of the energy sector."[63] With Australia, the relationship appeared stronger, with the president stating: "Australia and the United States look forward to working actively and constructively with all countries at the U.N. Climate Change Conference in Indonesia in December," toward "stabilizing greenhouse gas concentrations in the atmosphere at a level that would prevent dangerous anthropogenic interference with the climate system."[64] Finally there was the US joint statement issued with both Mexico and Canada whereby the three countries agreed to exchange "information and explor[e] opportunities for joint collaboration to further reduce barriers to expanding clean energy technologies, especially carbon dioxide capture and storage to mitigate greenhouse gas emissions."[65]

Although he will not be remembered as a leading advocate for the environment, George W. Bush knew how to appeal to those who supported his position, with whom he spoke frequently. In at least two State of the Union addresses, he mentioned climate change. In his 2007 State of the Union address, he talked about the need for increased reliance on alternative fuels, and the need also to reduce gasoline usage and restructure oil production in an "environmentally sensitive way." He stated that these measures would make the United States less dependent on oil and help to "confront the serious challenge of global climate change."[66] That same year, in a speech at a meeting on energy and climate change, Bush had this to say: "Energy security and climate change are two of the great challenges of our time. The United States takes these challenges seriously. . . . Our guiding principle is clear: We must lead the world to produce fewer greenhouse gas emissions, and we must do it in a way that does not undermine economic growth or prevent nations from delivering greater prosperity for their people."[67]

In his 2008 State of the Union address, Bush was more specific. He suggested that the United States needed to develop "technologies that can generate coal power while capturing carbon emissions," "emissions-free nuclear power," and "battery technology and renewable fuels to power the cars and trucks of the future." He also encouraged development of an "international clean technology fund" to help such nations as India and China to make greater use of clean energy, and surprisingly recommended that the United States should "complete an international agreement that has the potential to slow, stop, and eventually reverse the growth of greenhouse gases." Bush summarized his position by asserting that "the United States is committed to . . . confronting global climate change and the best way to meet these goals is for America to continue leading the way toward the development of cleaner and more energy efficient technology."[68]

The words he spoke were directed to the need to contain climate change and at first glance one would think he was a champion of the movement to stop global warming, but his statements did not fool political leaders at the state and local levels. A 2005 University of Vermont analysis found that as a result of the lack of federal leadership from the White House and Congress, a number of states and localities on their own were making an effort to reduce greenhouse gas emissions following standards set forth by the Kyoto Protocol.[69] During Bush's second term in office, "mayors from 158 American cities . . . formally acknowledged climate change as a major concern" and at least sixteen states, led by California governor Arnold Schwarzenegger, were making efforts to "reduce greenhouse gas emissions to the 1990 level or below."[70]

One of the more intriguing aspects of global climate change as it played out during the administration of George W. Bush was the politicization of climate science and at times the rejection of the research findings of the scientific community.[71] The Bush administration not only challenged the scientific outcomes, but also at times revised the scientific reports to support the White House position. According to the *New York Times*, Philip Cooney, then chief of staff for the White

House Council on Environmental Quality, "removed or adjusted descriptions of climate research that government scientists and their supervisors, including some senior Bush administration officials, had already approved. In many cases, the changes appeared in final reports." It was further reported that many of the changes were as subtle as inserting such phrases as "significant and fundamental" before the word "uncertainties." This tended to make the reports appear to be more scientifically uncertain in tone.[72] A number of critics accused the Bush administration of "deliberate and widespread distortion of climate science."[73] This was clearly further than any other president had gone in advocating their own approach to climate change.

After eight years of Republican control of the White House, the environmental community was encouraged once again when Democrat Barack Obama won the 2008 presidential election. Against a backdrop of economic distress at home and two wars abroad, global climate change was on the agenda of the new administration. In the election campaign, both Republican senator John McCain and Democratic senator Barack Obama agreed that climate change was a critical issue, and both supported strategies to encourage clean energy and reduction of emissions in the United States.[74] This represented a marked departure from the policies of the George W. Bush administration. The 2008 election of Barack Obama was highly welcomed by environmentalists who had been looking for a president willing to advocate policies to limit climate change. During his campaign, Obama had promised "a new chapter in America's leadership on climate change."[75]

The new president moved quickly on several environmental fronts. On March 28, 2009, for example, he announced that he would launch a major economies forum on energy and climate and invite delegates from the seventeen largest economies. The forum took place in Italy in July 2009. Obama announced at that time that he and the delegates had agreed to set a goal to "limit global warming to levels recommended by scientists" and that a commitment from emerging economies—including China—"to work for limiting global warming" had been secured, despite the fact that no particular target dates were set for these countries to fulfill their commitments.[76]

By the end of his first year in office, however, little meaningful progress had been made domestically on climate change. President Obama tried to convince Congress to agree to an energy and climate bill, but was not successful. A major reason for this was spelled out in the "2011 Environmental Scorecard," drawn up by the League of Conservation Voters, which suggested that the 2011 House of Representatives was the most "anti-environmental in our nation's history"—and had appeared just as resistant to Obama's efforts prior to 2011.[77]

The president's "cap and trade" legislation, first introduced in February 2009, failed to win congressional passage. The proposed system would place a nationwide limit on the amount of carbon dioxide emitted, while allowing industries to trade emissions permits in order to reach the overall goal. Similar proposals had been successfully implemented as recently as the 1990s, when George H. W. Bush sought to limit sulfur dioxide emissions to reduce acid rain.[78] Opposition to this "cap and trade" proposal emerged, however, because carbon dioxide was one of the pollutants that would be regulated under the program. The revised proposal was branded by opponents as "cap and tax." Given the recession, opponents were successful in stalling the bill's progress.[79]

Confronting such opposition in Congress against climate change legislation led Obama to begin stressing other policy options related to climate change domestically. The president chose to focus his efforts on clean energy legislation to avoid further confrontations with lawmakers. But this time he chose to rely on his own presidential authority. In 2010, for example, Obama signed a memorandum on improving fuel economy standards, a positive step forward in reducing greenhouse gas emissions.[80]

In the 2012 State of the Union address, Obama hinted at the strength of the Republican opposition to an all-inclusive climate change: "The differences in this chamber may be too deep right now to pass a comprehensive plan to fight climate change. But there's no reason why Congress shouldn't at least set a clean energy standard that creates a market for innovation. So far, you haven't acted. Well, tonight, I will."[81]

That same year, as commander in chief, Obama announced during a press conference that the US Navy, Air Force, and Marine Corps had been testing vehicles using a mixture of biofuels to reduce greenhouse gas emissions from military transports. He also praised Navy secretary Ray Mabus for setting a goal of "using 50 percent alternative fuels in all planes, vehicles, and ships in the next 10 years."[82] President Obama used this press conference to encourage action on a clean energy and climate bill that would further national security, economic stability, and protection of the environment. He encouraged leaders to "come together to pass comprehensive energy and climate legislation that [would] foster new energy, new industries, create millions of jobs, protect our planet, and help us become more energy independent."[83]

Obama has done other things to at least keep the issue of climate change visible domestically. As chief executive, for example, he issued two executive orders[84] that structured the National Economic Council and the Domestic Policy Council to include the position of assistant to the president for energy and climate change. Carol Browner, a career-long environmentalist who had first served under Bill Clinton, filled the post.

Moreover, as a result of constant resistance from the Republican Congress, Obama has placed increasing responsibility in the hands of the Environmental Protection Agency and its director, Lisa Jackson. With authority received from the 2007 Supreme Court case *Massachusetts v. Environmental Protection Agency*,[85] the administrator of the EPA is required under the Clean Air Act to set the emissions standards for any "air pollutant" from cars or any motor vehicle engines that contributes to pollution and may endanger public health. This provides Obama a way to enforce air quality if he so chooses.

Still, he has not always fully supported the EPA's actions or advice. Obama chose, for example, to keep in effect the Bush ozone standards until 2013, which EPA director Jackson considered legally indefensible given the available scientific evidence.[86] Obama also left intact the old smog regulations rather than move ahead, as the EPA had recommended, with stricter standards. Jackson had advocated reducing the ozone level from 75 parts per billion to 60–70 parts per billion. Hundreds of counties in the United States would have been out of compliance with the law had Obama consented. Moreover, Republicans complained that the ozone reduction effort would cost billions of dollars and a loss of thousands of jobs. Obama backtracked and rejected the EPA's advice, a move that may have enhanced his reelection efforts, but at the expense of disappointing many environmentalists. As John Broder wrote in the *New York Times,* "Somehow we need to get back the president we thought we elected in 2008."[87]

In the international arena, Obama has been more assertive. In May 2009, while visiting Canada, he and Prime Minister Stephen Harper announced in a joint press conference that they would collaborate in an effort to "advance carbon reduction technologies" and to "develop an electric grid that can deliver clean and renewable energy in the U.S. and Canada."[88] In July of the same year, Obama met with Mexican president Felipe Calderón and the two agreed to strengthen "bilateral cooperation by establishing the U.S.-Mexico Bilateral Framework on Clean Energy and Climate Change."[89]

Together with other nations, President Obama has had several opportunities to demonstrate strong leadership. He has not always taken these opportunities, however, nor always followed through on those he has. In his first speech before the United Nations General Assembly, for example, Obama emphasized the domestic programs that the United States was and would be developing to itself "move from a bystander to a leader in international climate negotiations."[90] Though in his rhetoric Obama tried to signal to the world that the United States would no longer impede progress in producing a climate agreement, resistance from Congress has prevented progress.[91]

Obama had a real opportunity to exert international leadership against climate change during the 2009 Copenhagen Conference, but he did not arrive until near its conclusion. His address would, nevertheless, have to be considered relatively successful, given its strong message and the potential for goodwill and progress that existed among the delegates from the 194 nations participating in the two-week summit sponsored by the United Nations. Obama indicated that "The time for talk is over. This is the bottom line: We can embrace this accord, take a substantial step forward, continue to refine it and build upon its foundation. . . . Or we can choose delay, falling back into the same divisions that have stood in the way of action for years. And we will be back having the same stale arguments . . . all while the danger of climate change grows until it is irreversible."[92] As Elizabeth Rosenthal noted, in an article for the *New York Times,* the delegates who attended Copenhagen became convinced that the United States was now serious about climate change, which "set off a flurry of diplomacy around the globe."[93]

President Obama saw the signing of the Copenhagen Accord as groundbreaking, because it was the first time in history that all of "the world's major economies have come together to accept their responsibility to confront the threat of climate change."[94] Despite Obama's optimism, however, others saw it differently. Radoslav Dimitrov, European Union delegate to the UN Climate Change negotiations since 2009, was among those who originally had high hopes for the massive Copenhagen meeting, which was attended by 37,000 registered persons, including more than 10,000 government delegates, 13,000 observers from civil society, and 3,000 journalists. Moreover, a thousand official and informal meetings were held over the two-week course of the conference, generating around 300 press conferences. However, Dimitrov concluded that, overall, the conference was a "failure whose magnitude exceeded our worst fears" and that the resulting Copenhagen Accord "was a desperate attempt to mask that failure." He thought that the weakened accord that was produced was a "face-saving device to 'greenwash' the absence of a substantive agreement." Dimitrov charged that China, India, and Brazil had prevented a stronger agreement, since "they consistently blocked substantive policy proposals and refused to reciprocate to Western concessions with any policy commitments of their own." But even Dimitrov admitted, however, that in order to judge success, one had to look at all levels of governance. He argued that "there is a sharp contrast between multilevel climate governance and 'aggregate' climate governance."[95] Nations that met in smaller groups had been able to accomplish much more than did the multinational Copenhagen gathering.

Immediately after the Copenhagen Accord was passed, President Obama, along with Australian prime minister Kevin Rudd and some of the other leaders, held press conferences to announce the news—even before the leaders of the conference had a chance to examine it. Thus the conference had to settle for an accord that was nonbinding, with little policy content, and, in Dimitrov's judgment, "of highly ambiguous legal status in international law."[96] It was the intention of this accord to provide $100 billion annually in climate aid for developing nations, but it lacked a timetable for emission limits.[97] The accord laid a framework for verification of emission commitments by developing countries, but did not include mandatory commitments. Without mandatory commitments, it is unlikely that sufficient action to reduce climate change will be taken by the signatory countries.

While Copenhagen was certainly the most eventful climate change conference of President Obama's tenure, several other negotiations have since taken place, including the 2010 Climate Summit in Cancun. The Cancun Accord represents "the first time all countries [were] committed to cutting carbon emissions under an official UN agreement."[98] While the Cancun agreement represents an additional step beyond the Copenhagen agreement, the commitments made by the signatories are still based on voluntary compliance, until a "legally binding global deal is achieved."[99] Unlike the Copenhagen Accord, the Cancun Accord requires the 194 signatory countries to ensure that average global temperature does not increase more than 2 degrees Celsius above the preindustrial global average.[100] The major carbon-emitting countries pledged to cut their emission levels and develop a monitoring system to track success or failure. Developed countries also agreed to deliver $30 billion in near-term climate aid while raising $100 billion annually by 2020 for vulnerable nations as part of the Green Climate Fund.[101] President Obama took a strong position at Cancun on the agreement and was a chief advocate for it. As US envoy Todd Stern noted: "This is very good from our point of view. . . . This was the U.S. strategic vision and plan we had in 2010 when we returned from Copenhagen."[102] But as with the Copenhagen Accord, details were not forthcoming on some aspects of the Cancun Accord. For example, it was unclear how the $100 billion for the Green Climate Fund would be raised, nor did the accord incorporate all of the changes that scientists indicate are necessary to protect the planet from global warming.[103]

And once again, the 2011 Climate Summit in Durban, South Africa, produced no immediate binding agreement that would result in halting global climate change. But after seventeen sessions, from November 28 to December 11, 2011, the summit produced a plan, the "Durban Platform for Enhanced Action," that brought together the 194 participant countries, and most importantly the top three major polluters—the United States, China, and India—in agreeing on the need to cut carbon emissions. The question, of course, became "How much, and when?"

The Durban Platform calls for a legally binding agreement from the 194 countries by 2015, to be implemented by 2020. It also calls for reducing greenhouse gas emissions, limiting global temperature increase, and helping developing countries make the transition to cleaner energy economies. Moreover, the agreement does not give preferential treatment to rich or poor countries, but rather applies the same standards to all.[104] Though European Union countries wanted a legally binding treaty, the rest of the world as represented at Durban was not ready to support this step.[105] The United Nations Framework Convention on Climate Change considered the Durban Platform to be a historic achievement, since it "accounted for the mitigation efforts of all countries under one agreement." It was also announced that "all developed country governments and 48 developing countries affirmed their emission reduction pledges up to 2020."[106] The participant countries further decided that the Kyoto Protocol would move to a new commitment period in 2013, in a seamless transition from the end of the previous commitment period in 2012. Some amendments were to be added to the protocol, the most important of which was to reexamine the "range of greenhouse gases covered."[107]

Obama joined with the European Union in promoting progress in Durban. As declared in a joint statement issued prior to the summit: "We stand fully behind the commitments we made last year in Cancun. We affirm that Durban should deliver on operationalizing the Cancun agreements and helping the international community move a step further towards a comprehensive, global framework with the participation of all, including robust and transparent greenhouse gas emission reduction commitments by all major economies, recalling the 2°C objective agreed upon in Cancun."[108]

A UN Climate Change Conference was held in Doha, Qatar, on December 8, 2012, where the countries agreed to adopt a draft of a universal climate agreement by 2015 to cover all countries by 2020. The primary goal is to curb world emissions so that they stay below 2 degrees Celsius. As before, there were plans for a number of workshops and smaller meetings in 2013 and 2014 to encourage nations to plan for the 2015 deadline. The next major UN Climate Change Conference is to be held at the end of 2013 in Warsaw, Poland.[109]

Meanwhile in the United States, President Obama has adopted a new program to reduce noncarbon pollution, again using the authority of the presidency and also seeking the involvement of other nations. In February 2012, Secretary of State Hillary Clinton announced the new program, the Climate and Clean Air Coalition, which proposes to reduce the emissions of common pollutants that contribute to rapid climate change and increased health problems.[110] The purpose of this program is to facilitate rapid action on climate change. According to Durwood Zaelke, president of the Institute for Governance and Sustainable Development, this initiative, "if expanded and adequately financed, would have more impact on the climate than the United Nations climate change negotiations, at least in the near term."[111] The initiative is aimed at reducing emissions of soot, methane, and hydrofluorocarbons. Scientists suggest that soot can be reduced by "installing filters on diesel engines, replacing traditional cookstoves with more efficient models, modernizing brick kilns and banning the open burning of agricultural waste. Methane can be captured from oil and gas wells, leaky pipelines, coal mines, municipal landfills, wastewater treatment plants, manure piles and rice paddies."[112] The State Department is claiming that such an initiative can reduce the global average temperature by half a degree Celsius by 2050. The United States has promised to contribute $12 million to get the program started.

Even though Obama has not always achieved tangible results in his efforts regarding climate change, and even though he has not always kept the environmental promises he made during his first campaign for the presidency, he has made a major effort to keep the issue of climate change salient for the American people. In his first three years as president, for example, he referenced "climate change" 229 times, in both major and minor speeches.[113] The vast majority of these references—193 of them—came during his first year as president. Since 2010, though, he has referenced "climate change" much more sporadically.

Although Barack Obama's presidency had been highly anticipated by environmentalists both within the United States and among the international community, his achievements have sometimes fallen short, particularly in the domestic arena. He has been more successful in the international arena, however, in trying to shape policy and influence other nations to take heed of the dangers of climate change if something is not done soon.

Conclusion

Presidential leadership is important in making air pollution and climate change key agenda issues and in identifying climate change, in particular, as a national priority. Although earlier presidents, beginning with Harry Truman, were concerned with air pollution, they did not have a sense of its global implications.

The transition from concern about air pollution to concern about climate change occurred during the presidency of Jimmy Carter and publication of the *Global 2000 Report*. In response to the threat of a warming planet, not all US presidents have been instrumental in seeking far-reaching, effective climate change policy. Like Carter, Bill Clinton also made a positive contribution. In contrast, Ronald Reagan and George W. Bush led the nation away from effectively responding to the dangers of climate change. George H. W. Bush's contribution, on the whole, was more positive than negative, as was Obama's during his first term. Obama, however, faced constraints of domestic politics that affected his role as diplomatic leader abroad.

Positive or negative contributions aside, all six of these presidents experienced the difficulties of leadership in confronting the issue of global climate change. A president's climate policy goals can be easily frustrated if he lacks support from Congress and the public. This was particularly the case during the tenure of Bill Clinton and during Barack Obama's first term.

Among these six presidents, those who exhibited less positive leadership often found that other elements of the political system were waiting to fill the leadership void—either Congress or state governments. This was particularly the case during the tenure of George W. Bush, when hundreds of cities and a number of states—California in particular—were going their own way in attempting to reduce greenhouse gas emissions.

These six presidents have also shown how rhetoric can both advance global climate change remedies through interacting with other heads of states and other domestic policymakers, as during Barack Obama's first term, and also frustrate that advance, as during the presidency of George W. Bush. These presidents have further shown that rhetoric must be accompanied by action if the president is to maintain his leadership role, internationally as well as domestically. Both forms of leadership are essential for adopting an effective and global approach to climate change. Concern regarding Obama's inability to secure congressional support for his climate policy during his first term was disappointing to leaders of other countries and posed a problem for the president.

When focusing on global climate change as an important policy issue, presidential leadership and presidential-congressional relations are linked together in the US system of government. When both are attuned, then progress, both nationally and globally, is more likely to occur on this transnational environmental problem.

Notes

1. Benoit Nemery, Peter H. M. Hoet, and Abderrahim Nemmar, "The Meuse Valley Fog of 1930: An Air Pollution Disaster," *Lancet* 357 (March 3, 2001): 704–708.

2. D. W. Dockery and C. A. Pope, "Acute Respiratory Effects of Particulate Air Pollution," *Annual Review of Public Health* 15 (May 1994): 107–132.

3. John A. Scott, "Fog and Deaths in London, December 1952," *Public Health Reports* 68, no. 5 (May 1953): 474–479.

4. Harry Truman, "Message to the United States Technical Conference on Air Pollution," May 3, 1950, in *Public Papers of the Presidents: Harry S. Truman, 1950* (Washington, DC: Government Printing Office, 1965), 281–282.

5. See Dwight D. Eisenhower, "Annual Message to the Congress on the State of the Union," January 6, 1955, online by John Woolley and Gerhard Peters, *The American Presidency Project*, www.presidency.ucsb.edu/ws/?pid =10416. See also Dwight D. Eisenhower, "Special Message to the Congress Recommending a Health Program," January 31, 1955, online by John Woolley

and Gerhard Peters, *The American Presidency Project,* www.presidency.ucsb
.edu/ws/?pid=10399.

6. John F. Kennedy, "Annual Message to the Congress on the State of the
Union," January 11, 1962, online by John Woolley and Gerhard Peters, *The
American Presidency Project,* www.presidency.ucsb.edu/ws/print.php?pid=9082.

7. John F. Kennedy, "Special Message to the Congress on Protecting the
Consumer Interest," March 15, 1962, online by John Woolley and Gerhard Peters, *The American Presidency Project,* www.presidency.ucsb.edu/ws/print
.php?pid=9108.

8. John F. Kennedy, "Special Message to the Congress on Improving the
Nation's Health," February 7, 1963, online by John Woolley and Gerhard Peters, *The American Presidency Project,* www.presidency.ucsb.edu/ws/?pid
=9549.

9. Lyndon B. Johnson, "Statement by the President in Response to Science Advisory Committee Report on Pollution of Air, Soil, and Waters," November 6, 1965, in *Public Papers of the Presidents: Lyndon B. Johnson, 1965*
(Washington, DC: Government Printing Office, 1966), 1101.

10. Lyndon B. Johnson, "Annual Message to the Congress on the State of
the Union," January 10, 1967, in *Public Papers of the Presidents: Lyndon B.
Johnson, 1967* (Washington, DC: Government Printing Office, 1968), 5.

11. Lyndon B. Johnson, "Special Message to the Congress: Protecting Our
Natural Heritage," January 30, 1967, in *Public Papers of the Presidents: Lyndon B. Johnson, 1967* (Washington, DC: Government Printing Office, 1968),
97.

12. Richard Nixon, "Annual Message to the Congress on the State of the
Union," January 22, 1970, in *Public Papers of the Presidents of the United
States: Richard Nixon, 1970* (Washington, DC: Government Printing Office,
1971), 13.

13. Clean Air Act, Public Law 91-604 (1970), in *Legislation: A Look at
U.S. Air Pollution Laws and Their Amendments.* www.ametsoc.org/sloan/clean
air/cleanairlegisl.html.

14. Richard Nixon, "Remarks on Signing the Clean Air Amendments of
1970," December 31, 1970, online by John Woolley and Gerhard Peters, *The
American Presidency Project,* www.presidency.ucsb.edu/ws/index.php?pid
=2874. See also Environmental Protection Agency, "The 40th Anniversary of
the Clean Air Act: Public Health Improvements, Technology Advancements,
and Remaining Air Quality Challenges," September 14, 2010, www.epa.gov
/oar/caa/40th.html.

15. Gerald Ford, "Special Message to the Congress Urging Enactment of
Proposed Energy Legislation," February 26, 1976, online by John Woolley
and Gerhard Peters, *The American Presidency Project,* www.presidency.ucsb
.edu/ws/?pid=5623.

16. Gerald Ford, "Remarks and a Question-and-Answer Session at a
Forum in Houston," April 28, 1976, online by John Woolley and Gerhard Peters, *The American Presidency Project,* www.presidency.ucsb.edu/ws/index
.php?pid=5892.

17. Council on Environmental Quality and US Department of State, *The
Global 2000 Report to the President,* vol. 1, preface, vii.

18. Ibid.

19. Council on Environmental Quality and US Department of State, *The Global 2000 Report to the President: Documentation on the Government's Global Sectoral Models: The Government's "Global Model,"* vol. 3, chapter 4, "The Climate Section," 174-207, www.geraldbarney.com/Global_2000 _Report/G2000-Eng-GPO/G2000-GPO-Vol3.pdf.

20. Ibid., 52–53, 257, 259.

21. Jimmy Carter, "Science and Technology Message to Congress," March 27, 1979, online by John Woolley and Gerhard Peters, *The American Presidency Project,* www.presidency.ucsb.edu/ws/print.php?pid=32109.

22. Jimmy Carter, "National Energy Plan: Address Delivered Before a Joint Session of the Congress," April 20, 1977, online by John Woolley and Gerhard Peters, *The American Presidency Project,* www.presidency.ucsb .edu/ws/print.php?pid=7372.

23. Rafe Pomerance, "The Dangers from Climate Warming: A Public Awakening," in Abrahamson, *The Challenge of Global Warming,* 265.

24. Neil E. Harrison, "Political Responses to Changing Uncertainty in Climate Science," in Harrison and Bryner, *Science and Politics in the International Environment,* 131.

25. John Jolusha, "Bush Pledges Aid for Environment," *New York Times,* September 1, 1988.

26. Byron W. Daynes and Glen Sussman, "Comparing the Environmental Policies of Presidents George H. W. Bush and George W. Bush," *White House Studies* 7 (2007): 167.

27. George H. W. Bush, "Letter to Congressional Leaders on Legislation to Amend Clean Air Act," September 26, 1990, online by John Woolley and Gerhard Peters, *The American Presidency Project,* www.presidency.ucsb.edu/ws /index.php?pid=18867.

28. George H. W. Bush, "Paris Economic Summit: Economic Declaration," July 16, 1989, in *Public Papers of the Presidents: George H. W. Bush, 1989* (Washington, DC: Government Printing Office, 1990), 965.

29. Marvin S. Soroos, "From Stockholm to Rio: The Evaluation of Global Environmental Governance," in *Environmental Policy in the 1990s,* edited by Norman J. Vig and Michael E. Kraft, 2nd ed. (Washington, DC: Congressional Quarterly, 1994), 313–314.

30. "US Acts the Spoiler in Global Climate Talks," *New York Times,* May 24, 1992.

31. Elizabeth Kolbert, "Comment: Leading Causes," *New Yorker,* October 5, 2009, www.newyorker.com/talk/comment/2009/10/05.

32. George H. W. Bush, "Message to the Senate Transmitting the United Nations Framework Convention on Climate Change," September 8, 1992, online by John Woolley and Gerhard Peters, *The American Presidency Project,* www.presidency.ucsb.edu/ws/index.php?pid=21432.

33. George H. W. Bush, "Remarks to the Intergovernmental Panel on Climate Change," February 5, 1990, online by John Woolley and Gerhard Peters, *The American Presidency Project,* www.presidency.ucsb.edu/ws/index.php ?pid=18117.

34. George H. W. Bush, "Remarks to Residents of Leiden, the Nether-

lands," July 17, 1989, online by John Woolley and Gerhard Peters, *The American Presidency Project,* www.presidency.ucsb.edu/ws/index.php?pid=17302.

35. Byron W. Daynes and Glen Sussman, *White House Politics and the Environment: Franklin D. Roosevelt to George W. Bush* (College Station: Texas A&M University Press, 2010), 108.

36. Elizabeth Kolbert, "Comment: Leading Causes."

37. Bill Clinton, "Remarks to the 52d Session of the United Nations General Assembly in New York City," September 22, 1997, in *Public Papers of the Presidents: William J. Clinton, 1997,* vol. 2 (Washington, DC: Government Printing Office, 1999), 1207.

38. "Mr. Gore's Mission in Kyoto," *New York Times,* December 4, 1997.

39. J. H. Price, "A Lukewarm Theory? Scientists Roast Global Warming's 'Uncertainties,'" *Washington Times,* November 30, 1997.

40. Bill Clinton, "Speech at City of Montreal Event Coinciding with the United Nations Climate Change Conference," 2005, www.clintonfoundation .org/120905-sp-cf-gn-env-can-sp-remarks-at-montreal-event-coinciding-with -un-climate-change-conference.htm.

41. Ibid.

42. W. Witter, "Gore Offers Flexibility on Emission Cuts; Attempts to Break Deadlock in Kyoto," *Washington Times,* December 8, 1997.

43. Cass R. Sunstein, "Of Montreal and Kyoto: A Tale of Two Protocols," *Harvard Environmental Law Review* 31, no. 1 (2007): 3–4, 25.

44. Bill Clinton, "Russia–United States Joint Statement on Cooperation to Combat Global Warming," June 4, 2000, in *Public Papers of the Presidents: William J. Clinton, 2000–2001,* vol. 1 (Washington, DC: Government Printing Office, 2001), 1074–75.

45. Charles Digges, "Putin Signals Russia Will Sign Kyoto Protocol for WTO Membership," Bellona, May 23, 2004, www.bellona.org/English_import _area/energy/34179.

46. Sunstein, "Of Montreal and Kyoto," 4.

47. Miranda Schreurs, "20th Anniversary of the Rio Summit: Taking a Look Back and at the Road Ahead," 2012, http://creativecommons.org/licenses /by/3.0.

48. Michael Bloch, "What Is the Kyoto Protocol?" Carbonify.com, February 12, 2013, www.carbonify.com/articles/Kyoto-protocol.htm.

49. T. A. Boden, G. Marland, and R. J. Andres, "Global, Regional, and National Fossil-Fuel CO_2 Emissions" (Oak Ridge, TN: Carbon Dioxide Information Analysis Center, Oak Ridge National Laboratory, US Department of Energy, 2010).

50. Tom Boden and T. J. Blasing, "Record High 2010 Global Carbon Dioxide Emissions from Fossil-Fuel Combustion and Cement Manufacture Posted on DCIAC Site" (Oak Ridge, TN: Carbon Dioxide Information Analysis Center, Oak Ridge National Laboratory, US Department of Energy, 2010), http://cdiac.ornl.gov/ftp/trends/co2_emis/Preliminary_CO2_emissions _2010.xlxs.

51. Ibid.

52. Bill Clinton, "Address Before a Joint Session of the Congress on the State of the Union," January 27, 2000, online by John Woolley and Gerhard

Peters, *The American Presidency Project,* www.presidency.ucsb.edu/ws/index
.php?pid=58708.

53. A list of President Clinton's references to "global warming" from 1993
to 2001 can be found through a database search online, namely, *The American
Presidency Project,* by John Woolley and Gerhard Peters, www.presidency
.ucsb.edu. At the bottom of the homepage, under "Opinion 1: search," one can
find these references by searching for "global warming" from January 1, 1993,
to January 20, 2001, under William Clinton.

54. A list of President Clinton's references to "climate change" from 1993
to 2001 can be found through a database search online, namely, *The American
Presidency Project,* by John Woolley and Gerhard Peters, www.presidency
.ucsb.edu. At the bottom of the homepage, under "Opinion 1: search," one can
find these references by searching for "climate change" from January 1, 1993,
to January 20, 2001, under William Clinton.

55. "Democratic Party Platform of 1992," online by John Woolley and
Gerhard Peters, *The American Presidency Project,* www.presidency.ucsb.edu
/ws/index.php?pid=29610.

56. "Democratic Party Platform of 1996," online by John Woolley and
Gerhard Peters, *The American Presidency Project,* www.presidency.ucsb.edu
/ws/index.php?pid=29611.

57. For a critical look at the George W. Bush administration's approach to
global warming, see Daynes and Sussman, "The 'Greenless' Response to
Global Warming."

58. George W. Bush, "President Calls for Conservation and Stewardship
on Earth Day," White House Office of the Press Secretary, April 22, 2002,
www.georgew-bush-whitehouse.archives.gov/news/releases/2002/04
/20020422-I.html.

59. Christopher Marquis, "Bush Energy Proposal Seeks to 'Clear Skies' by
2018," *New York Times,* July 30, 2002.

60. Douglas Jehl, "On Environmental Rules, Bush Sees a Balance, Critics
a Threat," *New York Times,* February 23, 2003.

61. "Bush and Gore Air Opposite Policies on Earth Day," Environmental
News Service, April 23, 2002, www.ens-newswire.com/ens/apr2002/2002-04
-23-01.html.

62. George W. Bush, "Joint Statement by the United States of America and
Japan on Energy Security, Clean Development, and Climate Change," April
27, 2007, online by John Woolley and Gerhard Peters, *The American Presidency Project,* www.presidency.ucsb.edu/ws/?pid=25226.

63. George W. Bush, "Joint Statement: U.S.-German Joint Actions on
Cleaner and More Efficient Energy, Development, and Climate Change," Feb-
ruary 23, 2005, online by John Woolley and Gerhard Peters, *The American
Presidency Project,* www.presidency.ucsb.edu/ws/?pid=63265.

64. George W. Bush and John Howard, "Joint Statement by President George
W. Bush and Prime Minister John Howard of Australia on Climate Change and
Energy," September 5, 2007, online by John Woolley and Gerhard Peters, *The
American Presidency Project,* www.presidency.ucsb.edu/ws/?pid=75735.

65. George W. Bush, Felipe Calderón, and Stephen Harper, "Joint Statement by President George W. Bush, President Felipe de Jesus Calderón Hino-

josa of Mexico, and Prime Minister Stephen Harper of Canada," April 28, 2008, online by John Woolley and Gerhard Peters, *The American Presidency Project,* www.presidency.ucsb.edu/ws/?pid=77160.

66. George W. Bush, "Address Before a Joint Session of the Congress on the State of the Union," January 23, 2007, online by John Woolley and Gerhard Peters, *The American Presidency Project,* www.presidency.ucsb.edu /ws/index.php?pid=24446.

67. George W. Bush, "Remarks During a Meeting on Energy Security and Climate Change," September 28, 2007, online by John Woolley and Gerhard Peters, *The American Presidency Project,* www.presidency.ucsb.edu/ws/index .php?pid=75839.

68. George W. Bush, "Address Before a Joint Session of the Congress on the State of the Union," January 28, 2008, online by John Woolley and Gerhard Peters, *The American Presidency Project,* www.presidency.ucsb.edu/ws /index.php?pid=76301.

69. "UVM Analysis of States' Greenhouse Gas Efforts Appears in 'Nature,'" University of Vermont, December 8, 2005, www.uvm.edu/news.

70. Daynes and Sussman, "The 'Greenless' Response to Global Warming," 442.

71. Norman Miller, *Environmental Politics,* 2nd ed. (New York: Routledge, 2009), 146–148.

72. Andrew C. Revkin, "Bush Aide Edited Climate Reports," *New York Times,* June 8, 2005.

73. Conway, *Atmospheric Science at NASA,* 307.

74. John McCain, "McCain's Speech on Climate Change," *New York Times,* May 12, 2008, www.nytimes.com/2008/05/12/us/politics.

75. Barack Obama, "Videotaped Remarks to the Bi-Partisan Governors Global Climate Summit," November 18, 2008, online by John Woolley and Gerhard Peters, *The American Presidency Project,* www.presidency.ucsb.edu /ws/index.php?pid=84875.

76. Paula Newton, "Obama: Leaders Will Work Together on Climate," CNN, July 9, 2009, www.cnn.com/2009/WORLD/europe/07/09/g8.summit /index.html?_s=PM:WORLD.

77. League of Conservation Voters, "Scorecard: 2011."

78. John M. Broder, "'Cap and Trade' Loses Its Standing as Energy Policy of Choice," *New York Times,* March 26, 2010.

79. Ibid.

80. Barack Obama, "Remarks on Signing a Memorandum Improving Energy Security, American Competitiveness and Job Creation, and Environmental Protection Through a Transformation of Our Nation's Fleet of Cars and Trucks," May 21, 2010, online by John Woolley and Gerhard Peters, *The American Presidency Project,* www.presidency.ucsb.edu/ws/index.php?pid=87932.

81. Barack Obama, "State of the Union 2012: Obama Speech Full Text," *Washington Post,* January 25, 2012, http://washingtonpost.com/politics.

82. Barack Obama, "Remarks on Energy at Andrews Air Force Base, Maryland," March 31, 2010, online by John Woolley and Gerhard Peters, *The American Presidency Project,* www.presidency.ucsb.edu/ws/index.php?pid=87685.

83. Ibid.

84. Executive Order no. 13499, 3 CFR 6979 (2009); Executive Order no. 13500, 3 CFR 6981 (2009).

85. *Massachusetts v. Environmental Protection Agency,* 549 US 497 (2007).

86. Juliet Eilperin, "Obama Pulls Back Proposed Smog Standards in Victory for Business," *Washington Post,* September 2, 2011, www.washington post.com/national/health-science.

87. John M. Broder, "Obama Administration Abandons Stricter Air-Quality Rules," *New York Times,* September 2, 2011, www.nytimes.com/2011/09 /03/science/earth.

88. Scott Horsley and Robert Siegel, "In Canada, Obama Pledges Stronger Ties," National Public Radio, February 19, 2009, www.npr.org.

89. White House, "US–Mexico Announce Bilateral Framework on Clean Energy and Climate Change," April 16, 2009, www.whitehouse.gov/the-press -office.

90. Barack Obama, "Address to the United Nations General Assembly in New York City," September 23, 2009, online by John Woolley and Gerhard Peters, *The American Presidency Project,* www.presidency.ucsb.edu/ws/index .php?pid=86659.

91. Barack Obama, "Remarks at the United Nations Climate Change Summit in New York City," September 22, 2009, online by John Woolley and Gerhard Peters, *The American Presidency Project,* www.presidency.ucsb.edu/ws /index.php?pid=86657.

92. Barack Obama, "Remarks at a Plenary Session of the United Nations Climate Change Conference in Copenhagen, Denmark," December 18, 2009, online by John Woolley and Gerhard Peters, *The American Presidency Project,* www.presidency.ucsb.edu/ws/index.php?pid=87011.

93. Elizabeth Rosenthal, "Obama's Backing Raises Hopes for Climate Pact," *New York Times,* March 1, 2009.

94. Barack Obama, "Remarks on Health Care Reform and Climate Change," December 19, 2009, online by John Woolley and Gerhard Peters, *The American Presidency Project,* www.presidency.ucsb.edu/ws/index.php ?pid=87007.

95. Radoslav S. Dimitrov, "Inside UN Climate Change Negotiations: The Copenhagen Conference," *Review of Policy Research* 27, no. 6 (2010): 796.

96. Ibid., 815.

97. William Matthias, "China and India Endorse Copenhagen Climate Accord," Environmental News Network, March 10, 2010, www.enn.com.

98. Louise Gray, "Cancun Climate Change Conference Agrees Plan to Cut Carbon Emissions," *The Telegraph,* December 11, 2010, www.telegraph.co.uk /earth/environment/climatechange.

99. Ibid.

100. United Nations Framework Convention on Climate Change, "Outcome of the Work of the Ad Hoc Working Group on Further Commitments for Annex I Parties Under the Kyoto Protocol at Its Fifteenth Session," 2010, http://unfccc.int.

101. Ibid.

102. Lisa Friedman, "A Near-Consensus Decision Keeps U.N. Climate

Process Alive and Moving Ahead," *New York Times,* December 13, 2010, www.nytimes.com/cwire/2010/12/13.

103. Ibid.

104. United Nations Framework Convention on Climate Change, "Establishment of an Ad Hoc Working Group on the Durban Platform for Enhanced Action," November 28–December 9, 2011, http://unfccc.int.

105. Louise Gray, "Durban Climate Change: Last Minute Talks Produce 'Historic Deal to Save the Planet,'" *The Telegraph,* December 11, 2011, www.telegraph.co.uk/earth/environment/climatechange.

106. Javier Amantegui, "Is Renewable Energy Still a Green Investment?" *CorporateLiveWire,* June 15, 2012, www.corporatelivewire.com/top-story .html?id=is-renewable-energy-still-a-green-investment (accessed April 4, 2013).

107. Ibid.

108. Barack Obama, "Joint Statement by the United States and the European Union," November 28, 2011, online by John Woolley and Gerhard Peters, *The American Presidency Project,* www.presidency.ucsb.edu/ws/index .php?pid=97341.

109. John M. Broder, "Qatar, a Greenhouse Gas Titan, to Host U.N. Climate Meeting," *New York Times,* November 29, 2011, http://green.blogs.nytimes .com; "Doha Climate Conference Opens Gateway to Greater Ambition and Action on Climate Change," December 9, 2012, www.unep.org/newscentre /default.aspx?DocumentID=2700&ArticleID=9353 (accessed April 5, 2013).

110. Hillary R. Clinton, "Remarks at the Climate and Clean Air Coalition to Reduce Short-Lived Climate Pollutants Initiative," US Department of State, February 16, 2012, www.state.gov/secretary/rm/2012/02/184061.htm.

111. John M. Broder, "U.S. Pushes to Cut Emissions of Some Pollutants That Hasten Climate Change," *New York Times,* February 15, 2012, www.ny times.com/2012/02/16/science/earth.

112. Ibid.

113. For the complete speeches of Obama and other presidents, see John Woolley and Gerhard Peters, *The American Presidency Project,* www.presidency .ucsb.edu.

5

The Role
of the Judiciary

Although interest in global climate change dates back to Aristotle, federal courts in the United States have been involved with this issue for only a few years. One reason for this is the fact that courts have resisted involvement because they have recognized their own limitations. As G. Gordon Davis indicated, for the courts, such issues as climate change may be "too abstruse and the remedies too recondite to kick off the kind of popular tide of opinion that spawned so much environmental legislation in the early 1970s."[1] While judges have always been reluctant to tackle environmental issues, admitting their lack of expertise, along with the complexity of the issue, global climate change poses even more concerns for the courts because of its massive reach. As David Hunter puts it, "The world's legal systems—both international and national—have never seen a challenge quite like climate change. The science involves complexities of global ecology that are of a scale new to the courts. Nearly all of our activities, whether as individuals, corporations, or governments, contribute to the problem and almost everyone is affected. The entire world is at once simultaneously both a potential plaintiff and defendant."[2]

Another problem courts have in responding to climate change was pointed out by Brent Newell, a legal specialist from the San Francisco Center for Race, Poverty, and the Environment, whose legal focus has been on the Clean Air Act.[3] Newell reminds us how uncertain the legal process is in terms of the time it takes a case to make it through to its final decision, as well as the unpredictability of what the global environment will look like once the case is decided.[4] As an example, he pointed to the *American Electric Power v. Connecticut* case, which was first filed in 2005 but was not finally decided until 2011.[5] In 2005, as Newell indicated, the *Massachusetts v. Environmental Protection Agency* case (discussed later) had not yet been taken up by the courts, and the George W. Bush administration was still in power and resisting efforts to deal with climate change.[6] The responses from the courts to global climate change tend to be less effective than responses from either the federal legislative or executive branch.

Because of the failure of both the president and the Congress to assume leadership in responding to global climate change, the courts have essentially been forced to respond to the climate crisis. Even Bill Clinton, who was supportive of most environmental goals, was reluctant to regulate carbon dioxide emissions near the end of his presidency in 1999, preferring instead to promote both "economic growth and environmental progress simultaneously" rather than promoting "retail competition in the electric power industry."[7]

Clearly climate change is a priority that needs attention, as James Gustave Speth, dean of the Yale School of Forestry and Environmental Studies contends; climate change is as serious a problem as terrorism, yet climate change has received far less attention. As Speth indicates, climate change is "both the number one challenge and the number one area where new U.S. attitudes and policies are needed."[8] As a result, the courts have found themselves open to all sides of the climate question and have become, in the words of John Schwartz, primary "battlefields" for "climate fights."[9]

But the courts have not been just passive arenas for the airing of others' arguments; they have established unique responses of their own to climate change. As Hunter indicates, they have become innovators, developing "creative new strategies internationally and domestically." Furthermore, he contends, the courts have made an effort to "push for the progressive development of the law and related institutions, emphasizing not only the differences but the similarities of climate change with more familiar issues."[10] Whether the courts' involvement will motivate and encourage the president and Congress to be more assertive in establishing a US response to climate change remains to be seen.

Judicial Involvement

To provide a complete assessment of how the US federal court has addressed climate change, the following discussion assesses three tiers of cases. In the top tier, we find only two cases—*Massachusetts v. Environmental Protection Agency* (2007) and *American Electric Power v. Connecticut* (2011)—through which the Supreme Court has generated new federal regulations regarding global climate change or has indicated in other ways its approach to the issue. In both of these cases, the authority of the Environmental Protection Agency (EPA) became increasingly important. All future decisions on climate change will have to take these two cases into account.

In the second tier, we find the largest number of cases. Most of these cases are decisions from the lower federal courts—from the district or appellate level, or cases waiting on appeal to the Supreme Court. Many of these cases are likely to have partial or indirect effects on aspects of global climate change, or illustrate unique circumstances wherein guidelines established by other federal cases and decisions can be applied. None of these cases are as significant as the two in the top tier, but they have potential significance as conflict over climate change continues.

In the third tier are cases in which climate change is a secondary concern. These cases are unlikely to have significant impact on the climate change debate or on the direction the courts will take in the future.

Top-Tier Cases

The most important top-tier case decided by the Supreme Court was *Massachusetts v. Environmental Protection Agency* (2007). It had been a hundred years since the Supreme Court had taken its previous and first case on global climate change, in 1907. The *Massachusetts* case was important because it opened the door for Court action in the twenty-first century. It was this case that challenged the environmental policies and views of President George W. Bush and his administration. In a 5-to-4 decision, the Court determined that state governments and environmental interest groups had a right to sue the Environmental Protection Agency, since it had refused to exercise its responsibility to regulate carbon dioxide (CO_2) as a pollutant under the Clean Air Act.

This case had its beginnings in 2003, when the Bush EPA decided to reject a petition demanding that the federal government restrict emissions of greenhouse gases, principally carbon dioxide. The EPA argued that carbon dioxide was not an air pollutant, the same argument used by the US Court of Appeals. In 2006, twelve states, three local governments, thirteen environmental interest groups, and six former directors of the EPA appealed the appellate court decision arguing that the EPA had "abdicated its responsibility under the Clean Air Act to regulate the emissions of four greenhouse gases, including carbon dioxide."[11] In the petition, two questions were asked: "whether the EPA had the statutory authority to regulate greenhouse gas emissions from new motor vehicles" and, if so, "whether its . . . reasons for refusing to do so are consistent with the statute."[12] Associate Justice John Paul Stevens of the Supreme Court, speaking for the majority, supported the appeal, ruling that carbon dioxide from new motor vehicles fit the definition of a greenhouse gas pollutant within the context of the Clean Air Act.

The Court majority took a firm stance in supporting the potential damage that might come from global warming. As Stevens wrote, "The harms associated with climate change are serious and well recognized." He then quoted a National Research Council report concerning those damages, including "the global retreat of mountain glaciers, reduction in snow-cover extent, the earlier spring melting of rivers and lakes [and] the accelerated rate of rise of sea levels during the 20th Century relative to the past few thousand years."[13] Stevens added that "the rise in sea levels associated with global warming has already harmed and will continue to harm Massachusetts." Stevens then emphasized potential harm, indicating that "the risk of catastrophic harm, though remote, is nevertheless real. That risk would be reduced to some extent if petitioners received the relief they seek."[14]

The Court was highly critical of the EPA's approach to air pollution during the George W. Bush administration. Alleging "scientific uncertainties" regarding carbon dioxide as a pollutant, the EPA's primary argument was that climate change was an "important foreign policy issue" that should be addressed by the president alone.[15] To this, Justice Stevens responded that the EPA "has offered no reasoned explanation for its refusal to decide whether greenhouse gases cause or contribute to climate change. . . . Its action was therefore 'arbitrary, and capricious . . . or otherwise not in accordance with law.'"[16] Justice Stevens ruled that the Clean Air Act does give the EPA authority to regulate greenhouse gas emissions from new motor vehicles. The Court then firmly stated that the EPA could avoid taking action against greenhouse gases only if it provided "some reasonable explanation as to why it cannot or will not exercise its discretion."[17]

The dissenting justices reiterated the EPA's argument about the essence of the policymaking process. Chief Justice John Roberts, for example, repeated that climate change could be better dealt with by Congress or the president than by the EPA or the Supreme Court. This is the same argument, in effect, that President Barack Obama has made: decisions to limit carbon dioxide and other greenhouse gases should come from Congress and not from the EPA or the Supreme Court. Roberts then made his most challenging charge to the majority, asking whether there was actually a discernable connection between "relevant greenhouse gas emissions" and global warming, and whether limiting new automobile emissions would prevent damage to the coastal lands of Massachusetts.[18]

Associate Justice Antonin Scalia, in his dissenting opinion, asked whether a government agency like the EPA has the right to refrain from rendering a decision on a controversy, since the EPA is not required to make a "judgment." Thus, since climate change is "extraordinarily complex and still evolving," the EPA, in Scalia's opinion, cannot be forced to act.[19] Scalia concluded his dissenting opinion by arguing that this case was about Congress having passed a "malleable statute giving broad discretion, not to us [the Court] but to an executive agency. No matter how important the underlying policy issues at stake, this Court has no business substituting its own desired outcome for the reasoned judgment of the responsible agency."[20]

What both the majority opinion and the dissenting opinion illustrate is that the *Massachusetts v. Environmental Protection Agency* case brings together all of the difficult questions the courts face when they attempt to resolve an issue as complex as climate change, and points to the need to develop a link for each aspect of climate change to the harm that is alleged. This reiterates the logic of why it is so important to examine US politics and its institutions and actors in assessing the importance of this global environmental concern.

The other top-tier climate change case is also the most recent heard by the Supreme Court, *American Electric Power v. Connecticut* (2011).[21] This case is significant for different reasons compared to the *Massachusetts v. Environmental Protection Agency* case. The judicial precedent set by the *American Electric* case effectively removed "public nuisance" as an actionable claim for anyone bringing a climate change case to court.

This case involved not only the state of Connecticut, but seven other states as well: California, Iowa, New York, New Jersey, Rhode Island, Vermont, and Wisconsin. In addition, the City of New York joined with these states, as did three land trusts—the Open Space Institute, the Open Space Conservancy, and the Audubon Society of New Hampshire—in suing six energy companies over pollutant emissions deemed damaging to these states, New York City, and the land trusts. The other five energy companies named in the suit, in addition to American Electric Power, were Cinergy Corporation, Southern Company, Xcel Energy, and the Tennessee Valley Authority. These energy companies were selected since they were considered "the largest emitters of carbon dioxide in the U.S., and were collectively responsible for 'ten percent of worldwide carbon dioxide emissions from human activities.'" The charge was that the emissions from these companies created a "public nuisance" for the parties named in the suit. The states and land trusts claimed to represent about 77 million people, as well as "their environments and their economies." It was demanded by the states and land trusts that the energy companies cap their "emissions of carbon dioxide and then reduc[e] those emissions by a specified percentage per year for at least a decade."[22]

The Supreme Court took only two months of deliberation before it rejected the demand of the states and land trusts that carbon dioxide emissions be capped. Instead, in a unanimous 8-to-0 decision (with Associate Justice Sonia Sotomayor abstaining) that reinforced the *Massachusetts v. Environmental Protection Agency* decision, the Court reiterated that any federal regulation of emissions of carbon dioxide would need to come under the Clean Air Act and be negotiated by the EPA and not through use of the judiciary's "public nuisance" standard. In the words of Associate Justice Ruth Bader Ginsburg, "We hold that the Clean Air Act and the EPA actions it authorizes displace any federal common law right to seek abatement of carbon-dioxide emissions from fossil-fuel fired power plants. *Massachusetts* made plain that emissions of carbon dioxide qualify as air pollution subject to regulation under the Act."[23]

For environmentalists, this decision was difficult to fully support, since it rejected the states' demand that "public nuisance" could be used for relief, which had appeared to be a promising alternative to the EPA setting standards and enforcing them. Although many environmentalists might well be against the ruling, a *New York Times* editorial contended that the decision is a "clarifying and positive decision vindicating the Clean Air Act, which is under siege in the House, and increasing pressure on the Environmental Protection Agency to carry out its authority to regulate greenhouse gases under that act." The editorial also acknowledged that with this decision the EPA's regulatory authority became one of the "last remaining regulatory weapons the government can use to combat global warming."[24] *American Electric Power* may thus be the last climate change case to pass through the courts, since the EPA has effectively now been identified by the Supreme Court as the primary actor in all matters related to climate change.

The problem with investing the EPA with this sort of authority is that when a president is elected who does not recognize the existence of global climate change, such as George W. Bush, the EPA will lie dormant, with the federal government doing little to respond to the climate crisis. On the other hand, Justice Ginsburg did indicate that in allowing the EPA to decide, the decision is not made by "a single federal judge overseeing a legal dispute."[25]

Second-Tier Cases

While only two Supreme Court decisions can be considered top-tier cases, a large number of cases are included in the second tier. Some of these cases have not yet come to the high court, but may in the near future. Some may never come to the high court, but the lower-court decisions in these cases may still have some impact on the future decisionmaking of the Supreme Court as it responds to global climate change. Still other cases have been rejected outright by the Supreme Court, or are highly unlikely to ever be decided at the high-court level given the decisions of previous courts. A few of the cases in this tier are included here merely because of their creative approach to global climate change. All are instructive in helping us understand the role of the courts and judicial decisionmaking in responding to global climate change.

One case that demands particular attention because of its potential impact on global climate change is *Coalition for Responsible Regulation v. Environmental Protection Agency* (2011).[26] This case involves twenty-six other climate change cases, all consolidated under the "coalition" title. It is important because of the potentially crippling effect it could have on the EPA's regulations regarding climate change. The "endangerment finding" is in question in this case, which is a cornerstone of every EPA regulation tied to carbon dioxide emissions.

The endangerment finding became a part of EPA regulations on December 15, 2009, when the EPA found that carbon dioxide was in fact dangerous to public health and safety and therefore required regulation.[27] The Coalition for Responsible Regulation is challenging the EPA's endangerment finding on the grounds that it is "arbitrary and capricious" and fails to "identify any criteria by which to judge endangerment." Further, the coalition charges that the levels of carbon dioxide emissions that endanger public health and welfare are unspecified in the regulation.[28] While this case has not yet been decided, it could become the basis for weakening the EPA's response to global climate change.

A second *Coalition for Responsible Regulation v. Environmental Protection Agency* (2012) case,[29] which also has not yet made its way to the Supreme Court, challenges two other EPA rules: "tailoring" and "timing," which govern how carbon dioxide regulations are applied to stationary sources of emission.[30] Title V of the Clean Air Act requires stationary sources that emit "100 tons per year or more of any air pollutant" to obtain a permit to operate. Title I of the Clean Air Act requires that a permit be obtained before building or modifying any source that emits "250 tons per year or more of any air pollutant." The Clean Air Act also allows the EPA to regulate stationary-source air pollutants that are "subject to regulation" under the act.[31] Because carbon dioxide is emitted at a greater rate than traditional pollutants, the EPA thought it necessary to "tailor" the amounts of pollutants that are emitted, as well as regulate the "timing" of these emissions. The Coalition for Responsible Regulation contends that the free market is sufficient to produce a solution for the emissions.

This case is important for the EPA's regulatory function when considering carbon dioxide. Since the EPA is now the principal actor in regulating carbon dioxide, if the Supreme Court were to disallow the EPA control over the "tailoring" and "timing" rules, this could greatly reduce its effectiveness. In February 2012, Brad Plummer, in an article for the *Washington Post* titled "Will the EPA's New Climate Rules Get Killed in the Court?" suggested that the "tailoring" rule is the rule to watch. The energy, mining, and farming industries want to challenge the rule to do away with it, which would throw the entire regulatory system into chaos. The tailoring rule, as Plummer explained, allows the EPA to insist that only the largest polluters (those that emit more than 100,000 tons of carbon dioxide) need permits to continue to operate. Industry wants to open this up so that all emitting facilities—large and small—would need permits, which would affect some 6 million facilities across the country and overwhelm state regulators.[32]

Another case, one that has been appealed to the Ninth Circuit Court of Appeals, may also have major consequences on how the United States responds to evidence of damage caused by global climate change. *Native Village of Kivalina v. Exxon Mobil* (2009) concerns a remote and isolated Alaskan village.[33] This case, if decided in favor of the village of Kivalina, could potentially have great impact on the US economy. Traditionally this coastal Alaskan village of fewer than 400 people has been protected from extreme winter weather by a buildup of ice that normally forms during the fall months. Due to rising global temperatures, this buildup of ice has decreased, leaving the village vulnerable to extreme weather. The Army Corps of Engineers estimated that the village will need to relocate at a cost of up to $125 million.[34] The village brought Exxon Mobil, in addition to the other large petroleum companies, to court as the primary offenders against the health and welfare of its people.

The US District Court for Oakland, California, at first dismissed the case, indicating that the village had no standing before the court. The village then filed an appeal before the Ninth Circuit Court of Appeals, seeking monetary damages for the injuries allegedly caused by Exxon Mobile and the other oil companies. The problem the village faces, however, is that the decision hinges upon federal common law and public nuisance claims. The Supreme Court has already rejected the claim of public nuisance in the *American Electric* case. The only possibility of success is if the Ninth Circuit Court finds a distinct difference between the monetary damages being requested by the village and the findings in the *American Electric* case. The possibility of such a difference, even though slight, makes the *Kivalina* case potentially significant.

A case with potential impact on global climate change that had a brief life was *Comer v. Murphy Oil* (2009).[35] This case began as a class action suit brought by those who suffered property damage as a result of Hurricane Katrina. Murphy Oil and other energy companies were charged with the following violations that exacerbated the severity of the hurricane:

1. *Trespass:* a claim that Murphy Oil's emissions enhanced the ferocity of the hurricane, causing water damage to the affected property.

2. *Public nuisance:* a claim that emissions from the energy companies enhanced the hurricane's "ferocity" and caused property damage.
3. *Negligence:* a charge based on the presumption that Murphy Oil and the other energy companies knew the risks associated with global climate change but did nothing to alter their behavior.
4. *Unjust enrichment:* an assertion dismissed by the court as "too general."
5. *Fraudulent misrepresentation:* a claim that Murphy Oil and the other energy companies embarked on a smear campaign to undermine the scientific findings that support the existence of global climate change.
6. *Civil conspiracy:* a charge based on government's inaction to do something about climate change.

Charges 4, 5, and 6 were each dismissed because they were considered "generalized grievances" best resolved by the political branches of government. The Supreme Court was then petitioned, but the petition was denied by the high court in January 2011. Had this case gone before the Supreme Court, and had the Court ruled in favor of those who lost property during Katrina, the decision could well have resulted in more stringent emission caps and a reduction in greenhouse gases.

The next set of cases of interest in this second tier are those that have targeted the EPA in order to weaken its decisionmaking authority regarding global climate change. One such case is *American Chemistry Council v. Environmental Protection Agency and Lisa Jackson* (2011).[36] This appellate court case is focused on undercutting the EPA's "deterioration" rule, which requires that pollution-emitting sources obtain permits to continue to operate. The EPA has included greenhouse gases and carbon dioxide as pollutants requiring such a permit. The challenge here came from the American Chemistry Council and other such organizations, which charged that the EPA's permit system has too broad a reach and unnecessarily increases the number of companies that require these permits. Since oral arguments have not yet been scheduled, it is far too early to assess the potential consequences of the case.

A number of automobile cases are also included in this tier, because of their potential air pollution consequences. The case that might have national significance is *Chamber of Commerce of the United*

States of America and National Automobile Dealers Association v. Environmental Protection Agency (2011).[37] Here the US Chamber of Commerce and the National Automobile Dealers Association (NADA) challenged the EPA's authority to allow states to adopt vehicle emission standards that are more stringent than the federal standards that regulate air pollution. The US Chamber of Commerce and NADA claimed that the Clean Air Act does not permit the EPA such authority. They argued that federal law preempts any state regulations for emissions. As of early 2013 there are thirteen states that wish to adopt California's emission standards, which would give car manufacturers a clear incentive to produce vehicles that meet these more stringent standards, since many of these states, particularly New York, Massachusetts, Pennsylvania, and New Jersey, have large populations.[38]

Despite the EPA's actions, the appellate court that heard the case indicated that the US Chamber of Commerce and NADA had no standing before the court, since the emissions standards did not have a direct impact on the chamber or the automobile dealers. The court dismissed the case because of a lack of concrete injury. Even though the case was dismissed, important considerations were raised regarding air pollution standards that may yet prove important in the future.

In another automobile emissions case, *Center for Biodiversity v. National Highway Traffic Safety Administration* (2008),[39] eleven states and four environmental groups challenged National Highway Traffic Safety Administration (NTSA) rules regarding national fleet averages for fuel economy. The Center for Biodiversity claimed that the NTSA's rules were not sufficiently calculated and that they were "arbitrary and capricious and contrary to the National Environmental Policy Act." The center also charged that the NTSA had not set emission standards at a "minimum feasible" level, had failed to give "consideration to the need of the nation to conserve energy," and had not assigned enough value to reducing carbon emissions. The center further asserted that there was a loophole in the NTSA's rules that allowed a lower fuel-economy standard for sport utility vehicles, minivans, and light trucks, and that the rules mentioned nothing about heavy vehicles. The Ninth Circuit Court of Appeals was sympathetic to the arguments of the Center for Biodiversity and its request for more stringent regulations from the NTSA, and eventually remanded the decision to the NTSA for further consideration, asserting that the current NTSA rules were "arbitrary and capricious." The court's judges further indicated that "the Environmental Assessment was inadequate and that the petitioners [the center] have raised a substantial question as to whether the Final Rule may have significant impact on the environment."[40]

The court's decision represented a victory for environmental activists as a precedent for judicial review of environmental regulations by the federal government. But the case appears less important than the others mentioned here since the final decision was made by the NTSA rather than the federal court. Yet the positive aspect of the case is that the Ninth Circuit Court of Appeals still recognized carbon dioxide as a pollutant.

Two other automotive cases that are important, but of more limited consequence, are *Green Mountain v. Crombie* (2007) and *Central Valley v. Goldstene* (2007).[41] These cases involved the Green Mountain and Central Valley automotive companies, among others. In the first case, Green Mountain filed suit against George Crombie, who at the time was secretary of the Vermont Agency of Natural Resources, as well as against other members of Vermont's government, over Vermont's implementation of California's stringent emissions standards. The auto firms alleged that this action would damage their businesses. The US District Court for Vermont ruled in favor of Crombie and the Vermont office-holders, allowing them to implement the California standards. This was a victory, of sorts, for climate change supporters, since the transportation sector is one of the largest air polluters in the United States. Enforcing strict emissions standards is a positive response to climate change.

In the second case, auto dealer Central Valley, along with the Association of International Automobile Manufacturers, sued James Goldstene, who was the executive officer of the California Air Resources board. The case was brought as a challenge to California's emissions standards on the grounds that those standards were preempted by the Clean Air Act. The California law imposed standards that would require all cars manufactured after 2009 to meet strict specifications for mileage per gallon. The US District Court for California upheld the state's emission standards. This decision is of consequence since it allows California, and other states that have patterned their emission standards after California's, to impose strict automobile specifications.

A final automotive case is the third case brought by the Coalition for Responsible Regulation, this one involving the National Highway Traffic Safety Administration and several other organizations. The Clean Air Act's requirement that the EPA establish vehicle emission standards brought about the EPA's Tailpipe Rule in 2010 for greenhouse gases, which sets emission standards for cars and light trucks. According to the rule, it automatically "triggers" regulation of stationary greenhouse gas emitters under two sections of the Clean Air Act. In *Coalition for Responsible Regulation v. Environmental Protection Agency* (2011),[42] the coalition is challenging the EPA's rule for light-duty vehicles, which has an important provision that triggers greenhouse gas regulation automatically from vehicles to stationary sources. The coalition wishes to dismantle this rule completely. The coalition also claims that the EPA unlawfully failed to analyze the cost and burdens that would be imposed on its members by stationary-source regulations. If the rule for light-duty vehicles is overturned by the appellate court, the impact could be similar to a court dismissal of the endangerment finding, since it would again weaken the EPA's ability to regulate efforts to address climate change.

The *Border Power Plant v. Department of Energy* (2003) case involved climate change concerns that were secondary from the outset.[43] Yet it became important because this was the first time that any court considered carbon dioxide as a pollutant. In this case, a California district court rejected a proposal for the construction of an electric line crossing the border between the United States and Mexico. The line was to connect new power plants in Mexico with the power grid in southern California. Once again, the court found that the environmental impact statement had failed to include assessments to "address the potential environmental impacts of carbon dioxide emissions," despite the fact that carbon dioxide had not yet been identified by the EPA as a pollutant.[44] The Border Power Plant group sued the US Department of Energy and the Bureau of Land Management for their failure to file such an impact statement prior to the approval of the electric-line construction project. The US District Court for San Diego ruled that the impact statement had in fact been filed, but that it was inadequate since it failed to assess the overall environmental consequences on the project.

One of the keys to establishing a workable strategy to counteract global climate change relies on generating accurate information over time. *Center for Biological Diversity v. Brennan* (2007) illustrates the importance of this standpoint.[45] In 1990, Congress passed the Global Change Research Act, which required two things: (1) submission of a research plan, with goals and priorities for information used to base policy decisions, and (2) submission of a Scientific Assessment analyzing the effects of global climate change. The US Climate Change Science Program was then created to carry out this research and analysis to "improve understanding of global change" and "analyze current trends in global [climate] change."[46] The results of the original research were published in 2000 and in 2003, but the 2006 report was not completed. The Center for Biological Diversity, Friends of the Earth, and Greenpeace filed suit against William Brennan, then–acting director of the Climate Change Science Program, to force completion of the 2006 report.

The US District Court for the case sided with the Center for Biological Diversity and ordered that the report be written and published "no later than March 1, 2008, and that the proposed Research Plan itself be submitted to Congress not later than 90 days thereafter."[47] This case is important because of the need for continued research in the field of climate change, since it is critical that actions taken to resolve global climate be based on science. Otherwise, any regulation that lacks scientific backing will be subject to skepticism. The court's ruling in this case is important because it represents an effort by the judiciary to ensure that mandated scientific research supports the laws it generates.

The issue of power companies violating EPA regulations is another aspect of the tier-two cases, and *Environmental Defense v. Duke Energy* (2007) is a good example.[48] The reason is that Duke Energy violated the EPA's 1980 regulations requiring that a permit be obtained prior to making any alterations to a facility that could result in increased emissions of pollutants.[49] Duke Energy made modifications to one of its coal-fired power plants that allowed the plant to operate longer each day, but without first obtaining the required permit. Duke Energy contended that since the modifications did not increase the hourly emissions from the plant, it was not required to obtain a permit.

When Duke Energy violated this EPA statute, the US government brought a lawsuit against the company. The Supreme Court ruled in favor of enforcing the EPA's regulations. Associate Justice David Souter, speaking for the Court, ruled that the law regarding the permits did not measure emissions on an hourly basis but on a yearly basis; and it was Duke Energy's yearly emissions that did increase as a result of the retrofit. Duke Energy was held liable for the violation. The case is important given the support the EPA received from the Court, without which it is unlikely that any EPA regulation could be enforced.

Also potentially important is the still-pending *Coke Oven Environmental Task Force v. Environmental Protection Agency* (2006) case, because of the demands it put on the EPA.[50] The Coke Oven Environmental Task Force took the EPA to court in order to force it to devise regulations governing coal-fired power plants and industrial boilers. But there were several problems affecting any actions that could be taken. First, the Supreme Court's ruling in *Massachusetts* had not yet identified carbon dioxide as a pollutant. Second, the George W. Bush administration was not encouraging action on the part of the EPA. And finally, as Barbara Underwood made clear in the *American Electric* case, "There is no Federal statute or regulation that currently regulates the emission of greenhouse gases by existing unmodified power plants. . . . The Clean Air Act doesn't regulate anything until the EPA makes findings and imposes restrictions."[51] This explains why, even though the *Coke Oven* case was first filed in 2006, it has yet to be resolved by the EPA and submitted again to the courts.

A negative precedent for climate change litigation emerged from the case of *California v. General Motors* (2007).[52] As one of the leading states in addressing the problem of climate change, California was unsuccessful in bringing a suit against six of the largest automakers in the United States—General Motors, Toyota, Ford, Honda, Daimler-Chrysler, and Nissan—for their contributions to air pollution.[53] California was initially seeking damages amounting to the cost of new infrastructure that would be necessary as a result of damages caused by global climate change. California attorney general William Westwood "Bill" Lockyer, who filed the original claim, stated: "Global warming is causing significant harm to California's environment, economy, agriculture and public health . . . costing millions of dollars and the price tag is increasing. Vehicle emissions are the single most rapidly growing source of the carbon emissions contributing to global warming, yet the federal government and automakers have refused to act. It is time to hold these companies responsible for their contribution to this crisis."[54]

The US District Court for the case dismissed the suit, indicating that it presented a "political question" that could be better handled by either the president or Congress. The case was then appealed to the Ninth Circuit Court of Appeals, but the new California attorney general, Jerry Brown, asked that the appeal be dropped, since the Obama administration had announced plans to address greenhouse gas regulation. The president, however, never followed through on this plan. While unsuccessful, the case is of interest because of the monetary redress that California sought for changes to the infrastructure to repair the potential damage caused by climate change.

Third-Tier Cases

Finally we come to the third-tier cases, beginning with one of the more interesting, *Gersh Korsinsky v. US Environmental Protection Agency* (2005).[55] As a citizen of New York, Gersh Korsinsky sued the EPA, the New York State Department of Environmental Conservation, and the New York City Department of Environmental Protection because of their failure to address climate change. The complaint was filed seeking relief under federal common law and under New York state law on public nuisance. Korsinsky accused the EPA and the New York environmental protection departments of contributing to global warming by failing to stop yearly emissions of "approximately 6,500 million tons of carbon dioxide" and by failing to implement "practical, feasible and economically viable options for eliminating carbon dioxide emissions."[56] Although each was a government agency and not directly responsible for the emissions, failure to regulate carbon dioxide was an accurate claim, but in 2006 carbon dioxide had not yet been labeled as a pollutant in need of regulation.

Korsinsky is a third-tier case because it was an unsuccessful attempt to force the EPA to regulate carbon dioxide as a pollutant. The US District Court reasoned that the climate change claim was a "generalized grievance" better suited for the political branches of government. The court also rejected Korsinsky's claims of emotional stress and other health concerns as insufficient to prove standing.[57] The Second Circuit Court of Appeals accepted the conclusion of the US District Court and dismissed the appeal.

In *Mayo Foundation v. Surface Transportation Board* (2006),[58] the Mayo Foundation (an organization concerned with animal and environmental welfare) filed a petition, along with the Sierra Club and several other organizations, to challenge a ruling by the Surface Transportation Board allowing the Dakota, Minnesota, & Eastern Railroad Corporation to construct approximately 280 miles of new rail line reaching into Wyoming's coal mines. The Mayo Foundation had a number of complaints about the building of the new railroad, but its primary concern was focused on a noise ordinance and the repercussions of the construction of the railroad. Increasing emissions through the increased use of coal by the railroad was a secondary concern. The Eighth Circuit Court of Appeals affirmed the Surface Transportation Board's new findings in December 2006, and ruled that the board had adequately considered the impact of increased coal consumption on the human environment.[59]

The final case that is relevant to third-tier issues is *Northwest Environmental Defense Center v. Owens Corning* (2006).[60] It is perhaps the most insignificant case with regard to climate change. Similar to the *Duke Energy* case, it concerned the need for permits to build a facility. Congress had already enacted a law requiring that permits be obtained prior to constructing any building that could result in additional emissions polluting the air. If the required permits were not obtained, the infraction would carry a $32,500 penalty. Northwest Environmental Defense Center sued construction company Owens Corning for a construction project that had failed to secure the proper permits. Owens Corning requested that the case be dismissed, but the US District Court for Oregon refused. Owens Corning later complied with the court order and obtained the permit, and the matter was settled.

Conclusion

While the judiciary has not been the primary actor in the United States in responding to global climate change, it could be reasonably argued that neither the president nor Congress have been actively engaged in responding to the global crisis as well. Thus it is not surprising that the Supreme Court might become the focal point of concern about climate change given the failure of Congress and the president to work together to craft a viable climate change bill.

Clearly the two top-tier case decisions—*Massachusetts v. Environmental Protection Agency* and *American Electric Power v. Connecticut* —were important in establishing significant guidelines for the Supreme Court and other decisionmakers. It was the Supreme Court that gave major support to the Clean Air Act and made this the most important piece of global climate change legislation in the United States. Further, these cases also established the Environmental Protection Agency as the primary institution to create limits and impose restrictions on pollutant emissions. And the president and Congress have not interfered with these Supreme Court decisions. In fact, they have not challenged the Court's leadership, except in passing. For example, Obama indicated during his 2008 presidential campaign that once in office he would assume leadership in responding to global warming and climate change, but this did not happen, at least during his first term in office.

The tier-two and tier-three cases surveyed in this chapter can be divided into three major categories:

1. Cases that challenged the EPA's regulations, permit system, and authority. The *Coalition* cases raised concerns regarding the endangerment finding, and the tailoring and timing rules. The *Korsinsky* case charged the EPA at the federal and state level with neglect of duty; and the *American Chemistry, Duke Energy,* and *Northwest Environmental Defense Center* cases, as well as the third *Coalition* case, raised questions about the EPA's permit system and its broadened authority.

2. Cases that found the petroleum industry to be chiefly responsible for global climate change, including the *Kivalina Village* and *Comer* cases.

3. Cases that showed a "federalism conflict" between those who were satisfied with federal standards and regulations on emissions and those who asserted that federal government restrictions on emissions were not nearly stringent enough and should be replaced by stricter state laws, as in the *Chamber of Commerce, Crombie, Goldstene,* and *General Motors* cases.

So far, the Environmental Protection Agency has withstood all efforts to undercut its legitimacy as established by the Clean Air Act and the *Massachusetts* and *Connecticut* cases. However, the central question remains: Will the many judicial decisions discussed here encourage the president and Congress to take matters into their own hands in response to climate change, or will the Environmental Protection Agency—backed by judicial sanctions—continue to provide the primary response to the global crisis?

Notes

1. G. Gordon Davis, "Essay Review: The Making of Environmental Law," *Perspectives in Biology and Medicine* 49, no. 2 (Spring 2006): 291.

2. David B. Hunter, "The Implications of Climate Change Litigation: Litigation for International Environmental Law-Making," in *Adjudicating Climate Change: State, National, and International Approaches,* edited by William C. G. Burns and Hari M. Osofsky (Cambridge: Cambridge University Press, 2009), 358.

3. The center is a nonprofit law firm that does advocacy for individuals and groups facing environmental issues.

4. Telephone interview with Brent Newell by Byron Daynes and Todd Gee, July 27, 2011.

5. *American Electric Power Co. et al. v. Connecticut et al.,* 564 US 131 S.Ct. 2527 (2011).

6. *Massachusetts v. Environmental Protection Agency,* 549 US 497 (2007).

7. Bill Clinton, "Memorandum on Carbon Dioxide Emissions," *Weekly Compilation of Presidential Documents* (April 15, 1999): 654–655.

8. Davis, "Essay Review," 292.

9. John Schwartz, "Courts as Battlefields in Climate Fights," *New York Times,* January 27, 2010, www.nytimes.com/2010/01/27/business/energy -environment.

10. Hunter, "The Implications of Climate Change Litigation," 358.

11. The states were California, Connecticut, Illinois, Maine, Massachusetts, New Jersey, New Mexico, New York, Oregon, Rhode Island, Vermont, and Washington. The local governments were New York City, Baltimore, the District of Columbia, and American Samoa. The interest groups were the Center for Biological Diversity, the Center for Food Safety, the Conservation Law Foundation, Environmental Advocates, Environmental Defense, Friends of the Earth, Greenpeace, the International Center for Technology Assessment, the National Environmental Trust, the Natural Resources Defense Council, the Sierra Club, the Union of Concerned Scientists, and the US Public Interest Research Group.

12. *Massachusetts v. Environmental Protection Agency* (2007).

13. National Research Council Report no. 16 in *Massachusetts v. Environmental Protection Agency* (2007).

14. *Massachusetts v. Environmental Protection Agency,* 549 US 497 (2007).

15. "Supreme Court: Arguments on Climate Change," *Environmental Policy and Law* 37, no. 1 (2007): 54.

16. *Massachusetts v. Environmental Protection Agency* (2007).

17. Ibid.

18. Ibid.

19. Ibid.

20. Ibid.

21. *American Electric Power v. Connecticut* (2011).

22. Hanna McCrea, "Why the Second Circuit 'Nuisance' Case Brings Good News, and Bad (Part II)," *Grist: A Beacon in the Smog,* September 25, 2009, http://grist.org/article/2009-09-24-why-second-circuit-nuisance-case-brings-good-news-and-bad-part-2/ (accessed April 18, 2013).

23. *American Electric Power v. Connecticut* (2011).

24. "The Carbon Ruling," *New York Times,* June 21, 2011, www.nytimes .com/2011/06/22/opinion/22wed2.html.

25. David G. Savage, "Supreme Court Kills Global Warming Suit," *Los Angeles Times,* June 21, 2011, http://latimes.com/news/nationworld/nation.

26. *Coalition for Responsible Regulation Inc. et al. v. Environmental Protection Agency,* 09-1322, US Court of Appeals for the District of Columbia Circuit (2011).

27. Ibid., 2.

28. Ibid., 4.

29. *Coalition for Responsible Regulation Inc. et al. v Environmental Protection Agency,* 10-1073, US Court of Appeals, District of Columbia Circuit, 684 F.3d 102 (2012).

30. *Prevention of Significant Deterioration and Title V Greenhouse Gas Tailoring Rule,* 75 Fed. Reg. 31,514 (June 3, 2010) (the "tailoring" rule); *Reconsideration of Interpretation of Regulations That Determine Pollutants Covered Clean Air Act Permitting Programs,* 75 Fed. Reg. 17,004 (April 2, 2010) (the "timing" rule). The EPA uses these rules to determine how to regulate carbon dioxide as a pollutant.

31. *Coalition for Responsible Regulation v. Environmental Protection Agency,* 10-1073, US Court of Appeals, District of Columbia Circuit, 684 F.3d 102 (2012), 2.

32. Brad Plummer, "Will the EPA's New Climate Rules Get Killed in Court?" *Washington Post,* February 27, 2012, www.washingtonpost.com/blogs.

33. *Native Village of Kivalina et al. v. Exxon Mobil Corp. et al.,* C 08-1138 SBA, US District Court, N.D. California, Oakland Division (2009).

34. Tribal Climate Change Project, "Climate Change: Realities of Relocation for Alaska Native Villages," University of Oregon, 2010, http://tribal climate.uoregon.edu/files/2010/11/AlaskaRelocation_04-13-11.pdf.

35. *Comer v. Murphy Oil,* 07-60756, US Court of Appeals, Fifth Circuit (2009).

36. *American Chemistry Council v. US Environmental Protection Agency and Lisa P. Jackson,* 10-1167, US Court of Appeals, District of Columbia Circuit (2011).

37. *Chamber of Commerce of the United States of America and National Automobile Dealers Association v. Environmental Protection Agency,* 09-1237, US Court of Appeals, District of Columbia Circuit (2011).

38. The thirteen states that have adopted California's emission standards are: Arizona, Connecticut, Maine, Maryland, Massachusetts, New Jersey, New Mexico, New York, Oregon, Pennsylvania, Rhode Island, Vermont, and Washington. Environmental Defense Fund, "13 States Adopting California Clean Car Standards Would Reap Significant Economic and Environmental Benefits," June 30, 2009, www.edf.org/news/13-states-adopting-california-clean-car-standards-would -reap-significant-economic-and-environme (accessed April 18, 2013).

39. *Center for Biodiversity v. National Highway Traffic Safety Administration,* 538 F. 3d 1172, US Court of Appeals, Ninth Circuit (2008).

40. Ibid., 9.

41. *Green Mountain Chrysler Plymouth Dodge Jeep v. George Crombie,* 2:05-cv-302, US District Court, Vermont (2007); *Central Valley Chrysler-Jeep Inc. et al. v. James Goldstene,* 529 F. Supp. 2d 1151, US District Court, Eastern California (2007).

42. *Coalition for Responsible Regulation Inc. et al. v. Environmental Protection Agency, Lisa P. Jackson, and National Highway Traffic Safety Administration,* 10-1092, US Court of Appeals, District of Columbia Circuit (2011).

43. *Border Power Plant Working Group v. Department of Energy,* 260 F. Supp. 2d 997, US District Court, San Diego, California (2003).

44. Gary Bryner, "The Rapid Evolution of Climate Change Law," *Utah Bar Journal,* April 30, 2007, http://webster.utahbar.org/barjournal/2007/04/the _rapid_evolution_of_climate.html.

45. *Center for Biological Diversity v. Dr. William Brennan,* C 06-7062 SBA, US District Court, Northern California, Oakland Division (2007).

46. *Center for Biological Diversity v. National Highway Traffic Safety Administration,* 538 F. 3d 1172, US Court of Appeals, Ninth Circuit (2008), 1. *Center for Biological Diversity v. Dr. William Brennan,* C 06-7062 SBA, US District Court, Northern California, Oakland Division (2007), 1–3.

47. Ibid., 37.

48. *Environmental Defense v. Duke Energy Corp.,* 549 US 05-848 (2007).

49. As regulated by 40 CFR 51.166 (b) (2).

50. *Coke Oven Environmental Task Force v. Environmental Protection Agency and Stephen L. Johnson,* 06-1131, US Court of Appeals, District of Columbia Circuit (2006).

51. Supreme Court oral arguments in *Connecticut v. American Electric Power Company,* 10-174 (2011).

52. *California v. General Motors Corp.,* C06-05755 MJJ, US District Court, Northern California (2007).

53. Environmental Law Institute, "California v. General Motors Corp.," in *Endangered Environmental Laws,* 2010, www.endangeredlaws.org/case _california.htm.

54. California Department of Justice, Office of the Attorney General, "Attorney General Lockyer Files Lawsuit Against 'Big Six' Automakers for Global Warming Damages in California," *In the News,* September 20, 2006, http://oag.ca.gov/news/press_release?id=1338.

55. *Gersh Korsinsky v. US Environmental Protection Agency,* 05 civ. 859 (NRB), US District Court, Southern New York (2005), 6.

56. Ibid., 4.

57. Ibid., 7.

58. *Mayo Foundation v. Surface Transportation Board,* 472 F. 3d 545, US Court of Appeals, Eighth Circuit (2006).

59. Ibid., 10.

60. *Northwest Environmental Defense Center et al. v. Owens Corning Corp.,* 04-1727-JE, US District Court, Oregon (2006), 13.

6

Interest Groups
and Public Opinion

In democratic societies, public policy is linked to citizens through interest groups, which play an integral role in shaping the policymaking process. Citizens are also linked to the political system in general and the policymaking process in particular as a result of public opinion polls. In the case of organized interests, as Steven Rosenstone and John Mark Hansen have described them, "interest groups urge people to take part in governmental politics because they want to accomplish something. . . . By participating, they hope to bring about policies that benefit them."[1] Or as Deborah Lynn Guber and Christopher Bosso have argued, "compared to their European cousins, . . . organized interest groups in the United States play disproportionately central roles in educating, organizing, and mobilizing into action relevant sectors of the mass public."[2]

In the case of public opinion, as Glen Sussman, Byron Daynes, and Jonathan West put it, "public opinion polls are conducted in order to obtain a portrait of the political orientations of American citizens" and "in a democratic society, the purpose of gaining a better understanding of public opinion is to determine the extent to which there is linkage between opinion and policy making."[3] Moreover, to paraphrase Elaine Sharp, who researched public opinion and social policy, "if we cannot find a close connection between public opinion and policy development . . . there is little reason to be sanguine about public knowledge and governmental responsiveness in other areas of public affairs."[4] In short, the extent to which there is congruence between

131

public opinion and policy outcomes remains an important aspect of modern democratic politics. Moreover, on the basis of research carried out over several decades, Robert Erickson and Kent Tedin have argued that in the United States "public opinion is far from inconsequential. At the national level, we find that opinion and national policy are in agreement more often than not."[5]

As we have discussed elsewhere in this book, the Intergovernmental Panel on Climate Change (IPCC), the US National Oceanic and Atmospheric Administration (NOAA), the US Environmental Protection Agency (EPA), the US National Aeronautics and Space Administration (NASA), environmental agencies in other countries, and numerous world leaders have stated officially that human activities are a major contributor to global climate change. In short, human actions are producing greenhouse gases, which have a profound impact on Earth's climate. Although the news media in the United States have framed an argument that suggests that the country has become polarized over the issue, the evidence indicates that the vast majority of the scientific community believe that global warming is anthropogenic, although a small but vocal group of "contrarians" or "deniers" continues to aggressively resist the science in favor of emphasizing natural climatic variability and the effects of the sun on Earth's climate. We begin this chapter by focusing on the role of organized interests, climate change, and policymaking, and then turn our attention to American public opinion, the environment in general, and global climate change in particular.

Organized Interests and Global Climate Change

Two major camps have organized around the issue of climate change, with one collection of groups committed to government action in response to the issue and the other collection of interests concerned more about government becoming too big and imposing too many regulations on business and industry. The division between the two camps has been well articulated by Erik Conway and Christopher Bosso, who highlight perceived threats to existing power and institutional relationships in the United States. On the one hand, Conway sets forth the following argument:

> The scientific findings made during the 1980s and 1990s threatened core American beliefs. Environmentalism had been divisive in the

United States because it threatened a host of traditional beliefs: in private property rights, in market capitalism, in the superiority of private over public enterprise, in technological progress, in American exceptionalism. To anyone who believed in the superiority of marketplace capitalism, and particularly to those who held the central tenet of late twentieth-century American conservative dogma, that human freedom and market capitalism were inextricably linked, the finding that human industry could cause global-scale damage had been ideologically shattering.[6]

He goes on to say that, "in the view of these political critics of late twentieth-century science, atmospheric scientists' efforts had led directly to government regulation, indeed elimination, of the chlorofluorocarbon (CFC) industry. . . . Atmospheric scientists had destroyed the comforting notion that humans could have no significant impact on Earth and its life-sustaining capabilities."[7] On the other hand, Christopher Bosso has offered additional insight into the conflict between the two camps as he highlights the importance of political culture in American society:

In the United States . . . the dominant political culture is built around core beliefs in individual liberty, limited government, private property, the Protestant work ethic, social mobility based on merit, and faith in progress and in the free market. Taken together, these beliefs make politics subordinate to the private sector and thus give business a privileged position in political debates. Because many environmentalists seek goals that question or challenge these core beliefs, their efforts to define or redefine problems have a tough time finding fertile ground.[8]

In short, due to the affirmative response of the federal government to the science of stratospheric ozone depletion (the danger posed by a hole in the ozone layer), what happened to the chlorofluorocarbon industry as a result of the commitment of the United States to the 1987 Montreal Protocol could and would, according to deniers of human-induced climate change, have the same impact on fossil fuel interests, resulting in more governmental regulation of the industry.

The importance of global warming and climate change for US politics was clearly revealed by two reports published by the Center for Public Integrity in 2009. In February the center reported that "more than 770 companies and interest groups hired an estimated 2,340 lobbyists to influence federal policy on climate change in the past year."[9] The following August, the center reported that an additional 460 "new businesses and interest groups jumped into lobbying Congress on global warming in the weeks before the House neared its historic [June 26] vote on climate change legislation."[10] Included among the leading organizations expressing support for government action on climate change are the Environmental Defense Fund, the Natural Resources Defense Fund, Greenpeace, the Sierra Club, and the National Wildlife Federation, while the US Chamber of Commerce, the National Association of Manufacturers, and the fossil fuel industry are among the groups that oppose government action on this issue.

Supporters of Government Action on Global Warming and Climate Change

As a result of an abundance of scientific research and evidence, the vast majority of the scientific community has supported the argument that government action is needed to combat global warming and climate change. The initial warning underlying the current position held by the scientific community can be found in a chapter in a 1965 report prepared by the President's Science Advisory Committee. This section of the report, authored by oceanographer Roger Revelle, highlighted two important aspects involving the global warming issue. First, he "put projections of fossil fuel use, the associated rise of atmospheric CO_2 and its climatic consequences together on a timeline for the first time"; and second, he "issued a warning that the greenhouse effect was slipping through the cracks of the Federal government's research and pollution control programmes" and had "made little substantive impression on policymakers."[11]

Policymakers were moved to consider the significance of the issue due to congressional testimony by James Hansen, director of NASA's Goddard Institute for Space Studies, who warned in 1988, that "global warming has reached a level such that we can ascribe with a high degree of confidence a cause and effect relationship between the greenhouse effect and the observed warming."[12] Twenty years after the initial warning set forth by Hansen, John Holdren, professor of environmental policy at Harvard University, asserted:

> The most important conclusions about global climate disruption—that it's real, that it's accelerating, that it's already doing significant harm, that human activities are responsible for most of it, that tipping points into really catastrophic disruption likely lurk along the "business as usual" trajectory, and that there is much that could be done to reduce the danger at affordable cost if only we would get started—have not been concocted by the Sierra Club or the enemies of capitalism.[13]

Both Hansen and Holdren were representing the scientific community in reaching out to public forums in order to inform policymakers and citizens alike of the dangers posed by global warming and climate change. Moreover, the conflict between science and politics (i.e., the science of global warming and climate change on the one hand, and political intrusion into the publication of scientific findings about the warming of the planet on the other) came to a head during the presidential administration of George W. Bush. Scientists began to complain publicly about White House interference in the form of distorting or misrepresenting their research on global warming and climate change.[14]

At about the same time that Hansen raised the issue of global warming during his congressional testimony in 1988, global warming also emerged as a top priority on the agenda of the environmental movement. As science historian Spencer Weart describes it: "The environmental movement, which had found only occasional interest in global warming, now took it up as a main cause. Groups that had other reasons for preserving tropical forests, promoting energy conservation, slowing population growth, or reducing air pollution could make common cause as they offered their various ways to reduce emissions of CO_2."[15] Over the next two decades, a variety of environmental groups with different foci, resources, sizes, tactics, and strategies became increasingly involved in the climate change issue. For instance, in 2006, two interesting changes occurred in the composition of the group of stakeholders who supported action on climate change. First, a coalition of "greens," including the Natural Resources Defense Council and the Sierra Club, joined with the Communications Workers of America and the United Steelworkers to focus their joint attention on "job-creating solutions to global warming" the same year that "over eighty evangelical Christian leaders . . . announced an 'Evangelical Climate Initiative' to fight global warming," which they saw as a "moral question sanctioned in the biblical injunction for Christians to be good stewards of the Earth."[16] Second, as Marvin Soroos points out, groups including Greenpeace, the Environmental Defense Fund, the Sierra Club, and the Union of Concerned Scientists, among others, lobbied "the administrative and legislative branches of the federal government to work for strong international agreements to address the problem."[17]

One of the interesting aspects of the movement in support of government action on global warming concerns the rapidly increasing number of groups involved in the global climate change issue as we move beyond the first decade of the twenty-first century. In addition to extant environmental groups, there is now a broad spectrum of interests involved in environmental affairs in general and climate change in particular. Among them are medical groups, religious groups, farmers, unions, and military veterans who have joined together in the Clean Energy Works coalition.[18] Moreover, this new coalition has been joined by business interests that have broken away from the coalition opposing government action on climate change. Included among the businesses that have separated from the opposition coalition are General Electric, Johnson & Johnson, Nike, British Petroleum, Shell, Xerox, Apple, Alcoa, and DuPont, a separation that led Eileen Claussen, president of the Pew Center on Global Climate Change, to state in 2009 that this change "moves the politics on this issue to a new place," while former Senate staffer Chelsea Maxwell, who worked on the climate change legislation, also remarked in 2009: "Five years ago, people saw climate change as an environmental issue, and it really goes beyond that. It's an energy issue. It's a national security issue. It's a tax issue."[19]

Before turning to the deniers of human-induced climate change, it is important to give attention to the critics of the environmental movement who have argued that it hasn't been as effective as it could be. Some have gone so far as to argue that the environmental movement has failed in its mission to protect the environment in general and find a resolution to the climate change issue in particular. In fact, two environmental activists, Michael Shellenberger and Ted Nordhaus, went so far as to argue in a paper with the ominous title "The Death of Environmentalism," presented at the 2004 meeting of the Environmental Grantmakers Association, that environmental groups themselves are responsible for the movement's "failure to mobilise and engage the wider public."[20]

The fact that two environmentalists launched such a critique of the environmental movement led numerous environmental observers to join the debate. For instance, noted political scientist Gary Bryner, in referring to climate change as the "primary environmental threat" today, argued that the existing model of interest group activism is not capable of "generating support for the kinds of broad-based policies required to address that issue."[21] So, what can be done? What should the US environmental movement do to be more effective in addressing global climate change? Philip Brick and R. McGreggor Cawley have suggested that we need to avoid pessimism about the role of environmental groups' inability to influence Congress to produce climate change legislation. Instead, more focus should be placed on how issues are framed, which would have the potential to produce a forum for new ideas and build new coalitions in support of climate change legislation.[22] In the end, climate change as an important global environmental issue will require not only traditional environmental groups but also new ideas, new alliances, and participation by national, state, and local governments along with business and industry.

Contrarians and Deniers

Among those who downplay the role played by human actions in global warming and climate change, their focus tends to be on natural climatic variability and solar radiation, among other factors. In his recent book *Hot, Flat, and Crowded,* Thomas Friedman argued that there are three types of deniers of human-induced climate change: "those paid by fossil fuel companies to deny that global warming is a serious human-induced problem; those scientists, a small minority, who have looked at the data and concluded for different reasons that the rapid and extensive increase in greenhouse gas emissions since the Industrial Revolution is not a major threat to the planet's livability; and, finally, those conservatives who simply refuse to accept the reality of climate change because they hate the solution—more government regulation and intervention."[23] Included among the contrarians are the fossil fuel, automobile, and chemical industries, some individual scientists and some corporations, members of Congress led by Oklahoma Republican senator James Inhofe, and media celebrities including Rush Limbaugh, Glenn Beck, and novelist Michael Crichton of *Jurassic Park* fame, as well as media bloggers.

We begin with the Global Climate Coalition, which represented the fundamental concerns of the contrarians. As reported by Spencer Weart, the Global Climate Coalition emerged in the late 1980s as a major voice on global warming. Throughout the 1990s, as Weart argued, "some of the biggest corporations in the petroleum, automotive, and other industries created the Global Climate Coalition (GCC), whose mission was to disparage every call for action against global warming. . . . Operating out of the offices of the National Association of Manufacturers, over the following decade the organization would spend tens of millions of dollars. It supported lectures and publications by a few skeptical scientists, produced slick publications and videos and sent them wholesale to journalists, and advertised directly to the public every doubt about the reality of global warming."[24] Moreover, the GCC used its influence and resources to oppose the requirements of the Kyoto Protocol. In doing so, it "launched an advertising campaign in the US against any agreement aimed at reducing greenhouse gases internationally," but by the late 1990s, with evidence of the role of human activities in producing greenhouse gases increasing, "several members of the GCC including Dow, DuPont, Royal Dutch Shell, Ford, General Motors among others began to drop out of the organization."[25]

The GCC attempted to exercise its influence in response to congressional debate over the 2001 Clean Power Act, which was introduced in the Senate. When the GCC testified to the Senate Committee on Environment and Public Works, it made clear its self-appointed role as the "voice for business in the climate change debate, representing every major sector of the U.S. economy—including agriculture and forestry, electric utilities, railroads, transportation, manufacturing, small businesses, mining, oil and natural gas, and coal" in arguing that the bill had "unreasonable targets and timetables that would cause immediate and long-term damage to the U.S. economy, workers, and consumers" and that it remained "committed to applying constructive approaches to voluntarily address the climate change issue."[26] When the GCC disbanded the following year, it stated that it had "served its purpose by contributing to a new national approach to global warming" and that the George W. Bush administration would "soon announce a climate policy that is expected to rely on the development of new technologies to reduce greenhouse emissions, a concept strongly supported by the GCC."[27] Given its role in opposing government action on global warming, it is interesting to note that the GCC supported the overall effort to reduce greenhouse emissions, albeit voluntarily. Moreover, as reported by the *New York Times,* scientists working in the affected industries were already well aware that human activities were largely responsible for the greenhouse gases that were warming the planet.[28]

The fossil fuel industry (petroleum, coal, natural gas) is one of the largest industries in the United States. As a result of the effort of the federal government to take action against climate change, this sector of the economy has pursued a vigorous effort to protect its interests. For instance, according to one observer of the industry, "the United States is a big advocate for coal because it has the geological good luck of having more than 25 percent of the world's recoverable coal reserves— buried within its borders. As coal industry executives never tire of pointing out, this is enough coal to fuel America at the current rate of consumption for about 250 years," so it is not surprising to discover that among the "prominent industry groups in the early years of the global warming debate was the Western Fuels Association, a group of coal-burning electric utilities and cooperatives. In the early 1990s, when the battle over global warming began to be engaged, Western Fuels began a campaign to undermine the science of climate change."[29] Moreover, the international impact of domestic interests has also been a conspicuous aspect of the climate change issue. As Robert Falkner characterized the problem, "the lobbying efforts by the U.S. fossil fuel industries . . . as well as a wide range of energy-intensive manufacturing firms (e.g., chemical manufacturers, car manufacturers) have had a powerful impact on the international negotiation position of the United States."[30] In short, as Ross Gelbspan has written, "the central argument that big coal and big oil have spent millions of dollars to amplify over the last decade is that the warming is a natural phenomenon on which human beings have little or no impact."[31]

Of course the environmental movement was also criticized from otherwise friendly actors who called on traditional environmental organized interests to embrace a new way of looking at environmental problems, particularly the climate change issue. Conservative think tanks played a role as well in their effort to act as a resource to oppose the successes of the environmental movement beginning in the 1970s.[32] Various tactics have been employed by conservative think tanks in order to induce skepticism among American citizens. As Peter Jacques, Riley Dunlap, and Mark Freeman inform us, "The central tactic employed by [conservative think tanks] in the war of ideas is the production of an endless flow of printed material ranging from books to editorials designed for public consumption to policy briefs aimed at policymakers and journalists, combined by frequent appearances by spokespersons on TV and radio."[33] Moreover, an important aspect of conservative think tank advocacy is securing legitimacy in the eyes of the larger society that is helpful in challenging the community of scientists in order to provide a sense of "balance" when addressing climate change.

The CATO Institute and the Heritage Foundation are salient examples of think tanks involved in the conservative countermovement against environmental organizations. They were actively involved in opposing any effort of the federal government to take action against human-induced global warming. For instance, in 1992, the CATO Institute published an article by Massachusetts Institute of Technology scientist Richard Lindzen in which he disagreed with the larger community of climate scientists about human-forced climate change. He asserted that the "hysteria formally began in the summer of 1988" and that, as far as he was concerned as a scientist, "there is no substantive basis for predictions of sizeable global warming due to observed increases in minor greenhouse gases such as carbon dioxide, methane, and chlorofluorocarbons."[34] More recently, the Heritage Foundation published an article in 2009 in which it provided a foundation for opposing government action on global warming. In response to the Environmental Protection Agency's decision to regulate greenhouse gases under the Clean Air Act, the authors of the article, Ben Lieberman and Nicolas Loris, provided five reasons to oppose EPA action, which they argued would be an "economy killer" with "negligible environmental benefit" based on a "lack of scientific consensus," and would result in a "backdoor policy" bypassing legislators and in "expanding bureaucracy" through which bureaucrats would increasingly manage economic activity.[35]

Numerous concerns have been raised by the deniers of human-forced climate change in response to government efforts to address the issue. While it is evident that affected industries are using their resources to protect their interests, this factor has received little, if any, salience in the arguments made by the fossil fuel industry and its allies. Instead, as Shardul Agrawala and Steinar Andresen point out, "the dominant theme of industry, labor, and conservative arguments against aggressive action on climate change has been that it would lead to loss of American jobs and trade competitiveness."[36] This is an assertion that increasingly lacks credibility.

In light of the preceding discussion, we would be remiss if we did not turn our attention to the progress being made by the private sector in addressing climate change. As David Levy argued in 2011, "After years of hostility to any carbon regulation, government incentives, competitive pressures and non-governmental organization (NGO) campaigns have led many firms in the last decade to craft business models that exploit potential market opportunities in low-carbon products and services."[37] It can be argued that there is potential in private sector or public-private cooperation in meeting the challenge of climate change. For instance, in the oil industry itself, several companies have set forth positions indicating acceptance of the science of climate change and initiatives that might be viable in response. British Petroleum, Shell, and Texaco, in particular, have been characterized as moving in a "green" direction, while Exxon remains the most adamant opponent of efforts to address anthropomorphic greenhouse gas emissions.[38]

In assessing the private sector and efforts to address climate change, CNN Money pointed out that "big business and environmentalists used to be sworn enemies and for good reason. General Electric dumped toxins into the Hudson River. Wal-Mart bulldozed its way across America. DuPont was named the nation's worst polluter."[39] Yet progress has been made as many companies have engaged in actions to reduce their carbon footprint.[40] For instance, Honda has committed to reducing its carbon output, Continental Airlines employs environmental consultants and has committed to increasing the fuel efficiency of its airplanes, S.C. Johnson (a family-owned company) has cut back on coal-fired energy, and Hewlett Packard has pledged to reduce its energy consumption. Moreover, some companies have engaged in innovative efforts to reduce greenhouse gases.[41] Examples include Honda and several other automobile companies that have focused on hydrogen fuel cells to power their vehicles, such as Toyota's Prius hybrid. General Motors's Volt, Ford's Focus, and Nissan's Leaf have opened the door to contemporary electric cars. Furthermore, efforts to promote solar, wind, and tidal power continue. And Boeing's 787 Dreamliner passenger aircraft made its debut with Chile's LAN airlines. The new 247-seat aircraft is sensitive to passenger needs, more fuel efficient, and reduces carbon dioxide emissions by 20 percent.[42]

The insurance industry has also become increasingly concerned about the impact of climate change on business, commercial, and residential interests. As explained by Sverker Jagers, Matthew Paterson, and Johannes Stripple, "The main worry of insurers has been that many of the projections of global warming have suggested it would involve increases in the incidence, severity, and location . . . of catastrophic weather events."[43] Consequently, given increased concerns about risks and payouts, US-based insurers such as State Farm and Allstate as well as global reinsurers such as Swiss Re and Munich Re have added a new dimension to the climate change issue. For instance, as Garreau, Larsen, and Mills et al. report, several insurance companies including Allstate, Traveler's Insurance, and State Farm established new criteria to offset potential losses, thus reducing their risk and payouts, while Allstate, MetLife, Farmers, and American International Group either dropped, would not renew, or no longer offered coverage in Florida, coastal New York, and North Carolina.[44] In short, coastal communities are not only vulnerable to hurricanes and flooding but increasingly lack access to insurance coverage.

Climategate and Climategate 2?

Just prior to the Copenhagen Conference, which was set to bring together representatives from almost two hundred countries in December 2009 to address global warming and greenhouse gas emissions, a political controversy arose over the unauthorized release of e-mails from the University of East Anglia's Climate Research Unit, which were posted on the Internet. As reported in the *New York Times* in January 2010, in what became known as the "Climategate" scandal, "critics seized on the messages as evidence that, in their view, climate scientists were manipulating data and colluding to keep contrary opinion out of scientific journals. But climate scientists and political leaders affirmed what they called a broad-based consensus that the planet is growing warmer, and on a consistent basis, although with measurable year-to-year variations."[45]

On the basis of the leaked e-mails, opponents of the human-induced global warming argument raised concerns about the "scientific objectivity" of climate scientists as well as the "credibility of climate science itself."[46] In response, climate scientists argued that the science is sound and that human activities have had a profound impact on the warming of the planet. The problem has included a focus on the gatekeeping process as it relates to publication of scientific papers. According to Gavin Schmidt at NASA's Goddard Institute for Space Studies, "The problem is [that] the climate field has become extremely politicized, and every time some nonsense paper gets into a proper journal, it gets blown out of all proportion."[47] And as Richard Harris of National Public Radio described it, "most of the papers Schmidt and his colleagues object to challenge the mainstream view of climate science. Schmidt says they may be wrong or even deceptive, but they are still picked up by politicians, pundits, and businesses who are skeptical of climate change."[48] James Hansen of NASA's Goddard Institute for Space Studies considers the controversy as one of global warming deniers engaged in "fishing expeditions" in an effort to "discredit climate science."[49]

On the one hand, Republicans "raised their concerns" about what they argued "appeared to show scientists discussing the manipulation of climate data."[50] On the other hand, Hansen, the scientist who testified about global warming to a Senate committee in 1988, responded in the following way: "The important point is that nothing was found in the East Anglia e-mails altering the reality and magnitude of global warming in the instrumental record. The input data for global temperature analyses are widely available," and if "those input data could be made to yield a significantly different global temperature change, contrarians would certainly have done that—but they have not."[51]

In early 2012, an unexpected release of documents from the conservative Heartland Institute made it clear that the organization "rejects the scientific underpinnings of climate change," and that it was engaged in an effort to "persuade federal and state lawmakers that manmade climate change is not harmful to society."[52] Moreover, as reported by the *New York Times,* the "leaked documents suggest [that] an organization known for attacking climate science is planning a new push to undermine the teaching of global warming in public schools, the latest indication that climate change is becoming a part of the nation's culture wars."[53]

American Public Opinion and Climate Change

While organized interests have played an important role regarding the climate change issue, it is also necessary to examine and assess public opinion among American citizens in order to ascertain the extent to which they are knowledgeable about the issue and what they think should be done about it. An assessment of public opinion polls over the last several decades reveals that Americans generally support environmental protection. Furthermore, as Walter Rosenbaum has written recently about American public opinion and the environment, "the strength of public support for environmental protection early in the twenty-first century, as measured by public opinion polls, certainly appears vigorous and widespread."[54] However, environmental concerns among the American public have rarely ranked high in public opinion polls, and generally rank quite low, when citizens are asked about what they consider to be the most critical policy issues. But at the same time, when Americans are asked specifically about environmental protection, they indicate strong support. Consequently, assessing Americans' attitudes toward the issue of environmental protection is somewhat difficult given this dichotomy.

There are two important points to be made regarding the disconnect between scientific knowledge and political orientation among Americans. First, as Sandra Marquart-Pyatt and her colleagues have recently argued, "there is strong scientific consensus concerning the reality of anthropogenic climate change . . . and its potential consequences. However, increased confidence among scientists has not translated into a public consensus within the United States."[55] Second, although the American public is not fully informed or knowledgeable about global climate change, citizens are open to some type of action even though they might not be convinced that the "science [is] settled, suggesting that public understanding and acceptance of climate science may not be a precondition for supporting action to reduce greenhouse gas emissions."[56] The problem involves what types of actions Americans are willing to accept given the potential economic impact of these actions on their families. But it is important to gauge Americans' opinions on climate change, since this environmental issue has had and will continue to have significant consequences for their lives. As Matthew Nisbet and Teresa Myers state at the outset of their assessment of trends in public opinion and climate change 1997–2007: "Spanning local, national, and international politics, global warming forces consideration of contentious policy measures that require major societal, economic, and lifestyle changes."[57]

Unlike many other environmental issues, climate change has a relatively short history of public awareness. As Nisbet and Myers inform us, although only four out of ten Americans reported in a survey in the mid-1980s that they had heard something about the issue, about nine out of ten Americans twenty years later indicated that they were aware of the issue.[58] During this time, poll data began to provide an insight into the climate change issue: that it was dividing Americans along sociodemographic lines. In short, Democrats more than Republicans, Independents, and Tea Party identifiers, women more than men, the college-educated more than those without a college education, and the young (eighteen to twenty-nine years old) more than seniors (sixty-five and older) were more likely to indicate they believed that climate change was occurring.[59]

In order to gain a better impression of Americans' attitudes about climate change, there are several important factors to consider: attitudes about the role of scientists, attitudes about the causes of climate change, and the role played by political orientation. It is also important to address the role of science, since all of us are dependent to some degree on the research provided by the scientific community. First, according to Gallup Poll data, as Table 6.1 shows, in 1998 slightly less than half (48 percent) of the American public held the view that scientists believed that global warming was occurring. By 2006 the proportion of Americans who held this view had increased to 65 percent, but it dropped to 52 percent by 2010. It is interesting to note that in 1998 45 percent of survey respondents were either unsure or did not express an opinion, but the number decreased to 38 percent in 2012. Second, in December 2011, the Pew Research Center published data about public opinion among Americans during a similar period. In this case, the proportion of Americans who believed that there was "solid evidence" that Earth was warming dropped from 77 percent in 2006 to 57 percent in 2009.[60] However, two years later, in 2011, the proportion of Americans who held this belief had increased to 63 percent. Taken together, it is safe to conclude that a majority of Americans are convinced that global warming is occurring and that a majority of Americans believe that the scientific community holds this view as well.

Americans are divided, however, on the causes of global warming, as Table 6.2 shows. In 2003, 61 percent of Americans believed that human activities were responsible for the warming of the planet; however, by 2010, the proportion of Americans holding this view had dropped to 50 percent, while 46 percent of Americans were convinced that warming was due to natural causes.[61] In comparison, in 2003, while one-third of Americans believed that natural causes were responsible for global warming, this number increased to 46 percent by 2010. Global climate change is a complex issue that is difficult for the layperson to understand. Moreover, the consequences for addressing the issue of curbing greenhouse gas emissions threaten sectors of business and industry in the United States. In short, it would involve more rather than less governmental intervention, more rather than less exercise of regulatory power, and more rather than less reduction in fossil fuels as a major source of energy.

Table 6.1   Americans' Views of the Scientific Consensus on Global Warming, 1998–2010 (percentages)

	1998	2001	2006	2008	2010
Scientists believe that global warming is occurring	48	61	65	65	52
Scientists believe that global warming is not occurring	7	4	3	7	10
Gap	+41	+57	+62	+58	+42

Source: Adapted from Frank Newport, "Americans' Global Warming Concerns Continue to Drop," *Gallup World,* March 11, 2010, www.gallup.com/poll/126560 /Americans-Global-Warming-Concerns-Continue-Drop.aspx.

Table 6.2   Americans' Views of the Causes of
            Global Warming, 2003–2010 (percentages)

	2003	2006	2007	2008	2010
Human activities	61	58	61	58	50
Natural causes	33	36	35	38	46
Gap	+28	+22	+26	+20	+4

Source: Adapted from Frank Newport, "Americans' Global Warming Concerns Continue to Drop," *Gallup World,* March 11, 2010, www.gallup.com/poll/126560 /Americans-Global-Warming-Concerns-Continue-Drop.aspx.

What might account for this variation in Americans' views about the causes of global warming and climate change? On the one hand, as Steven Kolmes argues, "there is no longer any real debate among qualified scientists about the reality of human-caused climate change. The mainstream of scientific opinion, the conclusions of 97 percent of climate scientists, and the opinion of virtually all of the most qualified climate scientists concur: Climate change is real and we are causing it."[62] On the other hand, some observers argue that a disinformation campaign has been under way by those who fear more government intervention in regulating greenhouse gas emissions. Thus, "the low percentage of Americans who really understand climate change science is the product of a long-term, well-funded, and well-documented corporate disinformation campaign" and some corporations have generously "funded disinformation campaigns in the United States that seek to spread uncertainty, slow climate change legislation, and confuse the public."[63] Despite the scientific consensus and given the complexity of the issue and the politicization of the environmental policymaking process, it is not surprising that we find Americans at odds over the causes of global warming—whether primarily human-induced or the result of natural climatic conditions.

Given this background, political orientation seems to be a major influence that divides Americans on the climate change issue. Tables 6.3 and 6.4 compare Americans' views about the causes of global warming considering partisanship. As of 2011, as Table 6.3 shows, slightly more than six out of ten Democrats believe that global warming is caused by human activities, while slightly more than one-third of Republicans hold this view. While only one in five Tea Party identifiers believed that the warming of the planet is caused by human activities, 43 percent of Independents hold this view. Table 6.4 shows the partisan gap between the two major parties and Independents on the one hand, and those who identify with the Tea Party on the other hand. The gap between Democrats and those who identify themselves as Tea Party adherents is greatest, followed by the gap between Independents and Tea Party supporters, with a smaller gap between Republicans and those who support Tea Party philosophy. In short, Tea Party identifiers who are more likely to vote Republican appear to be pulling the Republican Party to the right on the issue of the causes of climate change.

We have seen that Democrats and Independents are less likely than Republicans and Tea Party identifiers to believe that global warming is a result of natural climate cycles and more likely to view human activities as the primary influence on the warming of the planet. In a similar pattern, as shown in Tables 6.5 and 6.6, Democrats and Independents are considerably more likely than Republican and Tea Party identifiers to argue in favor of substantive efforts to address greenhouse gas emissions regardless of the actions of other countries. Among all four partisan groupings, only a small minority prefers ac-

Table 6.3 Partisanship and the Causes of Global Warming, 2011 (percentages)

	Democrats	Independents	Republicans	Tea Party
Human activities	62	43	36	19
Natural causes	25	35	43	50

Source: Adapted from A. Leiserowitz, E. Maibach, C. Roser-Renouf, and J. D. Hmielowski, *Politics and Global Warming: Democrats, Republicans, Independents, and the Tea Party* (New Haven: Yale Project on Climate Change Communication, 2011), http://environment.yale.edu/climate/files/PoliticsGlobalWarming2011.pdf.

Table 6.4 Partisan Gap on the Causes of Global Warming, 2011 (percentages)

	Gap Between Democrats and Tea Party Supporters	Gap Between Independents and Tea Party Supporters	Gap Between Republicans and Tea Party Supporters
Human activities	+43	+24	+17
Natural causes	−25	−15	−7

Source: Adapted from A. Leiserowitz, E. Maibach, C. Roser-Renouf, and J. D. Hmielowski, *Politics and Global Warming: Democrats, Republicans, Independents, and the Tea Party* (New Haven: Yale Project on Climate Change Communication, 2011), http://environment.yale.edu/climate/files/PoliticsGlobalWarming2011.pdf.

tion by the United States only if other countries take action as well. Although about half of Republicans and Tea Party identifiers support action to reduce greenhouse gas emissions regardless of the efforts of other countries, there remains a clear gap between Democrats and Independents on the one hand, and Republicans and Tea Party identifiers on the other. Among the four partisan groupings, Tea Party identifiers remain the outlier: while about half of them accept the proposition that the planet is warming, only one out of five believe that the reason is related to human activities.

Table 6.5 Partisanship and Actions to Reduce Greenhouse Gases, 2011 (percentages)

	Democrats	Independents	Republicans	Tea Party
Reduction should be pursued regardless of actions taken by other countries	71	68	54	46
Reduction should be pursued only if other countries take action	8	12	15	12

Source: Adapted from A. Leiserowitz, E. Maibach, C. Roser-Renouf, and J. D. Hmielowski, *Politics and Global Warming: Democrats, Republicans, Independents, and the Tea Party* (New Haven: Yale Project on Climate Change Communication, 2011), http://environment.yale .edu/climate/files/PoliticsGlobalWarming2011.pdf.

Table 6.6 Partisan Gap on Actions to Reduce Greenhouse Gases, 2011 (percentages)

	Gap Between Democrats and Tea Party Supporters	Gap Between Independents and Tea Party Supporters	Gap Between Republicans and Tea Party Supporters
Reduction should be pursued regardless of actions taken by other countries	+25	+22	+8
Reduction should be pursued only if other countries take action	–4	0	+3

Source: Adapted from A. Leiserowitz, E. Maibach, C. Roser-Renouf, and J. D. Hmielowski, *Politics and Global Warming: Democrats, Republicans, Independents, and the Tea Party* (New Haven: Yale Project on Climate Change Communication, 2011), http://environment.yale .edu/climate/files/PoliticsGlobalWarming2011.pdf.

Global Attitudes About Climate Change

It is important to compare the United States with other countries in assessing beliefs about climate change. Here we assess attitudes about climate change in North America, comparing the United States to Canada, and then examine these attitudes in a global perspective compared to beliefs in several other countries.

The United States and Canada

The United States and Canada, two postindustrial democracies, share a 5,000-mile border and common policy concerns about the North American continent. Among these policy concerns is climate change, which has national, regional, and international consequences. On the one hand, as Kenneth Curtis and John Carroll describe the relationship between the United States and Canada, the two countries share common values and a high level of economic interdependency, while on the other hand, as described by Lynton Caldwell, "whatever ways that Canadians and Americans can be said to 'share a common continental environment,' they unavoidably share responsibility for the impact of their respective activities upon that environment."[64] After all, as Carroll argued in the early 1990s, the United States and Canada "lead the world by a wide margin in terms of gross national resource consumption and environmental impact" and the "people of both Canada and the United States contribute a vastly disproportionate share of global contamination, leading to such developments as climate change," among other regional and global environmental threats.[65]

Against this background, the unique nature of transboundary, binational relations suggests that nations that share borders might be characterized as relatively distinct in the global environmental policymaking process. For instance, Caldwell characterized environmentalism in the Canadian-US framework in the following way in 1985: "The ecological perspective on life and the world for North Americans tends to be continental in a global context."[66] Moreover, a decade later, Caldwell highlighted the importance and impact of democratic politics in the United States and Canada as it related to environmental affairs. Caldwell maintained that, "especially in the leading industrial democracies—Canada, . . . and the United States—organized and active citizen groups had pressured their government for legislative and administrative action to protect and restore the quality of the environment."[67]

Given the close relationship between the two countries in general and their similar approach to environmental affairs in particular, how do the American and Canadian publics assess the climate change issue? Table 6.7 compares Americans and Canadians on three issues related to climate change—the seriousness of climate change, the existence of solid evidence about the warming of the planet, and attitudes toward scientific opinion.

Canadians and Americans have both similar and different views about these three issues. First, on the one hand, a majority of Americans (53 percent) and of Canadians (71 percent) agree that climate change is a serious problem. On the other hand, a gap of almost 20 percent divides Americans and Canadians on this question. Second, on the one hand, a majority of Americans (58 percent) and of Canadians (80 percent) are convinced that solid evidence exists that the planet is warming. Yet, once again, a gap of about 20 percent divides the two publics on this issue. Third, on the one hand, almost half of Americans (47 percent) and about one-third of Canadians (36 percent) believe that scientists have overstated the evidence about human-induced climate change. But a gap of over 10 percent divides the two publics on this issue.

Given this background, it is useful to explore "the nature of the opinion-policy relationship in Canada," which Stuart Soroka and Christopher Wlezien have done in a study linking public opinion and

Table 6.7 Comparing Americans' and Canadians' Views on Climate Change, 2010 (percentages)

Agree That Climate Change Is a Serious Problem		Agree That Solid Evidence for Climate Change Exists		Agree That Scientists Overstate the Evidence	
United States	Canada	United States	Canada	United States	Canada
53	71	58	80	47	36

Sources: Adapted from Anita Pugliese and Julie Ray, "Fewer Americans, Europeans View Global Warming As a Threat," Gallup World, April 20, 2011, www.gallup.com/poll/147203/Fewer-Americans-Europeans-View-Global-Warming-Threat.asp; Christopher Borick, Erick Lachapelle, and Barry Rabe, "Climate Compared: Public Opinion on Climate Change in the United States and Canada" (Ann Arbor: Center for Local, State, and Urban Policy [Gerald Ford School of Public Policy, University of Michigan] and Institute of Public Opinion [Muhlenberg College], February 23, 2011), www.sustainableprosperity.ca/article911.

policy outcomes in the country. "There is evidence of policy representation in Canada—public policy does regularly follow public preferences, across a number of policy domains," but it is also the case that,
"as in many other advanced industrial democracies, there has been a
steady increase in disaffection with governments and leaders in
Canada—particularly an increase in the number of people who feel
that government does not represent their interests."[68] Given the large
proportion of Canadians who believe that climate change is a serious
problem and that solid evidence for climate change exists, the fact that
in December 2011 Canada became the first country to announce that it
was withdrawing from the Kyoto Protocol might be considered surprising. However, ideology can be seen as playing a major role in
Canadian politics on this issue. In short, as reported by *BBC News,*
where "Canada's previous liberal government signed the accord . . .
current Prime Minister Stephen Harper's Conservative government
never embraced it."[69] Moreover, Canadian environment minister Peter
Kent "broke the news on his return from talks in Durban [that] delegates to the climate change summit agreed to extend Kyoto for five
years and hammer out a new deal forcing all big polluters for the first
time to limit greenhouse gas emissions."[70]

An International Perspective

A variety of public opinion polls have been conducted to ascertain political orientations about climate change among citizens in countries
around the globe.[71] It has become apparent that there are similarities
and differences between countries on issues relating to climate change,
and that the differences are particularly apparent when comparing
wealthy and poor countries.

Table 6.8 compares the opinions of citizens in the top five greenhouse gas–emitting countries—China, India, Japan, Russia, and the
United States. In two surveys, the first in 2007–2008 and the second in
2010, citizens in these five countries were asked whether they considered climate change to be a serious threat. Several conclusions can be
drawn from the survey findings. First, for 2007–2008, the five countries can be divided into three tiers of citizen concern about climate
change, with India and Japan showing the greatest concern, followed
by the United States showing more moderate concern, and with Russia
and China showing the least concern. Second, the 2010 follow-up survey revealed a similar pattern, with India and Japan showing the great-

est concern, Russia and the United States showing more moderate concern, and China alone showing the least concern. Third, in the period between the two surveys, concern about climate change increased slightly in Russia and India, but decreased slightly in China, Japan, and the United States. The United States exhibited the largest decline in concern about the seriousness of climate change, while Russia exhibited the largest increase.

Characteristics of American Public Opinion on Climate Change

Notwithstanding the abundance of information produced by academics, scientists, and the news media about climate change as an important environmental issue both nationally and globally, the American public remains decidedly different compared to citizens in both wealthy and newly industrializing economies. In short, Americans have become less likely to accept climate change as a serious issue having severe consequences. Moreover, current opinion among Americans on climate change can be used by opponents to engage in delaying tactics and also provides the US government with a justification to act as a constraint on global attempts to address climate change in a substantive way. In other words, it has become increasingly difficult for the United States to remain engaged in multilateral efforts to secure viable climate change policy. Consequently, the credibility of the role of the United States in climate change policymaking has been put into question.

What might explain the nature and characteristics of the American public and its political orientations toward climate change? Let us set

Table 6.8   Is Climate Change a Serious Threat? Comparing Citizen Concern in the Top Five Greenhouse Gas–Emitting Countries, 2007–2008 and 2010 (percentages)

	China	India	Japan	Russia	United States
2007–2008	34	82	80	47	64
2010	32	83	77	55	55
Percentage change	−2	+1	−3	+8	−9

Source: Adapted from Julie Ray and Anita Pugliese, "World's Top-Emitters No More Aware of Climate Change in 2010," Gallup World, August 26, 2011, www.gallup.com/poll/149207/world-top-emitters-no-aware-climate-change-2010.aspx.

forth the following, as we have suggested elsewhere.[72] First, the state of the US economy remains the preeminent influence on contemporary American opinion. Arguably, it has become more difficult for Americans to view climate change with a sense of urgency since the 2007–2009 financial crisis and recession, given the increase in home foreclosures, unemployment, budget deficits, and national debt. Second, and similarly, it is understandable that Americans are reluctant to accept the urgency of climate change given their weariness from supporting two wars (Iraq and Afghanistan) while other potential international threats remain (e.g., leadership changes in North Korea and Russia, potential threats from Iran, and a continued focus on the war on terrorism). Third, partisan divisiveness over the issue of climate change has led to gridlock within Congress and between Congress and the president, and was particularly evident during President Barack Obama's 2012 reelection campaign as Republican contenders sought to exploit this divisiveness.

Fourth, solutions to climate change will not be easy, and will challenge the resolve of the American public, business and industry, and government at all levels. In the pursuit to secure viable solutions, business and industry, including the fossil fuel industry, will likely see any proposed solution as a threat to their interests and argue publicly that any efforts to address climate change will threaten the economy and job creation. It is interesting to note that business and industry, the scientific community, the environmental movement, and the US Senate during the presidency of Ronald Reagan were able to work together in support of the Montreal Protocol, which encouraged reduction of ozone-depleting chemicals in the late 1980s. President George H. W. Bush was able to organize a similar coalition in support of the Clean Air Act amendments in 1990. But more recently, it has been difficult to organize such a viable coalition in support of efforts to address climate change.

Fifth, ideology has become the prism through which supporters and opponents view climate change. Liberals and conservatives within and outside government view the issue from completely different perspectives. For instance, former Democratic vice president Al Gore referred to climate change as an "inconvenient truth," while *New York Times* journalist Thomas Friedman lamented in his book *Hot, Flat, and Crowded* about the muddy question of "whether humans are causing dangerous climate change" and "the impression that any assertion that human actions are changing the climate is merely a political opinion, not a scientific fact."[73] In contrast, as noted in Chapter 1, both media celebrity Rush Limbaugh and Oklahoma senator James Inhofe have pushed the notion that climate change is a "hoax." More recently, former Pennsylvania senator Rick Santorum, in seeking the Republican nomination for president in 2012, echoed both Limbaugh and Inhofe by referring to climate change as a "hoax" during a debate in Jacksonville, Florida.

Sixth, it is clear that the political rhetoric about climate change has confused and divided the American people about an important and complex issue involving the warming of the planet. In short, the argument that has been advanced by those who are convinced that global warming is caused by human activities has been opposed by those who argue that natural climate cycles are the primary cause.

Seventh, poll data indicate that even when Americans believe that climate change is human-induced, they are less likely than their European counterparts to accept sacrifices in order to address the problem. As Christopher Borick has argued, "the willingness of the public to pay for alternative energy development significantly outpaces its support for using taxes to reduce consumption of fossil fuels."[74] But despite Americans' aversion to tax-based solutions, they are more accepting of tax incentives to assist those who might consider purchasing energy-efficient products. For example, on the basis of a series of surveys, Borick found in 2010 that three out of four Americans were in favor of tax incentives to support the purchase of hybrid fuel–powered vehicles.[75]

Finally, the climate change issue, as it has evolved in the United States, demonstrates unequivocally the "science and politics" problem, whereby once an issue becomes politicized, it becomes more difficult for the scientific community to educate the American public about that issue. At the same time, there have been strong efforts by business and industry and lawmakers to thwart government action on climate change.

Conclusion

In a democratic society such as the United States, citizens are connected to policymaking through a variety of linkages, including interest group activism and public opinion. As we have seen, organized interests have been an integral part of the debate and discussions on climate change. Whereas environmental groups have advocated for substantive climate change policy to reduce greenhouse gas emissions, business and industry, and especially the fossil fuel sector, have used their considerable resources to oppose increased governmental intervention and the imposition of new regulations to curb these emissions. Moreover, some observers have argued that business and industry have not only used their influence to shape climate change policy, but also have engaged in a disinformation campaign to sway or confuse the American public. Given the politicization of the issue, it remains likely that divisiveness rather than cooperation on climate change policy will continue to characterize the actions of interest groups in the US political setting.

The impact of public opinion on the policymaking process in the United States has long been debated. While some observers have argued that lawmakers should not take into account the views of a malleable or uninformed electorate, others argue that policymakers are likely to consider public opinion when it is salient, intense, and stable over time, while still others see public opinion as providing the parameters for government action.[76] In the end, public opinion gives us a portrait of the American public at a given time and, more importantly, over time. American public opinion about climate change illustrates a mixed picture of both stability and variation.

While most Americans believe that climate change is occurring, the proportion of Americans who believe that human activities are a major factor has declined, despite the scientific consensus that global warming is anthropogenic. Among the explanations set forth for understanding Americans' views on climate change, partisanship plays a major role. Democrats more than Independents, Independents more than Republicans, and Republicans more than Tea Party identifiers are more likely to believe that climate change is occurring and that human activities are a major contributor to this environmental phenomenon. Another way to put it, according to Jeffrey Jones, is that public opinion polls have shown that "environmental concerns tend to take a back seat to economic matters when the economy is in poor shape" and that "Americans worry less about environmental concerns under Democratic presidents, who are generally rated higher on environmental protection than Republican presidents."[77] However, as other observers have argued, there is a difference in how climate change has been reported in the news media in the United States compared to other countries. In short, as several news media observers inform us, the scientific consensus on climate change has not been adequately communicated to the American public at the same time that the vocal minority of skeptics and deniers of climate change have been given more coverage than merited by their numbers.[78] Furthermore, "Climategate" may well have added additional confusion to Americans' understanding of global climate change.

Across the US border to the north, Canadians have exhibited more concern, overall, about climate change than have their American counterparts. They are more likely than Americans to view it as a serious problem, more likely to believe that solid evidence exists, and less likely to hold the opinion that scientists are overstating the evidence about climate change. However, near the end of 2011, despite the opinions about climate change held by Canadian citizens, the Canadian government renounced the Kyoto Protocol and made it clear that it would not engage in a post-Kyoto multilateral agreement.

As a result of the 2012 election, a Democratic presidential incumbent defeated former Republican Massachusetts governor Mitt Romney. The presidential election was consequential because the two candidates had differing views about how to address the climate change issue. However, despite President Obama's attempt to keep the climate change issue on his second term agenda, and despite the fact that Democrats maintained control of the US Senate, the president has been thwarted on this issue as Republicans retained control of the House of Representatives. Moreover, Tea Party adherents and groups opposed to action on climate change flexed their muscles during the 2012 campaign in order to influence climate change policy in Washington, as well as in state capitals around the country.

Environmentalists along with their allies in the Congress, as well as state and local political actors and the scientific community, have pushed strategies to address the threat posed by climate change and the warming of the planet. In contrast, deniers have questioned the science undergirding the arguments of those who seek government action; they have stressed uncertainties in order to delay action, and they have argued that even if climate change is occurring, it is more likely that it is a result of natural climate patterns rather than human activities. There has been a recent surge in the number of groups and their lobbyists involved in the climate change issue. From the National Wildlife Federation to the US Chamber of Commerce, from the Sierra Club to the National Association of Manufacturers, the climate change issue has involved all sectors of society—economic, social, political, and scientific. It has also been an emotional issue, with some opponents calling global warming a "hoax" and government action a direct threat to the economy and jobs.

We argue that a fundamental schism dividing the two sides rests with the perceived impact of government action. Environmentalists, for instance, express concern that humanity is heading toward a tipping point where it might be too late to reverse climate change. For deniers, government action means more "big government"—more government intervention in the affairs of business and industry.

In addition to the role of organized interests in the climate change issue is American public opinion, which provides a portrait of the view of citizens regarding this global phenomenon. As shown in this chapter, public opinion in the United States has been affected by the conflict between interest groups, partisanship, and ideology. Moreover, opinion in the United States differs compared to opinion in its neighbor to the north, Canada, as well as in other countries.

The American public can be characterized, on the whole, as accepting the argument that climate change is happening and that the scientific evidence of a warming planet is solid. Still, the size of this majority opinion has fluctuated. Furthermore, Americans are divided on the causes of climate change. As we have seen, they are almost evenly divided as to whether human activities or natural phenomena are responsible for a warming planet.

These differences in the beliefs of the American public can be found in their partisanship and ideology. Where Democrats and Independents are more likely to accept the scientific community's assessment that climate change is resulting from human activities, Republicans and especially Tea Party identifiers are more likely to reject this idea. A related factor involves ideology, where liberals and conservatives diverge, with liberals accepting the reality of the impact of human activities on the planet and conservatives less likely to accept this fact. Given that the United States and Canada share the North American continent, have been longtime allies and trade partners, and share the longest undefended border in the world, it is interesting to note the variation in opinions between Americans and Canadians. For example, despite majority opinion in both countries, poll data reveal that Canadians are much more likely than Americans to view climate change as a serious problem and to view the scientific evidence for a warming planet as solid.

There are also differences of opinion on climate change between the United States and China, India, Japan, and Russia—the other top greenhouse gas–emitting countries. India and Japan show the greatest concern for climate change as a threat, Russia and the United States show less concern, and China shows the least. More important, whereas Russians have become more concerned about climate change recently, Americans have become less concerned about the seriousness of this global environmental threat.

Notes

1. Steven J. Rosenstone and John Mark Hansen, *Mobilization, Participation, and Democracy in America* (New York: Macmillan, 1993), 101.

2. Deborah Lynn Guber and Christopher J. Bosso, "Past the Tipping Point? Public Discourse and the Role of the Environmental Movement in a Post-Bush Era," in *Environmental Policy: New Directions for the Twenty-First Century,* edited by Norman J. Vig and Michael E. Kraft, 7th ed. (Washington, DC: Congressional Quarterly, 2010), 61.

3. Glen Sussman, Byron W. Daynes, and Jonathan P. West, *American Politics and the Environment* (New York: Longman, 1992), 59.

4. Elaine Sharp, *The Sometime Connection: Public Opinion and Social Policy* (Albany: State University of New York Press, 1999), 3.

5. Robert S. Erickson and Kent L. Tedin, *American Public Opinion,* 7th ed. (New York: Longman, 2007), 331.

6. Conway, *Atmospheric Science at NASA,* 314–315.

7. Ibid.

8. Robert J. Duffy, *The Green Agenda in American Politics* (Lawrence: University of Kansas Press, 2003), 41.

9. Marianne Lavelle, "The Climate Change Lobby Explosion," Center for Public Integrity, February 25, 2009, www.publicintegrity.org/investigations /climate_change/articles/entry/1171.

10. Marianne Lavelle, "Tally of Interests on Climate Bill Tops a Thousand," Center for Public Integrity, August 10, 2009, www.publicintegrity.org /investigations/climate_change/articles/entry/1608.

11. David M. Hart and David G. Victor, "Scientific Elites and the Making of US Policy for Climate Change Research, 1957–74," *Social Studies of Science* 23 (November 1993): 657.

12. James Hansen, "The Greenhouse Effect: Impacts on Current Global Temperature and Regional Heat Waves," Testimony to the US Senate, Committee on Energy and Natural Resources, June 23, 1988, Washington, DC.

13. Thomas L. Friedman, *Hot, Flat, and Crowded* (New York: Farrar, Straus, and Giroux, 2008), 124.

14. Miller, *Environmental Politics,* 146.

15. Spencer Weart, "The Public and Climate Change," American Institute of Physics, February 2013, www.aip.org/history/climate/public2.htm.

16. Guber and Bosso, "Past the Tipping Point?" 62–63.

17. Marvin S. Soroos, "Negotiating Our Climate," in *Global Climate Change,* edited by Sharon L. Spray and Karen L. McGlothlin (Lanham: Rowman and Littlefield, 2002), 140.

18. Lisa Lerer, "New Climate Coalition Launches," *Politico,* September 8, 2009, http://dyn.politico.com/news/stories/0909/26873.html.

19. Lavelle, "The Climate Change Lobby Explosion."

20. David Schlosberg and Elizabeth Bomberg, "Perspectives on American Environmentalism," *Environmental Politics* 17 (April 2008): 190. For the full paper, see http://grist.org/article/doe-reprint.

21. Gary Bryner, "Failure and Opportunity: Environmental Groups in US Climate Change Policy," *Environmental Politics* 17 (April 2008): 323.

22. Philip Brick and R. McGreggor Cawley, "Producing Political Climate Change: The Hidden Life of US Environmentalism," *Environmental Politics* 17 (April 2008): 200–218.

23. Friedman, *Hot, Flat, and Crowded,* 114–115.

24. Weart, "The Public and Climate Change."

25. Sourcewatch, "Global Climate Coalition," www.sourcewatch.org/index .php?title=Global_Climate_Coalition.

26. Global Climate Coalition, "Statement of the Global Climate Coalition Before the Senate Committee on Environment and Public Works Hearing on S.556, the Clean Power Act," November 1, 2001, US Senate Committee on Environment and Public Works, http://eps.senate.gov/107th/Global_Climate_Coalition.htm.

27. Sourcewatch, "Global Climate Coalition."

28. Andrew C. Revkin, "Industry Ignored Its Scientists on Climate," *New York Times,* April 24, 2009.

29. Jeff Goodal, *Big Coal* (Boston: Houghton Mifflin, 2006), xv–xvi, 180.

30. Robert Falkner, "Business Conflict and US International Environmental Policy: Ozone, Climate, and Biodiversity," in *The Environment, International Relations, and US Foreign Policy,* edited by Paul G. Harris (Washington, DC: Georgetown University Press, 2001), 166.

31. Gelbspan, *Boiling Point,* 24.

32. Aaron McCright and Riley E. Dunlap, "Defeating Kyoto: The Conservative Movement's Impact on US Climate Change Policy," *Social Problems* 50 (2003): 348–373.

33. Peter J. Jacques, Riley E. Dunlap, and Mark Freeman, "The Organisation of Denial: Conservative Think Tanks and Environmental Skepticism," *Environmental Politics* 17 (June 2008): 355.

34. Richard S. Lindzen, "Global Warming: The Origin and Nature of the Alleged Scientific Consensus," CATO Institute, 1992, www.cato.org/pubs /regulation/regv15n2/reg15n2.html.

35. Ben Lieberman and Nicolas D. Loris, "Five Reasons the EPA Should Not Attempt to Deal with Global Warming," Heritage Foundation, April 23, 2009, www.heritage.org/Research/EnergyandEnvironment/wm2407.cfm.

36. Shardul Agrawala and Steinar Andresen, "Indispensability and Indefensibility? The United States in the Climate Treaty Negotiations," *Global Governance* 5 (1999): 471–472.

37. David L. Levy, "Mobilizing the Private Sector on Climate Change," Climate Inc., June 14, 2011, http://climateinc.org/2011/06/ti_bus_models.

38. David L. Levy, "Business and the Evolution of the Climate Regime: The Dynamics of Corporate Strategies," in *The Business of Global Environmental Governance,* edited by David L. Levy and Peter J. Newell (Cambridge: Massachusetts Institute of Technology Press, 2005), 83–86.

39. Marc Gunther, "Green Is Good," CNN Money, March 22, 2007, http://money.cnn.com/magazines/fortune/fortune_archives/2007/04/02/8403418.

40. "Going Green: 10 Green Giants," CNN Money, July 3, 2007, http://money.cnn.com/galleries/2007/fortune/0703/gallery.green_giants.fortune/index.html.

41. Bryan Walsh et al., "Global Warming: The Causes, the Perils, the Solutions," *Time,* special edition, 2012.

42. "Dreamliner Makes Its Debut in Chile," *New York Times,* September 16, 2012.

43. Sverker C. Jagers, Matthew Paterson, and Johannes Stripple, "Privatizing Governance, Practicing Triage: Securitization of Insurance Risks and the Politics of Global Warming," in Levy and Newell, *The Business of Global Environmental Governance,* 253.

44. J. Larsen, "Hurricane Dangers Soar to New Levels," 2007, Environmental News Network, www.enn.com/archive.html?id=1629&cat=net; J. Garreau, "Batten Down the Hatches: Climate Change Already Has a Chilling Effect on Coastal Homeowners," *Washington Post National Weekly* 24 (2006): 4, 6; E. Mills et al., "Insurance in a Climate of Change: Availability and Affordability," 2013, http://insurance.lblgov/availability-affordability.html.

45. Broder, "Past Decade Warmest on Record."

46. Fred Guterl, "Iceberg Ahead," *Newsweek,* March 1, 2010.

47. Richard Harris, "Stolen E-Mails Raise Questions on Climate Research," Environmental News Network, November 16, 2009, www.enn.com/top_stories/article/40759.

48. Ibid.

49. James Hansen, "The Temperature of Science," December 16, 2009, www.columbia.edu/~jehl/mailings/2009/20091216_TemperatureOfScience.pdf.

50. "EPA Issues Greenhouse Gas Warning Despite Concerns over Leaked E-Mails," *Fox News,* December 7, 2009, www.foxnews.com/politics/2009/12/07/republicans-slam-epa-decision-declare-public-health-danger.

51. Hansen, "The Temperature of Science."

52. Evan Lehmann, "Claiming That It Is a Hoax Victim, Skeptic Group Insists Climate Change Will Be Only a 'Bad Memory,'" *ClimateWire,* February 16, 2012.

53. Justin Gillis and Leslie Kaufman, "In Documents, a Plan to Discredit Climate Teaching," *New York Times,* February 16, 2012.

54. Walter A. Rosenbaum, *Environmental Politics and Policy,* 8th ed. (Washington, DC: Congressional Quarterly, 2011), 60.

55. Sandra T. Marquart-Pyatt et al., "Understanding Public Opinion on Climate Change: A Call for Research," *Environment* 53 (July–August 2011): 38.

56. Ted Nordhaus and Michael Shellenberger, "Apocalypse Fatigue: Losing the Public on Climate Change," *Environment* 360 (November 16, 2009), http://e360.yale.edu/content/feature.msp?id=2210.

57. Matthew C. Nisbet and Teresa Myers, "The Polls: Trends—Twenty Years of Public Opinion About Global Warming," *Public Opinion Quarterly* 71 (Fall 2007): 444.

58. Ibid., 444–445.

59. Christopher Borick, Erick Lachapelle, and Barry Rabe, "Climate Compared: Public Opinion on Climate Change in the United States and Canada" (Ann Arbor: Center for Local, State, and Urban Policy, University of Michigan, 2001), www.sustainableprosperity.ca/article911.

60. Pew Research Center for the People and the Press, "Modest Rise in Number Saying There Is 'Solid Evidence' of Global Warming," December 1, 2011, http://pewresearch.org/pubs/2137/global-warming-environment-partisan -divide-?src=prc-headline.

61. Ibid.

62. Steven Kolmes, "Climate Change: A Disinformation Campaign," *Environment* 53 (July–August 2011): 34.

63. Ibid.

64. Kenneth M. Curtis and John E. Carroll, *Canadian-American Relations* (Lexington, MA: Lexington Books, 1983), 1; Lynton Keith Caldwell, "Binational Responsibilities for a Shared Environment," in *Canada and the United States,* edited by Charles F. Dornan and John H. Siglar (Englewood Cliffs, NJ: Prentice Hall, 1985), 205–206.

65. John E. Carroll, "Environmental Issues and Future Canadian Policy," in *Canada and the United States in the 1990s,* edited by William Winegard et al. (Washington, DC: Brassey's, 1991), 29.

66. Caldwell, "Binational Responsibilities for a Shared Environment," 27.

67. Lynton Keith Caldwell, *International Environmental Policy: From the Twentieth to the Twenty-First Century,* 3rd ed. (Durham, NC: Duke University Press, 1996), 35.

68. Stuart Soroka and Christopher Wlezien, "Public Opinion and Public Policy," in *Oxford Handbook of Canadian Politics,* edited by John Courtney and David Smith (Oxford: Oxford University Press, 2010), 13, 1.

69. "Canada to Withdraw from Kyoto Protocol," *BBC News,* December 13, 2012, www.bbc.co.uk/news.

70. David Ljunggren and Randall Palmer, "Canada First Nation to Pull Out of Kyoto Protocol," Environmental News Network, December 13, 2011, www.enn.com/top_stories/article/43704.

71. See, for instance, Anita Pugliese and Julie Ray, "Fewer Americans, Europeans View Global Warming As a Threat," *Gallup World,* April 20, 2011, www.gallup.com/poll/147203/Fewer-Americans-Europeans-View-Global -Warming-Threat.asp; World Bank, "Public Attitudes Toward Climate Change: Findings from a Multi-Country Poll," in *World Development Report 2010* (Washington, DC, 2010); Tara Burghart, "Survey Finds Widespread Agreement Across Globe That Climate Change Is a Pressing Problem," March 14, 2007, www.worldpublicopinion.org.

72. Daynes and Sussman, "Global Warming,"198, 215.

73. Friedman, *Hot, Flat, and Crowded,* 115.

74. Christopher P. Borick, "American Public Opinion and Climate Change," in Rabe, *Greenhouse Governance,* 51.

75. Ibid., 52.

76. See, for instance, V. O. Key Jr., *Public Opinion and American Democracy* (New York: Knopf, 1964); Jeff Manza and Fay Lomax Cook, "A Democratic Polity: Three Views of Policy Responsiveness to Public Opinion in the United States," *American Politics Research* 30 (2002): 630–667; John Kingdon, *Agendas, Alternatives, and Public Policies* (New York: Longman, 2003).

77. Jeffrey M. Jones, "In US, Concerns About Global Warming at Lower Levels," *Gallup World,* March 14, 2011, www.gallup.com/poll/146606 /Concerns-Global-Warming-Stable-Lower-Levels.aspx?version=print.

78. L. Antilla, "Climate of Skepticism: US Newspaper Coverage of the Science of Climate Change," *Global Environmental Change* 15 (2005): 338–352; M. Boykoff and J. Boykoff, "Balance as Bias: Global Warming and the US Prestige Press," *Global Environmental Change* 14 (2004): 125–136; J. M. Dispensa and R. J. Bruille, "Media's Social Construction of Environmental Issues: Focus on Global Warming—A Comparative Study," *International Journal of Sociology and Social Policy* 23 (2003): 74–105.

7

The States Weigh In

Prior to passage of the National Environmental Policy Act (NEPA) in 1969, the environmental policy process in the United States was linked primarily to state politics, wherein policymakers were inclined to support economic development over protection of the environment. Subsequent to the adoption of NEPA, for the first time, the federal government was brought into the environmental policy process as a dominant player. But although the laws and regulations emanating from Washington set the tone for the rest of the country, it is up to the fifty states to carry out the mandate of the federal government. As Norman Miller has argued,

> Since states and local governments are closer to the problems, they had a better grasp of their sources, and of the available options for addressing those issues. They can thus tackle them in the most efficient and effective way and in a manner that minimizes adverse economic and social consequences, especially since most of these laws have quite a different impact on the various jurisdictions. To that extent, devolution of implementation to levels of government closer to the people is a practical allocation of authority and action, but such power sharing is not without its challenges—and its politics.[1]

And while Evan Ringquist confirmed that the states play an important role in environmental policymaking, James Lester reminded us that the actions of the individual states are influenced by a variety of factors that can result in some states taking substantive action while others might delay action, with some states having commitment but no capacity while others have the capacity but not the commitment to act.[2] In short, as Susanne Moser points out in her study of inaction on climate change, "countless sub-national governmental and non-governmental entities have stepped into this federal vacuum. The question is whether this growing mitigation activity in the U.S. amounts to anything of substance."[3]

An examination of actions in response to global climate change at the state and local level since 2000 shows us that federalism works and that it is a vital part of structuring effective environmental regulatory policy. When, for example, the Bill Clinton administration reluctantly refused to submit the Kyoto Protocol to the Senate for ratification, and when Clinton's successor, George W. Bush, pulled out completely from any commitment to this international environmental agreement, a number of states and cities adopted Kyoto standards on their own. These actions encouraged Sharen Begley to suggest that it is fruitful, when it comes to remedies for greenhouse gas emissions in the United States, to "think subnational."[4] Against this background, and given the reluctance of the federal government to offer a substantive effort to address greenhouse gas emissions, a *New York Times* editorial argued that US states and cities have "quietly been making serious commitments to curb emissions. Instead of finding reasons to do nothing, Congress should build on these actions to fashion a national response to climate change."[5]

In 2009, in a joint report, the Pew Center on the States and the Pew Center on Global Climate Change observed that "two trends are apparent with regard to state and regional efforts to address climate change: (1) more states are taking action and (2) they are adopting more types of policies. In this way, states and regions are acting as both leaders and innovators of climate change policy."[6] What stands out when assessing these trends is that despite political differences that divide the states, red and blue states alike have been engaged in efforts to address climate change in response to inaction by the national government. The Pew Report suggested that "since many individual states are major sources of greenhouse gas (GHG) emissions, state-level policies have the potential to produce significant reductions" and that by "acting as policy laboratories, states have been able to tailor policies to their own circumstances, test innovative approaches, and build experience with program design and implementation."[7] Moreover, the underlying rationale for the states and regions to engage in efforts to regulate greenhouse gas emissions in the face of inaction at the federal level centers on two primary reasons—first, state leaders have become concerned about the "projected economic and environmental toll of climate change on their states," and second, many of the states view climate change as an "economic opportunity" for them in new markets with increasing chances for "producing and selling alternative fuels, ramping up renewable energy exports, attracting high-tech business, and selling GHG emission reduction credits."[8]

State innovation in environmental policymaking can be important for three reasons. First, the action of one state can encourage policy diffusion as multiple states decide to join forces with the original state that adopted climate change regulation, as happened when Iowa in 1983 implemented a renewable electricity standard that set minimum thresholds on electricity produced by renewable energy sources. By the 1990s, Connecticut, Massachusetts, Maine, Nevada, New Jersey, and Wisconsin had all adopted the Iowa standard, and by 2008 there were twenty-nine states and the District of Columbia that had eventually followed Iowa's lead.[9] Second, state innovation can be important by encouraging the federal government to adopt environmental standards that reflect those of the states, as occurred when Governor Ronald Reagan of California in 1974 signed a law on appliance efficiency standards. Other states followed California's lead and by 1986 a similar standard had been set at the federal level.[10] Third, state innovation can be important because, if state environmental policies succeed, they may encourage action by the private sector to reduce greenhouse gas emissions. For example, Siemens, Coca-Cola, and Dow Chemical created "sustainability" programs, although they did so for different reasons. As Sharen Begley suggests: "For biofuels companies, averting climate change is only one selling point. . . . Breaking free of dependence on foreign oil and creating jobs that can't be exported . . . are arguably more important."[11] Businesses may be interested in addressing climate change, Begley indicates, because by "selling green tech, the market for their wares remains strong thanks to regional and state laws, such as Europe's requirements for greenhouse-gas reductions under the Kyoto treaty . . . and the twenty-nine state requirements that some percentage of electricity be generated by zero-carbon fuels."[12]

Innovation and Obstructionism in the States

In 1995, James Lester organized US states into four types as they relate to performance on environmental policymaking.[13] By using two dimensions—commitment and capacity—he was able to show graphically how and why some states perform well while others underperform. For instance, a state with high commitment and high capacity is much more capable of exhibiting progress in the environmental domain compared to a state that has low commitment and low capacity.

The discussion that follows is framed along the lines of Lester's approach. California, for example, can be categorized as a state that has the resources and the intention of taking action to improve the quality of its environment. In contrast, regardless of state capacity, partisanship has guided the actions of Utah's lawmakers. Using Lester's policy types, California might be categorized as a "progressive" state in responding to climate change, while Utah would be classified as a "regressive" state where lawmakers are inclined to reject the science on climate change and instead remain guided by ideology and the fear of regulatory policy set in Washington.

State Innovation:
California and Governor Arnold Schwarzenegger

As Barry Rabe has informed us in his authoritative account of the role of US states in climate change policy, a number of states have been proactive and sought solutions to the greenhouse gas problem. For example, legislation was passed in Minnesota in 1993 that included the "environmental and economic impacts of carbon dioxide releases as a formal component of decisions on energy development," while in the Pacific Northwest a 1997 law passed in Oregon "established carbon dioxide emissions standards for any new electrical power plants opened in the state."[14]

We believe that a critical part of state innovation has come from the leadership of state governors and other state leaders in support of governors' policies. This certainly is the case in California. Governor Arnold Schwarzenegger worked with both Democrats and Republicans in the state to gain the support he needed in taking innovative steps toward limiting greenhouse gases. As a result of his efforts, California sought to implement a state law to cut "greenhouse-gas emissions 25 percent by the year 2020" and, as Schwarzenegger pointed out, encouraged the federal government and the Barack Obama administration, in particular, to adopt the state's standards for low-carbon fuels' tailpipe emissions, which it did.[15]

In addition, California, under Schwarzenegger's leadership, instituted independent measures to reduce greenhouse gases, such as switching to low-sulfur fuel in 2006 and implementing an emissions performance standard for all retail providers of electricity in the state.[16] Moreover, in August 2006, the California state legislature passed the Global Warming Solutions Act, which established "the first-in-the-world comprehensive program for regulatory and market mechanisms to achieve real, quantifiable, cost-effective reductions in greenhouse gases."[17] Governor Schwarzenegger signed the bill the following month. During the same month, the governor signed an agreement with then–British prime minister Tony Blair to work in partnership to develop climate change initiatives.[18] Five months later, the California governor signed an executive order that would "reduce dependence on oil, boost clean technology efforts, and reduce greenhouse gas emissions by at least 10%."[19] Moreover, subnational activity within California has spread beyond the United States through its international agreements with cities in Canada, China, Europe, and Mexico.[20]

Notwithstanding these strong initiatives to address global climate change at home and abroad, Schwarzenegger eventually ran into trouble over vehicle emission standards with Stephen Johnson, the administrator of the Environmental Protection Agency (EPA) under President George W. Bush. As Walter Rosenbaum describes the process, "The federal Clean Air Act entitles California to set its own vehicle emissions standards, provided these exceed federal rules and the EPA administrator grants California a waiver to set the standards. If the waiver exists, other states may adopt similar standards."[21] Although California along with a dozen or so other states expected the waiver to be issued, Johnson refused to provide the waiver, resulting in acerbic political conflict as both sides tried to make their case and prevail amid congressional hearings. As discussed further in Chapter 4, in 2007 the Supreme Court issued a ruling that set the stage for the EPA to determine whether and to what extent carbon dioxide (CO_2) was a public and environmental threat. It would be up to the EPA to then establish appropriate regulatory measures to address threats posed by greenhouse gases. Due to continued obstruction by Johnson, the Bush administration was sued during the spring of 2008 by a coalition of eighteen states, two cities, and eleven environmental organizations. The suit argued that the administration had refused to comply with the Supreme Court's 2007 ruling.[22]

In 2008, a change in presidents also meant new leadership at the EPA. Lisa Jackson, who was appointed EPA administrator by newly elected president Barack Obama, determined that carbon dioxide was indeed a threat to the environment and a threat to public health. On June 30, 2009, the EPA granted the waiver to California for its "greenhouse gas emission standards for motor vehicles beginning with the 2009 model year."[23]

State Obstructionism: The Case of Utah

Some states have been equally concerned about the federal government's role regarding the regulatory process and greenhouse gas emissions, which has encouraged legal actions against the federal government. For instance, in February 2010 the Republican-dominated Utah state legislature passed a nonbinding joint resolution on climate change demanding that the Environmental Protection Agency immediately "halt its carbon dioxide reduction policies and programs and withdraw its 'Endangerment Finding' and related regulations until a full and independent investigation of the climate data conspiracy and global warming science can be substantiated."[24]

A sampling of some of the clauses in the legislation provides a sense of how intensely the state legislators felt about the issue. In the bill were allusions to the "climate change 'gravy train,' estimated at more than $7 billion annually in federal government grants that may have influenced the climate change research focus." Furthermore, there was the assertion in the bill that "there has been a concerted effort by climate change alarmists to marginalize those in the scientific community who are skeptical of global warming by manipulating or pressuring peer-reviewed publications to keep contrary or competing scientific viewpoints and findings on global warming from being reviewed and published" as well as the argument that the "'hockey stick' global warming assertion has been discredited and climate alarmists' carbon dioxide–related global warming hypothesis is unable to account for the current downturn in global temperatures."[25] Along with the hyperbole in the resolution was a deep concern among lawmakers that Utah might have to submit to new regulations imposed on the state by the federal government.

Multistate Obstructionism

While California under the leadership of Governor Schwarzenegger demonstrated a strong commitment to engage in efforts to reduce greenhouse gas emissions, a different response emanated from several states in the late 1990s due to concerns that state interests would be negatively impacted by new climate change regulations. Rabe informs us that as the decade of the 1990s was coming to a close, "sixteen states (Alabama, Arizona, Colorado, Idaho, Illinois, Indiana, Kentucky, Michigan, Mississippi, North Dakota, Ohio, Pennsylvania, South Carolina, Virginia, West Virginia, and Wyoming) passed legislation or resolutions that were critical of the Kyoto Protocol."[26]

The actions of Michigan and West Virginia are illustrative of this period. Against a background of historical support for environmental protection, during the period 1991–2003 the governor of Michigan, John Engler, viewed environmental regulation as being at odds with economic development.[27] He used his executive and legislative powers in support of economic development at the expense of protecting the environment. But in the gubernatorial election of 2002, Engler's lieutenant governor lost to Democrat Jennifer Granholm, who "emphasized a renewed commitment to environmental protection as one of her major campaign issues."[28] In West Virginia, lawmakers opposed unilateral action by the states and instituted a policy to enforce this philosophy; in 1998, legislation was passed that "prevented state agencies from entering into any agreement with any federal agencies intended to reduce the state's greenhouse gas emissions."[29] Moreover, under New Mexico's newly elected governor, Susana Martinez, her southwestern state was viewed as "bucking EPA's efforts to regulate emissions."[30]

More recently, other states have opposed the trend to reduce greenhouse gas emissions. For instance, as reported in the *Washington Post,* six southeastern states—Alabama, Georgia, North Carolina, South Carolina, Tennessee, and Virginia—would constitute the "world's seventh-biggest emitter" of greenhouse gases "if they were a single country."[31]

State Efforts to Address Global Climate Change

As a result, in part, of inaction by the federal government to implement substantive measures to address climate change, state governments have engaged in a variety of actions to fill the gap. According to the Council of State Governments, the states have taken the lead in addressing global climate change by drafting climate action plans, encouraging participation in regional alliances, enacting standards for renewable energy and energy efficiency, reducing emissions in the transportation sector, and generating green jobs.[32]

Climate Action Plans

The issue of climate change has been politicized in the United States, but it doesn't have to be this way. The scientific community has demonstrated unequivocally that human activities contribute to the warming of the planet and other climate changes. While delay and obstruction characterize policymaking at the federal level, one of the changes that has occurred at the state level is the development of climate action plans in a majority of the fifty states. The action plans are in response to the accumulation of greenhouse gases, especially carbon dioxide, in the atmosphere, and the goal is to reduce emissions of these pollutants, which are linked to climate change. The Environmental Protection Agency describes a state-level climate action plan as

> a comprehensive document that outlines a state's response to climate change, tailored to the state's specific circumstances. It typically includes a detailed emissions inventory; baseline and projected emissions; a discussion of the potential impacts of climate change on the state's resources; opportunities for emissions reductions; emission reduction goals; and an implementation plan. It also usually identifies and recommends policy options based on criteria such as emission reduction potential, cost-effectiveness, and political feasibility.[33]

In short, a climate action plan "lays out a strategy, including specific policy recommendations that a state will use to address climate change and reduce its greenhouse gas emissions."[34] An examination of greenhouse gas emission data at the state level illustrates the problem.

Table 7.1 shows CO_2 emissions in the fifty states from 1990 to 2008. Among the fifty states, only eight reduced their carbon dioxide emissions during the period. All of the other forty-two states increased their carbon dioxide emissions. Among the states that achieved a significant decrease in the period were Massachusetts (–10 percent), Hawaii (–9 percent), and New York (–9 percent). Among the states that have significantly increased their CO_2 emissions were Arizona (64 percent), Colorado (50 percent), Iowa (48 percent), South Carolina (45 percent), and Nebraska (42 percent). Moreover, nine states increased their carbon dioxide emissions by approximately one-third, while eleven states increased their emissions by about one-fourth.

In 2009 the Energy Information Administration (EIA) published an updated profile of the fifty states and their CO_2 emissions.[35] This

Table 7.1 Carbon Dioxide Emissions by State, 1990 and 2008 (million metric tons)

	1990	2008	Percentage Change
Alabama	109.2	139.1	+27.4
Alaska	34.6	39.4	+13.9
Arizona	62.7	103.0	+64.3
Arkansas	50.5	64.8	+28.3
California	364.4	392.3	+7.7
Colorado	65.1	97.5	+49.8
Connecticut	41.0	38.1	−7.1
Delaware	17.4	16.4	−5.9
Florida	189.0	240.4	+27.2
Georgia	138.8	174.4	+25.7
Hawaii	21.7	19.7	−9.2
Idaho	11.2	15.6	+39.3
Illinois	193.7	241.7	+24.8
Indiana	206.3	232.0	+12.5
Iowa	59.9	88.1	+47.8
Kansas	69.7	77.3	+10.9
Kentucky	117.6	154.9	+31.7
Louisiana	179.8	174.8	−2.8
Maine	19.0	18.8	−1.1
Maryland	70.3	74.4	+5.8
Massachusetts	83.9	75.5	−10.0
Michigan	180.3	176.2	−2.3
Minnesota	78.5	103.8	+32.2
Mississippi	47.9	63.7	+33.0
Missouri	104.3	137.8	+32.1
Montana	27.6	36.0	+30.4
Nebraska	32.6	46.2	+41.7
Nevada	30.5	41.0	+34.4
New Hampshire	14.7	18.9	+28.6
New Jersey	113.9	127.8	+12.2
New Mexico	53.2	57.6	+8.3
New York	209.4	190.9	−8.8
North Carolina	110.7	150.1	+35.6
North Dakota	44.3	53.0	+19.6
Ohio	246.2	262.3	+6.5
Oklahoma	88.2	112.1	+27.1
Oregon	30.6	43.0	+40.5
Pennsylvania	264.4	265.1	+0.3
Rhode Island	8.7	10.7	+23.0
South Carolina	59.2	86.0	+45.3
South Dakota	11.7	14.9	+27.4
Tennessee	104.0	120.1	+15.5
Texas	554.5	622.7	+12.3
Utah	54.2	69.9	+29.0
Vermont	5.5	6.1	+10.9
Virginia	94.8	118.4	+24.9
Washington	70.4	79.4	+12.8
West Virginia	107.7	112.9	+4.8
Wisconsin	85.4	105.9	+24.0
Wyoming	56.4	66.9	+18.6

Source: Adapted from the Energy Information Agency, Department of Energy, "State Energy-Related Carbon Dioxide Emissions Estimates," October 2010, www.eia.doe.gov/oiaf/1605/state_emissions.html.

Note: States that reduced carbon dioxide emissions are shown in italic.

study, however, used a shorter time frame (2000–2009) compared to that in Table 7.1. In this case, the EIA indicated that forty-seven states decreased their CO_2 emissions during the period, while the other three increased their CO_2 emissions. One way to understand the difference between these two studies is to account for the rapid expansion of industry during the 1990s along with the added increase in consumption of fossil fuels, which resulted in an increase in the production of greenhouse gases. In contrast, during the first decade of the twenty-first century, the 2007–2009 financial crisis and recession had a negative impact on the economy and on business and industry that led to a decrease in the use of fossil fuels and therefore a reduction in greenhouse gas emissions.

It is important to note that in a large country such as the United States, there are a variety of factors that can result in an increase or decrease in greenhouse gas emissions in the fifty states, including the type of fuels used, the types of businesses operating, the climate, and the population density.[36] For instance, a sparsely populated state such as Wyoming, with just over half a million residents, had the highest production of greenhouse gases in the United States in 2009 on a per capita basis, while the state's neighbor to the west, Idaho, benefited from the increased use of hydroelectric power and reduced its carbon-based fuel usage. Moreover, states with large metropolitan populations, such as New York, benefit from mass transportation in serving their densely structured residential areas, as well as from "efficiencies of scale in terms of energy use for heating and cooling."[37]

A study published in October 2010 indicated that geography may have an impact on how individual states approach the problem of greenhouse gas emissions.[38] According to the study, states that voted for Obama in the 2008 presidential election (the blue states of the coastal west, the upper midwest, and the northeast) were more likely to support EPA rules intended to reduce greenhouse gases, while states that voted against Obama (the red states of the Rocky Mountain west, the plains, and the south) were more likely to oppose EPA rules. An example of this geographical conflict has been seen in Utah, where much effort is expended in protecting the state's rights against the demands of the federal government. As University of California at Los Angeles professor Matthew Kahn put it, there is a "divide between wealthier, more educated states that are sympathetic to green causes and blue-collar, more carbon-intensive states that would stand to lose the most if greenhouse gas regulations ended up imposing heavy costs on the economy."[39] The point is that a variety of factors are at work (from partisanship to type of energy used to variability in regional climate) that differently influence the behavior of lawmakers and citizens in different states, resulting in actions put forth in support of or in opposition to regulatory efforts to address greenhouse gas emissions.

As noted earlier, California has taken the lead on climate change. In 2006 it passed the first enforceable climate change legislation, the Global Warming Solutions Act. More important, this set a standard for the other states for developing comprehensive climate action plans. According to the Pew Report, by January 2009, six states either had revised or were developing a climate action plan, and by August 2010, the EPA reported that thirty states had completed a climate action plan.[40] These plans are an important step in determining the seriousness of the climate change problem in each of the fifty states, what procedures will be needed to implement such plans, and what incentives will be needed to encourage reduction of greenhouse gas emissions.

Virginia's climate action plan, for example, illustrates this effort. In September 2007, Virginia governor Tim Kaine issued an executive order that established a commission on climate change as part of his overall energy plan.[41] Included among members of the commission were scientists, economists, environmentalists, representatives from the energy, transportation, building, and manufacturing sectors, along with state and local lawmakers. The commission had the responsibility to inventory the amount and sources of greenhouse gas emissions; evaluate expected impacts of climate change on the state's natural resources, public health, and economy; identify what was needed in order to prepare for climate changes; identify actions needed to reduce emissions by 30 percent; and finally, learn more about the actions being taken by other states, regions, and the federal government.

After spending almost the entire year of 2008 studying the problem, the commission set forth the following findings. First, sea-level rise was considered a major threat to coastal Virginia, affordable and available insurance might be lost, and climate change was considered a threat to national security. Second, climate change would have a significant impact on the state's ecosystems, and Chesapeake Bay was subject to a variety of threats including loss of marine species due to a reduction in oxygen levels in the bay as well as loss of coastal wetlands. Third, as a result of severe weather events (e.g., floods, droughts, hurricanes, heat waves), public health was at risk either directly or indirectly, including through the spread of illnesses such as the West Nile virus and Lyme disease. Fourth, a substantial financial investment was deemed a necessity to address greenhouse gas reductions along with moving toward a carbon-reduced economy, conserving and increasing existing natural carbon sinks, and reducing emissions from major sources of pollution. It is important to note that the US Energy Information Administration had determined that on a per capita basis, Virginia consumed more energy than most European countries, including the United Kingdom, Germany, France, and Italy. Finally, a significant and quantifiable goal was set forth—a 30 percent reduction of greenhouse gas emissions by 2025, which would remove 69 million metric tons of carbon dioxide from the atmosphere.

After assessing these important concerns, the commission made these recommendations, among others: Virginia would reduce greenhouse gas emissions by increasing energy efficiency and improving conservation efforts; state representatives would encourage federal actions to reduce emissions; emissions from cars and trucks would be reduced by increasing efficiency and use of alternative fuels, while more reliance on renewable energy sources would be encouraged; Virginia would expand state capacity to ensure implementation of the action plan; citizens would be educated by the state about climate change and efforts to address it; and the state would continually monitor, track, and report on greenhouse gas emissions and the impact of climate change.

This brief account of Virginia's climate change commission illustrates the complexity of the climate change issue in general and as it relates to politics and policymaking in the states. It is important to note that although the commission's final report was adopted on a unanimous vote, not all members agreed on all of the findings, nor on all of the recommendations. Nevertheless, a framework was created that eventually resulted in Virginia being included among the thirty states that had produced a climate change action plan as of August 2010.

Regional Alliances

Effective regional alliances have emerged in the United States in an effort to reduce greenhouse gas emissions, including the Conference of New England Governors, the Regional Greenhouse Gas Initiative, the Midwestern Initiative, and the Western Climate Initiative. Although the New England alliance resulted in a nonbinding agreement, which also involved five eastern Canadian provinces, all parties agreed to voluntarily pursue similar reductions in greenhouse gas emissions beginning in 2001.[42] The Regional Greenhouse Gas Initiative was established in 2005 by seven northeastern and mid-Atlantic states: Connecticut, Delaware, Maine, New Hampshire, New Jersey, New York, and Vermont. The purpose of this initiative was to implement a "cap and trade" program to reduce carbon dioxide emissions from power plants.[43] By 2011, three additional states—Maryland, Massachusetts, and Rhode Island—had became members of this initiative. The increase in membership is an important step in addressing greenhouse gas emissions, since, as the Pew Report informs us, "emissions are recorded and tracked through The Climate Registry, an independent greenhouse gas registry."[44]

As part of the Midwest Initiative, in late 2007 six states—Illinois, Iowa, Kansas, Michigan, Minnesota, and Wisconsin—joined with the Canadian province of Manitoba and drew up the Midwestern Greenhouse Gas Reduction Accord, wherein all parties agreed to reduce greenhouse gas emissions by up to 80 percent of their levels at that time. This process was to be implemented through a "cap and trade" agreement that was to begin in 2010.[45] And as part of the Western Climate Initiative, in 2007 five governors in the western United States committed to reducing greenhouse gas emissions in an effort to respond to climate change. As of 2011, the initiative included Arizona, California, New Mexico, Montana, Oregon, Washington, and Utah, as well as four Canadian provinces—British Columbia, Manitoba, Ontario, and Quebec. The initiative's goal is to reduce collective greenhouse gas emissions by 15 percent of their 2005 levels by 2020.[46] Moreover, six states in Mexico—Baja California, Chihuahua, Coahuila, Nuevo Leon, Sonora, and Tamaulipas—have assumed observer status, indicating that they are giving serious consideration to joining the Western Climate Initiative at some point in the near future.

Finally, a note regarding the evolving importance of regional alliances where US states have reached out to their neighbors across the country as a means to reduce greenhouse gas emissions. In March 2012, three existing groups—Midwestern Greenhouse Gas Reduction Accord, the Regional Greenhouse Gas Initiative, and the Western Climate Initiative—merged into the new North America 2050 alliance, with the following goals: "move their jurisdictions toward a low carbon economy while creating jobs, enhancing energy independence and security, protecting public health and the environment, and demonstrating climate leadership."[47] This new alliance includes sixteen states

(Arizona, California, Connecticut, Delaware, Illinois, Maine, Maryland, Massachusetts, Minnesota, Montana, New Jersey, New Mexico, Oregon, Rhode Island, Vermont, and Washington) and four Canadian provinces (British Columbia, Manitoba, Ontario, and Quebec). Based on the proposition that multistate initiatives can be effective and efficient, it is expected that North America 2050 can succeed in its combined effort.

Renewable Energy Portfolio and Energy Efficiency

Complementing action plans and regional alliances, states have also adopted standards for renewable energy and energy efficiency. While the former are concerned with increasing the use of renewable, nonfossil fuels, the latter involve maximizing and conserving energy sources that are already available.

Renewable electricity has become an important means of addressing climate change. Renewable electricity standards, according to the Council of State Governments, "require a certain percentage or amount of electricity generation [to come] from eligible renewable sources by a given state"; the overall purpose of the standards is to reduce "emissions of greenhouse gases—chiefly carbon dioxide—by incorporating a greater diversity of renewable energy into a state's energy portfolio, especially by supplementing coal-fired generation in areas where coal is heavily used."[48] Sources of renewable energy include geothermal, solar, wind, and biomass.

According to the US Energy Information Administration, renewable energy generation has increased conspicuously in most states during the period 2001–2011, with wind identified as the "largest driver of this increase across the states."[49] While Texas has been leading the way on wind power, hydropower remains a major source of renewable energy particularly in western states. Given the continuing delays at the federal level, this bodes well for the country as a whole, as states continue their effort to move, albeit slowly, from traditional energy sources in general to renewable electricity sources in particular. Table 7.2 ranks the fifty states in terms of their renewable electricity generation. The states of the coastal west—Washington, California, and Oregon—are the top three producers of electricity using renewable energy sources, with the second and third largest states—New York and Texas—placing fourth and fifth respectively. At the bottom end of the renewable electricity generation spectrum are New Jersey, Nebraska,

Hawaii, Rhode Island, and Delaware. Table 7.2 shows that, on a regional basis, six of the top ten states taking the lead in utilizing renewable sources of energy to produce electricity are western states (including Montana, Idaho, and Arizona in addition to the others just mentioned).

Along with increased use of renewable energy sources, states are also making an effort to conserve energy and to increase energy efficiency. According to Steven Nadel, executive director of the nonprofit American Council for an Energy-Efficient Economy, "The overall story here is one of states getting done what Congress has failed to do while noting that the federal government's allocation of $11 billion from the federal Recovery Program provided financial assistance to the states in their effort to promote energy efficiency."[50] Many of the states have made considerable progress on this front, having spent almost twice as much on energy efficiency in 2010 compared to 2007, and

Table 7.2　State Renewable Electricity Generation Rankings, 2010

1	Washington	26	Virginia
2	California	27	Wisconsin
3	Oregon	28	Kentucky
4	New York	29	Illinois
5	Texas	30	Louisiana
6	Alabama	31	Wyoming
7	Idaho	32	New Hampshire
8	Tennessee	33	Kansas
9	Montana	34	Maryland
10	Iowa	35	Massachusetts
11	Maine	36	Missouri
12	Minnesota	37	West Virginia
13	North Carolina	38	Indiana
14	Arizona	39	Vermont
15	Oklahoma	40	New Mexico
16	Georgia	41	Mississippi
17	Pennsylvania	42	Alaska
18	Arkansas	43	Utah
19	Colorado	44	Connecticut
20	South Dakota	45	Ohio
21	Florida	46	New Jersey
22	North Dakota	47	Nebraska
23	Nevada	48	Hawaii
24	South Carolina	49	Rhode Island
25	Michigan	50	Delaware

Source: Adapted from the Energy Information Agency, Department of Energy, "State Renewable Electricity Profiles," March 2012, www.eia.gov/renewable/state.

have also made important progress in utilizing the latest technology in construction of energy efficient homes and commercial properties.[51]

Table 7.3 categorizes the fifty states into three groups in terms of energy efficiency. Once again, the states of the coastal west—California, Oregon, and Washington—rank at the top in their commitment to energy efficiency. Rounding out the top ten, the states of the northeast—including Massachusetts, New York, Vermont, Connecticut, and Rhode Island—also perform well, as do Maryland in the mid-Atlantic and Minnesota in the upper Midwest. With the exception of West Virginia and Alaska, the states with the worst performance on energy efficiency are from the south and upper plains, including Nebraska, Louisiana, Missouri, Kansas, South Dakota, Wyoming, North Dakota, and Mississippi.

Texas in particular, as a large state in terms of both geography and population, has assumed an interesting and important role through its commitment to clean energy. As noted, Texas leads the nation in terms of wind power and ranks fifth on renewable electricity generation, but ranks thirty-second in terms of energy efficiency. It also remains a major producer of greenhouse gas emissions. Moreover, Texas (along with neighboring New Mexico under Governor Susana Martinez) has actively opposed EPA efforts to regulate greenhouse gas emissions emanating primarily from coal-fired power plants and oil refineries. In fact, in January 2011, Texas lost its third attempt to stop the EPA from exercising its right to regulate greenhouse gas emissions when a federal appellate court ruled against the

Table 7.3   State Energy Efficiency Rankings, 2012

Top 10	Massachusetts, California, New York, Oregon, Vermont, Connecticut, Rhode Island, Washington, Maryland and Minnesota (tied)
Middle 30	Iowa, Arizona, Michigan, Colorado, Illinois, New Jersey, Wisconsin, Hawaii, New Hampshire, Pennsylvania, Utah, Idaho, North Carolina, Ohio, Maine, Montana, Delaware, New Mexico, Florida, Nevada, Tennessee, Georgia, Indiana, Texas, Kentucky, Arkansas, Virginia, Oklahoma, Alabama, South Carolina
Bottom 10	Nebraska, Louisiana, Missouri, Kansas, Alaska, South Dakota, Wyoming, West Virginia, North Dakota, Mississippi

Source: Adapted from the American Council for an Energy-Efficient Economy, "ACEEE 2012 State Energy Efficiency Scorecard Ranking," 2012, www.aceee.org /energy-efficiency-sector/state-policy/aceee-state-scorecard-ranking.

state.[52] Texas reflects a dual and perhaps contradictory approach to clean energy—making a profound effort in development of wind power while at the same time attempting to protect its longtime petroleum industry as well as the numerous coal-fired power plants in the state. Texas will remain a state to watch as the United States moves forward on issues of energy and environment.

The Transportation Sector

Transportation accounts for approximately 28 percent of greenhouse gas emissions in the United States, with 62 percent of these emissions resulting from trucks and passenger vehicles.[53] There have been several state agreements negotiated in an effort to reduce greenhouse gas emissions arising from the transportation sector. In 2002, with the passage of the Pavley Global Warming Bill, California became one of the first states to attempt to reduce emissions from light-duty vehicles (passenger cars and trucks), with a 30 percent reduction goal by 2016.[54] Although the automobile industry attempted to block implementation of this legislation, the effort failed when the lawsuit was dismissed. As of 2011, fifteen states—Arizona, Colorado, Connecticut, Delaware, Maine, Maryland, Massachusetts, New Jersey, New Mexico, New York, Oregon, Pennsylvania, Rhode Island, Vermont, and Washington—had indicated either that they would follow the lead of California or that they intended to do so.[55] If all of the states do follow California's lead in reducing tailpipe greenhouse gas emissions, this would result in a reduction of at least 200 million tons of atmospheric carbon dioxide pollution annually.[56]

A related effort to address greenhouse gas emissions in the transportation sector involves new fuel standards. In May 2009, President Obama announced that a new fuel efficiency goal for light-duty trucks and passenger vehicles—35.5 miles per gallon—would take effect for new models beginning in 2016.[57] Moreover, as the Council of State Governments reported in 2009, the governors of eleven mid-Atlantic and northeastern states joined together in signing a memorandum of understanding to develop low-carbon vehicle fuel standards, an action taken by California in January 2010.[58]

Several states have pushed other measures to reduce vehicle-related impacts on climate change. For instance, in the midwest, Illinois "requires state agencies to purchase flexfuel vehicles that run on E85 (fuel that contains up to 85 percent ethanol)," while in the Pacific northwest,

Washington provides "various tax exemptions, credits or rebates for alternative fuels and vehicles" and Oregon and Washington "have the oldest . . . complete streets policies" (a program initiated by the Obama administration whereby "bicycles and pedestrian projects" are placed on an "equal footing with road and transit work").[59] Furthermore, Oregon and Washington have made significant strides in encouraging the use of mass transportation through investment in public transit, road pricing, ride sharing, and building of additional cycling lanes.[60]

Given this background, how well have the states performed in terms of aligning their transportation policies with their goals to address climate change and reduce greenhouse gas emissions? In December 2010, Smart Growth America and the National Resources Defense Council published a report that ranked the states in terms of their transportation policies as related to performance on climate change goals. As Table 7.4 shows, while a few states achieved positive results, more rather than less work needs to be done. The overall portrait of state action shows that California, Connecticut, Maryland, and New Jersey performed the best. However, not one of the states received an "A" grade. Moreover, the fact that four states fell into the "D" category, while forty-two states received a failing grade, reflects a sad state of affairs for the states in terms of aligning their transportation policies with their goals to reduce greenhouse gas emissions and deal seriously with climate change. However, as reported in October 2012, a positive trend concerns a twenty-two-state effort, led by Virginia, to begin conversion to cleaner, alternative fuels for fleets of state vehicles.[61]

The Smart Growth America and National Resources Defense Council report offers several suggestions for the federal government and the states to consider.[62] States are encouraged to promote public transportation, make highway repair and safety a higher priority than new construction, promote smart growth patterns linking transportation with land use, and commit to appropriate reductions in greenhouse gas emissions. The federal government is encouraged to set specific greenhouse gas emission targets, assess emission impacts from transportation, reform financing and funding formulas to reward reductions in driving and fuel consumption, and allocate revenue received from greenhouse gas fees to support investment in clean transportation modes. In short, the states have to do much more to ensure a sustainable transportation sector that is shaped to reduce greenhouse gas emissions and the resulting impact of climate change.

Table 7.4   Transportation Policy and Performance on
             Climate Change Goals Among the States, 2010

Climate Change Performance Grade	States
A	None
B	California
C	Connecticut, Maryland, New Jersey
D	Massachusetts, Oregon, Rhode Island, Washington
F	Alabama, Alaska, Arizona, Arkansas, Colorado, Delaware, Florida, Georgia, Hawaii, Idaho, Illinois, Indiana, Iowa, Kansas, Kentucky, Louisiana, Maine, Michigan, Minnesota, Mississippi, Missouri, Montana, Nebraska, Nevada, New Hampshire, New Mexico, New York, North Carolina, North Dakota, Ohio, Oklahoma, Pennsylvania, South Carolina, South Dakota, Tennessee, Texas, Utah, Vermont, Virginia, West Virginia, Wisconsin, Wyoming

Source: Adapted from Smart Growth America and Natural Resources Defense Council, "Getting Back on Track: Aligning State Transportation Policy with Climate Change Goals," December 14, 2010, www.nrdc.org/smartgrowth/files/GettingBackon Track_4pgr.pdf.

Note: Grades represent the extent to which states' transportation policies reduce greenhouse gas emissions. The goal is to align transportation policy with climate change goals.

Green Jobs

According to Pew Charitable Trusts, "A clean energy economy generates jobs, businesses and investments while expanding clean energy production, increasing energy efficiency, reducing greenhouse gas emissions, waste and pollution, and conserving water and other natural resources."[63] During the period 1998–2007, for instance, clean energy jobs—a mix of white- and blue-collar positions varying from scientists and engineers to electricians, machinists, and teachers—grew by 9.1 percent, while overall job growth was only 3.7 percent.[64] This is an unprecedented and profound employment factor with important implications for the future.

An increasing number of states have acted proactively to address climate change through the development of "green jobs." By 2007, about 770,000 green jobs had been created, with over 125,000 of them located in California and 55,000 in Texas.[65] California, as a leader in job creation, has posted gains from green jobs in a variety of sectors in the overall state economy. As reported in the *Los Angeles Times,* California's "core green economy" includes several important occupational fields such as research and advocacy, finance and investment, energy efficiency, recycling, and building.[66] In addition to the environmentally friendly job growth in California and Texas, the largest growth in green jobs has occurred in Pennsylvania (39,000 green jobs created by 2007), Ohio (35,000), New York (34,000), Florida (31,000), Illinois (28,000), Massachusetts (27,000), New Jersey (25,000), and Michigan (23,000). Overall, in 2007, "more than 68,000 green businesses in the fifty states and the District of Columbia generated 770,000 jobs. By way of comparison, utilities, coal mining, and the oil and gas industry employed 1.27 million workers."[67] Despite the difference between number of jobs in the clean energy economy and number of jobs in the utilities and fossil fuel industries, what stands out as important is the growth rate of jobs in the clean energy economy.

Table 7.5 illustrates several important aspects about job growth in the green economy compared to job growth in the overall economy. First, in forty-one states in the period 1998–2007, the green employment growth rate was positive, with Idaho (126 percent growth), Nebraska (109 percent), and South Dakota (93 percent) setting the pace for the rest of the country. Seven states had a green job growth rate ranging from 30 to 56 percent, while another six states had a growth rate ranging from 20 to 29 percent. Only nine states (18 percent) had a negative green job growth rate. Second, green job growth outpaced overall job growth in thirty-six (70 percent) of the states. Moreover, the growth in green jobs was especially helpful in several states where overall traditional employment declined. In the twelve states that suffered negative overall employment growth (Connecticut, Delaware, Illinois, Indiana, Kansas, Massachusetts, Michigan, Nebraska, New Jersey, New York, Ohio, and Pennsylvania), seven of them (Nebraska, Kansas, Indiana, Michigan, Ohio, Connecticut, and Massachusetts) experienced positive growth in green jobs. Third, in only a few states (Alaska, Florida, Georgia, Montana, New Hampshire, Washington, and Wisconsin) did growth of traditional jobs significantly outpace growth of green jobs, with Utah as the conspicuous anomaly, since green employment growth there was quite low (–12.4 percent) while the state's overall employment growth was relatively high (11 percent) in comparison to growth in most other states.

Table 7.5 Green Employment Growth vs.
Overall Employment Growth, 1998–2007

	Green Employment Growth (percentage)	Overall Employment Growth (percentage)	Growth Rate Gap[a]
Idaho	126.1	13.8	+
Nebraska	108.6	–4.9	+
South Dakota	93.4	4.9	+
Wyoming	56.4	14.0	+
Kansas	51.0	–0.3	+
Oregon	50.7	7.5	+
New Mexico	50.1	1.9	+
Hawaii	43.6	7.3	+
South Carolina	36.2	2.2	+
North Dakota	30.9	9.4	+
Nevada	28.8	26.5	+
Iowa	26.1	3.6	+
Mississippi	24.8	3.6	+
Maine	22.7	3.3	+
Arizona	21.3	16.2	+
Louisiana	19.5	3.0	+
Colorado	18.2	8.2	+
Tennessee	18.2	2.5	+
Indiana	17.9	–1.0	+
Texas	15.5	6.7	+
North Carolina	15.3	6.4	+
Vermont	15.3	7.4	+
Minnesota	11.9	1.9	+
Georgia	10.8	15.7	–
Michigan	10.7	–3.6	+
Kentucky	10.0	3.6	+
Alaska	9.4	15.7	–
Florida	7.9	22.4	–
Arkansas	7.8	3.5	+
California	7.7	6.7	+
Ohio	7.3	–2.2	+
Connecticut	7.0	–2.7	+
Oklahoma	6.8	2.4	+
Virginia	6.0	6.6	–
Missouri	5.4	2.1	+
Massachusetts	4.3	–4.4	+
Alabama	2.2	1.6	+
New Hampshire	2.0	6.8	–

continues

Table 7.5   continued

	Green Employment Growth (percentage)	Overall Employment Growth (percentage)	Growth Rate Gap[a]
Rhode Island	0.7	0.6	+
Washington	0.5	1.3	–
Montana	0.2	12.7	–
New York	–1.9	–2.6	+
Delaware	–2.3	–8.9	+
Maryland	–2.4	1.3	–
Illinois	–2.5	–2.5	–
West Virginia	–4.1	0.7	–
Wisconsin	–5.2	3.4	–
Pennsylvania	–6.2	–3.1	–
New Jersey	–9.6	–2.7	–
Utah	–12.4	10.8	–

Source: Adapted from Pew Charitable Trusts, "The Clean Energy Economy," June 2009, www.pewcenteronthestates.org/uploadedFiles/Clean_Economy_Report_Web.pdf.

Note: a. A plus (+) indicates better performance in green employment growth, and a minus (–) indicates better performance in overall employment growth.

Despite the overall small number of green jobs in the United States, the growth rate for this sector of the economy has clearly outpaced that for the traditional job market. This trend suggests an increasing impact of green industries in the US economy. Moreover, in states that are experiencing low overall employment growth, green jobs can help offset the poor economy. As Pew Charitable Trusts argued in its 2009 study of the emerging green economy:

> The clean energy economy, still in its infancy, is emerging as a vital component of America's economic landscape. Across the country, jobs and businesses in the clean energy economy are being driven by consumer demand, venture capital infusions by private-sector investors eager to capitalize on new market opportunities, and policy reforms by federal and state lawmakers who want to spur economic growth while sustaining the environment. . . . Today, every state has a piece of the clean energy economy. But there will be winners and losers going forward. Policy makers who act quickly and effectively could see their states flourish, while others may lose opportunities for new jobs, businesses and investments. State leaders recognize this, and a growing number are pursuing measures such as financial incentives for clean energy generation and energy efficiency, renewable energy and energy efficiency standards, and laws to reduce vehicle emissions. . . . [F]ederal and state policies, together with private-sector support, will position the United States as a leader in the global clean energy economy.[68]

Conclusion

We conclude this chapter where we began, by arguing that when states have exhibited a commitment to responding to climate change, two primary reasons emerge for taking action: in response to inaction on the part of the federal government, or as part of a proactive approach to address global climate change. For instance, in 2006, California was the first state to pass legislation that enabled the establishment of mandatory caps on statewide greenhouse gas emissions from all sectors, with the goal of cutting greenhouse gas emissions to 1990 levels by 2020.[69] Within two years, five other states—Hawaii, New Jersey, and Washington in 2007, and Connecticut and Massachusetts in 2008—joined California in this effort. Moreover, in April 2008, New York and several other states filed a joint lawsuit against the EPA, insisting that it observe the instructions of the Supreme Court in 2007 in *Massachusetts v. Environmental Protection Agency* (see Chapter 5 for more discussion regarding the role of the judiciary in addressing climate change). In short, it was expected that the EPA, under the leadership of Stephen Johnson, would begin regulating greenhouse gas emissions under the authority of the Clean Air Act. However, as New York governor Andrew Cuomo argued, "There is no justification for [the] EPA's continu[ed] flouting of the Supreme Court's decision other than the Bush administration's deliberate inaction. The EPA must finally end its foot-dragging, do its job, and move forward to address global warming pollution."[70] Moreover, Doug Myers, writing for the Council of State Governments, observed in July 2010:

> It's obvious that the feds have neither the ability nor the will to pass climate change legislation, and that has left the states in a position to take charge in reducing greenhouse gas emissions, something they have endeavored to do admirably on all fronts, from implementing renewable portfolio standards to requiring state fleets run on E85, an ethanol/gasoline mix composed of 85% ethanol. . . . And aside from mitigating greenhouse gas emissions, such policies also serve to balance out our nation's transportation portfolio and moderate our dependence on foreign sources of oil, both of which have positive economic and foreign policy implications.[71]

In his assessment of the value of renewable portfolio standards, in particular, Myers argued:

> The trend toward implementing and strengthening state renewable portfolio standards is increasing and is likely to continue. A state renewable portfolio standard can have several important benefits for the state that implements it, including stabilized energy rates,

job creat[ion] and reduced emissions of greenhouse gases. Regulating carbon dioxide emissions—via a carbon tax or a cap-and-trade program as some states are attempting and as the federal government [is] likely to do—will raise the rates of electricity from coal-fired power plants relative to electricity generated from renewable energy.[72]

In the long run, renewable energy appears to have the potential to provide adequate, safe, and efficient supplies of electricity for American consumers.

As we have found, there are numerous instances of state innovation (e.g., California) as well as state obstructionism (e.g., Utah) in addressing climate change. In California during the first decade of the twenty-first century, Governor Arnold Schwarzenegger engaged in several initiatives to reduce the production of greenhouse gases. While this was a positive step, the governor was opposed by EPA administrator Stephen Johnson during the second term of the George W. Bush administration when California sought a waiver to go beyond the requirements of the Clean Air Act and set better emission standards. The conflict between Johnson and the governor was not resolved until Barack Obama took office in 2008 and appointed a new EPA administrator, Lisa Jackson, who then granted the waiver. In contrast, two years later, legislators in Provo, Utah, questioned the climate science and passed legislation demanding that the EPA engage in more studies about the role of carbon dioxide in the warming of the planet. In short, lawmakers in Utah sought to delay efforts in support of the EPA's "endangerment finding" as required by the 2007 Supreme Court ruling.

While much attention is directed to the role of the federal government —Congress, the president, the Supreme Court—in addressing climate change, there have been numerous attempts at the state level to reduce greenhouse gases, including climate action plans, regional alliances, adoption of renewable energy and energy efficiency standards, and creation of green jobs. These efforts are important because they allow us to compare the fifty states on several dimensions and assess the success or delay in achieving productive results. Although our focus in this volume has been on federalism and the role of the states, at a more local level several cities have also engaged in initiatives to address climate change. For instance, Henrik Selin and Stacy VanDeveer inform us that "well over 800 mayors from all fifty states . . . signed Seattle Mayor Greg Nickel's initiative calling on cities to meet or exceed the U.S. commitments under the unratified Kyoto Protocol" and that "many cities also use the U.S. Mayors Climate Protection Center as a mechanism for exchanging best practices and lobbying state and federal governments to enact more stringent [greenhouse gas] legislation."[73] Individual examples of city-level climate action range from Boston and New York City in the northeast, where the former switched "to hybrid vehicles in its city vehicle fleet" and the latter "hosted a Large Cities Climate Summit in 2007";[74] the mid-Atlantic, where President John Broderick of Old Dominion University began an initiative in 2012 to address future threats to the university due to the rising sea level along the state's southeastern coast; to Salt Lake City, Utah, in the west, where Mayor Rocky Anderson, despite the state's history of obstructionism, established Salt Lake City's Green Program, which included reducing the city's greenhouse gas emissions from municipal operations in order to reduce the city's carbon footprint and committed the city to the goals of the Kyoto Protocol.

Where climate action plans take into consideration the specific characteristics of a given state, regional alliances reflect the efforts of states joining together to engage in strategies to reduce greenhouse gases. As we have seen, not all states have produced viable action plans, and among those that have, many have experienced difficulty in reducing greenhouse gases. At the same time, coalitions of states have emerged, including the ten-state Regional Greenhouse Gas Initiative, the six-state Midwestern Initiative, and the seven-state Western Climate Initiative. Moreover, several Canadian provinces have joined these coalitions. Together, these groups offer hope to the effort to reduce greenhouse gases at the state and regional level.

The enactment of renewable energy and energy efficiency standards is yet another example of efforts to reduce greenhouse gas production and increase energy conservation. Renewable energy represents a rather small proportion of the overall use of energy resources in the United States, lagging behind petroleum, coal, and natural gas. In fact, fossil fuels account for about 80 percent of energy use in the United States. Nevertheless, renewable sources of energy remain an important component in ensuring a diversity of resources available for energy production. Among the fifty states, the states of the coastal west—Washington, California, and Oregon—along with New York and Texas, produce the most electricity using renewable energy sources. In contrast, New Jersey, Nebraska, Hawaii, Rhode Island, and Delaware produce the least electricity through renewable energy. In conjunction with use of renewable sources of energy to meet the nation's electricity needs, energy efficiency and conservation add a crucial element to the equation.

Once again, the states of the coastal west—California, Oregon, and Washington—along with several states in the northeast—New York, Vermont, Rhode Island, Connecticut, and Maine—perform well in terms of energy efficiency and conservation.

Finally, the states have begun moving toward a clean energy economy, with over 80 percent of them having experienced positive growth in green jobs since the turn of the twenty-first century. And although green jobs constitute only a fraction of all jobs in the US economy, they are increasing at a faster rate compared to the overall job market.

In 2009, Tony Dutzik and his colleagues at the Environment America Research and Policy Center concluded that

> power over environmental and energy policy is actually dispersed throughout various levels of government. Individual states have the power to reduce global warming pollution within their borders, to develop innovative policy solutions that can be honed and implemented elsewhere, and even to spur the development of clean technologies that can benefit people and the environment around the world. . . . Over the past decade, state governments have begun to use that power to drive globally significant reductions in America's contribution to global warming.[75]

As Environment America has observed based on these patterns at the subnational level, the "clean energy movement in the states is widespread and it is significant."[76] It has concluded that altogether, when considering state policies that regulate greenhouse gas emissions, state policies that have been adopted by the federal government, and other recent federal actions that will be implemented by the states, the emission reductions are "significant on a global scale, exceeding the annual energy-related carbon dioxide emissions of all but eight nations of the world."[77]

Given recent history, the achievement of a substantive international environmental agreement in support of reducing greenhouse gas emissions remains a distant goal. Notwithstanding the positive actions taken by other countries, the obstructionist posture of the United States ensures that the conflict over climate change between the president and the Congress will continue into the foreseeable future. US leadership is desperately needed in the attempt to negotiate a viable post–Kyoto Protocol treaty, but this will require the United States to overcome domestic constraints of ideology, partisanship, and pressure from organized interests.

Notes

1. Miller, *Environmental Politics*, 60–61.

2. Evan Ringquist, *Environmental Protection at the State Level* (Armonk, NY: Sharpe, 1993), 43–45; James Lester, "Federalism and State Environmental Policy," in *Environmental Politics and Policy*, 2nd ed., edited by James Lester (Durham, NC: Duke University Press, 1995), 49–53.

3. Susanne C. Moser, "In the Long Shadows of Inaction: The Quiet Building of a Climate Protection Movement in the United States," *Global Environmental Politics* 7 (May 2007): 124.

4. Sharen Begley, "Leaders of the Pack," *Newsweek*, November 30, 2009.

5. "Where the Action Is on Climate," *New York Times*, January 4, 2010, www.nytimes.com/2010/01/02/opinion.

6. Pew Center on the States and Pew Center on Global Climate Change, "Climate Change 101: State Action" [hereafter Pew Report], January 2009, www.c2es.org/docUploads/climate-101-state.pdf.

7. Ibid., 1, 8.

8. Ibid., 1.

9. Tony Dutzik et al., "America on the Move: State Leadership in the Fight Against Global Warming and What It Means for the World" (Boston: Environment America Research and Policy Center, December 2009), 17.

10. Ibid.

11. Begley, "Leaders of the Pack," 50.

12. Ibid.

13. Lester, "Federalism and State Environmental Policy," 53–56.

14. Rabe, *Statehouse and Greenhouse*, 20.

15. Arnold Schwarzenegger, "Schwarzenegger: Beyond Copenhagen, Global Warming Requires Grassroots Action," *Christian Science Monitor*, December 14, 2009, www.csmonitor.com.

16. California Climate Change Portal, "History of California's Involvement in Air Pollution and Global Climate Change," State of California, 2012, www.climatechange.ca.gov/background/history.html.

17. Ibid.

18. Ibid.

19. Miller, *Environmental Politics*, 68.

20. Schwarzenegger, "Schwarzenegger: Beyond Copenhagen."

21. Walter A. Rosenbaum, "Science, Politics, and Policy at the EPA," in Vig and Kraft, *Environmental Policy*, 163–164.

22. "States Sue EPA to Move on Global Warming," April 2008, www.nbcnews.com.

23. Environmental Protection Agency, "California Greenhouse Gas Waiver Request," 2009, www.epa.gov/otaq/climate/ca-waiver.htm.

24. Climate Change Joint Resolution, HJR 12, State of Utah, 2010 General Session, http://le.utah.gov/~2010/bills.

25. Ibid.

26. Rabe, *Statehouse and Greenhouse*, 21.

27. Ibid., 41.

28. Ibid., 41–44.

29. Ibid., 20.

30. Wendy Koch, "States Take Lead in Efforts to Fight Climate Change," *USA Today,* January 23, 2011, http://content.usatoday.com/communities/green house.

31. Juliet Eilperin, "Fighting Global Warming Block by Block," *Washington Post,* May 4, 2008, www.washingtonpost.com.

32. Council of State Governments, "Climate Change: States with Measures to Combat Climate Change," 2009, www.csg.org/knowledgecenter/docs/TIA _FF_ClimateControl.pdf.

33. Environmental Protection Agency, "State and Local Climate and Energy Program: Climate Change Action Plans," August 23, 2010, www.epa.gov /statelocalclimate/state/state-examples/action-plans.html.

34. Ibid.

35. US Department of Energy, Energy Information Administration, "State-Level Energy-Related Carbon Dioxide Emission, 2000–2009," January 9, 2012, www.eia.gov/environment/emissions/state/analysis.

36. Ibid.

37. Ibid.

38. Gabriel Nelson, "It's Red States vs. Blue in Legal War over EPA Rules," *Greenwire,* October 12, 2010.

39. Ibid.

40. Environmental Protection Agency, "State and Local Climate and Energy Program"; Pew Report, 7.

41. This discussion is drawn from State of Virginia, Governor's Commission on Climate Change, "Final Report: A Climate Change Action Plan," December 15, 2008.

42. Rabe, "Second Generation Climate Policies in the States," 76.

43. Pew Report, 2.

44. Ibid.

45. Ibid., 3.

46. Ibid., 2; Center for Climate and Energy Solutions, "Regional Initiatives," May 13, 2011, www.pewclimate.org/sites/default/modules/USmap.

47. "Multi-State Climate Initiatives," Center for Climate and Energy Solutions, 2012, www.c2es.org/print/us-states-regions/regional-climate-initiatives.

48. Doug Myers, "Overview of State Renewable Portfolio Standards," Council of State Governments, December 1, 2008, http://knowledgecenter .csg.org.

49. US Department of Energy, Energy Information Administration, "Shares of Electricity Generation from Renewable Energy Sources Up in Many States," www.eia.gov/todayinenergy/detail.cfm?id=5750.

50. Wendy Koch, "Which U.S. States Are Most Energy Efficient?" *USA Today,* October 13, 2010, http://content.usatoday.com/communities/green house.

51. Ibid.

52. "Texas Loses Third Try at Blocking EPA Greenhouse Gas Controls," Environmental News Service, January 12, 2011, www.ens-newswire.com/ens /jan2011/2011-01-12-091.html.

53. Sean Slone and Doug Myers, "Climate Change and Transportation," Council of State Governments, February 22, 2010, http://knowledgecenter.csg .org/drupal/content/climatechange-and-transportation.

54. Pew Report, 5.

55. Slone and Myers, "Climate Change and Transportation."

56. Council of State Governments, "Trends in America: Climate Change Mitigation," November 2007, www.csg.org/knowledgecenter/docs/TIA_Climate ChangeMitigation.pdf.

57. Steven Mufson, "Vehicle Emission Rules to Tighten," *Washington Post,* May 19, 2009, www.washingtonpost.com.

58. Council of State Governments, Eastern Regional Conference, "U.S. State and Regional Efforts to Address Climate Change," *Green Matters,* February 2010, http://greenmatters.csgeast.org/climate-change.

59. Doug Myers and Sean Slone, "Green Transportation," Council of State Governments, July 27, 2010, http://knowledgecenter.csg.org/drupal/content/green-transportation.

60. Dutzik et al., "America on the Move," 27.

61. Julian Walker and Scott Harper, "State Vehicles Set for a Conversion," *Virginian-Pilot,* October 3, 2012.

62. Smart Growth America and the Natural Resources Defense Council, "Getting Back on Track: Aligning State Transportation Policy with Climate Change Goals," December 14, 2010, www.nrdc.org/smartgrowth/files/Getting BackonTrack_4pgr.pdf.

63. Pew Charitable Trusts, "The Clean Energy Economy," June 2009, www.pewenvironment.org/uploadedFiles/PEG/publications/Report/clean%20 Energy%20Economy.pdf.

64. Ibid.

65. Ibid.

66. Tiffany Hsu, "Job Growth in California Is Going Green," *Los Angeles Times,* December 9, 2009, http://articles.latimes.com/print/2009/dec/09/business /la-fi-green-jobs9-2009dec09.

67. Ron Scherer, "Report: 'Green' Jobs Outpacing Traditional Ones," *Christian Science Monitor,* June 10, 2009, www.csmonitor.com/Business.

68. Pew Charitable Trusts, "The Clean Energy Economy."

69. Council on State Governments, Eastern Regional Conference, "U.S. State and Regional Efforts."

70. "NY Sues EPA over Global Warming Regulations," *North Country Gazette,* April 2, 2008, www.northcountrygazette.org/2008/04/02/global _warming_suit.

71. Doug Myers, "Take Your State's Transportation to the Next Level," Council of State Governments, July 27, 2010, http://knowledgecenter.csg.org /drupal/content/take-your-state%E2%80%99s-transportation.

72. Myers, "Overview of State Renewable Portfolio Standards."

73. Henrik Selin and Stacy D. VanDeveer, "Climate Leadership in Northeast North America," in Selin and VanDeveer, *Changing Climates in North American Politics,* 123.

74. Ibid., 124.

75. Dutzik et al., "America on the Move," 14.

76. Ibid., 34.

77. Ibid., 36–37.

8

Assessing the US Response to Climate Change

> The scientific consensus is far stronger today than at any time in the past. Here is the truth: The Earth is round; Saddam Hussein did not attack us on 9/11; Elvis is dead; Obama was born in the United States; and the climate crisis is real. It is time to act.
>
> —*Al Gore*[1]

The conflict over climate change in the United States transcends several domains—environmental, political, economic, and social. It also transcends different levels of government—the US relationship with the global community, relations between the three branches of the federal government, and US federalism. The divisiveness of this conflict clearly shows that political leadership in the complex system of separation of powers and US federalism can just as easily come from the subnational level as it can emerge at the national level. As we have seen, despite the accumulating scientific evidence of human-induced climate change, leadership at the national level—congressional, presidential, judicial—has been problematic at best. When we observe action at the subnational level, we often see more innovation compared to efforts coming from the Congress or the presidency.

Climate change has been framed as a complex and difficult issue that, similar to many other social issues, including abortion, gun control, and same-sex marriage, excites confrontation and creates an ideological divide between liberals, who tend to support policy change, and conservatives, who tend to defend the status quo. Moreover, the problems involved in obtaining a domestic and global commitment to address climate change in a substantive way result from the transnational nature of the issue. For instance, while the United States can and often has offered leadership on a global level, domestic political actors and economic interests have used their resources to shape policy at home in a way that directly affects US external affairs. As Elizabeth DeSombre reminds us, "domestic actors play an important role in determining the shape of the international regulation sought and the means by which it is pursued."[2]

The Challenges Ahead

At the outset of this book we offered several research questions to help structure our analysis of climate change policy in the United States: (1) Why should Americans be concerned about climate change, and what might be the consequences of climate change for Americans? (2) Why has there been difficulty establishing cooperation among key players, and why has climate change been politicized? (3) How has science impacted the policymaking process? (4) Have policy agendas been helpful in confronting climate change? and (5) What does the future hold for climate change policymaking in the United States? In the discussion that follows, we attempt to answer these questions.

Public Interest in Climate Change

Climate change is a global environmental problem that has potentially serious consequences for the entire world. Why should Americans be concerned about it? This normative question can be answered by highlighting, empirically, several tangible implications of climate change for the United States.[3] While self-interest plays a role in Americans' concerns, moral considerations are also relevant, because US emissions of greenhouse gases and failure of the federal government to take action will affect other countries and other peoples. In short, climate change is a transnational environmental challenge that has implications beyond the United States.

First, the threat of extinction of terrestrial and marine life is a serious consideration. This could include rainforest plants, which are a source not only of food but also of a variety of medicines and potentially new medical discoveries. Second, changing precipitation patterns may cause droughts that will affect the production of agricultural products and increase the possibility of "water wars" at home and abroad. Third, increases in the intensity, if not the frequency, of hurricanes in the Atlantic and along the Gulf Coast may affect millions of Americans. Moreover, regionally as well as globally, many countries, including China, India, and Taiwan, are concerned about the threat posed by cyclones. Fourth, waterborne diseases are likely to increase as mosquitoes become an increasingly dangerous threat to the American population. Fifth, heat waves and droughts will have dire consequences for public health as well as agricultural production. Sixth, a warming planet will result in melting glaciers, rising sea levels, and flooding, posing dangerous conditions for island nations as well as coastal residential and commercial properties in the United States. This will create physical, emotional, political, economic, and social problems for Americans and extreme hardship for citizens of low-income countries such as Bangladesh. Seventh, in response to melting glaciers and ice sheets in the Northern Hemisphere, transnational security concerns are likely to arise, including territorial disputes involving several countries of the Northern Rim, such as the United States, Russia, Canada, Norway, Greenland, and Iceland. Melting glaciers and ice sheets might result in conflict over newly formed summer shipping lanes, competition over fishing rights, and conflict over access to and territorial jurisdiction over immense reserves of energy resources.[4]

Individually, but more importantly collectively, these implications of climate change can and will have a profound impact on Americans and fellow citizens around the world. But to what extent can the key players and institutions in the United States contribute to subnational, national, and international efforts to confront global climate change?

The Difficulty in Achieving Political Cooperation

A serious problem for policymakers within the US political setting involves the diversity of opinion and interests about climate change. On the one hand are those who believe that it is imperative to respond immediately to the human-induced warming of the planet. This position is grounded in the research findings of a variety of scientific organizations, both governmental and nongovernmental, as well as environmental organizations such as the National Wildlife Federation, the Sierra Club, the Environmental Defense Fund, and Greenpeace, which have taken an activist approach to supporting government action to address climate change. Moreover, the environmental movement has been joined by coalitions of Evangelical Christians, farmers, medical professionals, as well as businesses that have broken away from the deniers of human-induced climate change.

On the other hand are the opponents, who not only deny that global climate change is occurring but also refer to the proposition of a warming planet as a "hoax." There are also opponents who accept the notion of climate change but not the finding that human activities are the primary cause of climate change. These opponents argue instead that global warming is due to natural phenomena. Regardless of their beliefs, these opponents play a central role in the discord over climate change policy in the United States. Powerful, well-entrenched economic interests have employed a variety of tactics in an effort to influence and politicize the climate change debate. Political tactics have included questioning the validity of scientific research, lobbying to influence decisionmaking in the executive, legislative, and judicial branches of government, lectures by skeptical scientists, some of whom have been funded by the fossil fuel industry, and advertising campaigns.

As discussed in Chapter 6, individual industries, industry organizations, and think tanks have used their considerable resources to forcefully advocate their position on climate change policy. For instance, the US coal industry has run televised advertisements informing the American public that the United States is a storehouse of the coal that is used to produce electricity for American homes and businesses and that any effort to restrict its use would have a negative effect on the economy and jobs. At the same time, a new organization has emerged in support of continued use of coal, the American Coalition for Clean Coal Electricity. Comprised of power-generating companies (e.g., manufacturing and mining interests), this coalition supports mandatory limits on carbon dioxide, but only "as long as legislation encourage[s] 'robust utilization of coal.'"[5]

The Global Climate Coalition, funded by an array of industries during the 1990s, employed a variety of tactics to oppose climate change policy, while the Western Fuels Association, supported by coal-burning electric utilities, challenged the science of climate change. Finally, think tanks such as the Heritage Foundation and the CATO Institute have employed their resources to argue their forceful position that any effort to respond to the notion of human-induced climate change will undermine the economy and job creation.

Notwithstanding the conflict between those who want government action on climate change and those who oppose it, the seeds of divisiveness among the deniers themselves have become increasingly evident. Fissures have arisen that pose problems for the alliance of affected industries in their effort to protect their interests. For instance, as reported by the Center for Public Integrity, a new organization, America's Natural Gas Alliance, argues that it should be fueling a much larger share of the nation's electricity production, since natural gas is the least-carbon-intensive fossil fuel. In contrast, the coal industry has argued that such fuel-switching could be costly.[6]

Clearly it will be difficult for the key players to cooperate in crafting a viable resolution to the climate change problem. But this is necessary if the United States is to offer leadership abroad. Against a background of conflict rather than cooperation, "climate change has been politicized in American politics but it doesn't have to be that way. . . . Despite the role played by natural cycles, solar activity, cosmic rays, and volcanic activity, the scientific community has dismissed these factors as viable alternative explanations for contemporary global climate change."[7] The Intergovernmental Panel on Climate Change (IPCC), the World Meteorological Organization (WMO), the National Oceanic and Atmospheric Administration (NOAA), the Environmental Protection Agency (EPA), the National Aeronautics and Space Administration (NASA), and the Pew Center for Global Climate Change "all accept the proposition that human activities through the burning of fossil fuels (oil, coal, natural gas) play a major role in the warming of the planet and climate change."[8]

In the end, however, opponents of climate change policy have been relatively successful in their effort to prevent government-mandated controls that would fundamentally alter the landscape of climate change politics. Economically entrenched industries, in particular, have used their considerable resources to protect their financial interests and delay or prevent more demanding governmental regulation. For example, although the United States signed the Earth Summit's convention on global warming, it did so only on condition of voluntary rather than mandatory requirements. And although President Bill Clinton signed the Kyoto Protocol, the US Senate failed to ratify it, which allowed President George W. Bush to later renounce it.

The "Science and Politics" Problem

In many ways, the climate change problem can be framed within the "science and politics" problem. As Daniel Sarewitz wrote in the *Amer-*

ican Scientist in 2006, "Science should be able to cut through political controversy and enable beneficial action," yet we find instead that the climate change issue is "characterized by long-term intractability and periodic resurgence of bitter partisan dispute—all in the face of a continual expansion of scientific understanding."[9] And to apply to the climate change issue what former director of the Centers for Disease Control William H. Foege said about science, politics, and health decisions when referring to the smoking issue, while every environmental decision involves political decisions and should be based on the best available science, there are factors beyond science (e.g., partisanship and ideology) that "continue to contribute to public policy decisions."[10]

Even though climate research continues to move forward, and beyond uncertainties, by building on existing scientific knowledge, the climate change policymaking process has been criticized by members of the scientific community who have become frustrated with the slow pace of political progress in the United States. Richard Alley, one of the authors of the IPCC's fourth assessment report, of 2007, made his frustration clear in lamenting that "policy makers paid us to do good science, and now we have very high scientific confidence in this work—this is real, real, real. So now act, the ball's back in your court."[11]

Despite the evidence and the scientific community's efforts to present it to political actors around the world, political action has either been delayed or stagnated, particularly in the United States. In 2005, James Gustave Speth, founder of the World Resources Institute, environmental adviser to Presidents Jimmy Carter and Bill Clinton, and chief executive officer of the United Nations Environment Programme, reminded us of the environmental problems facing the global community. As he lamented by analogy, the question facing us today concerns to what extent we will be mindful of the need to take action now: "President John F. Kennedy often told the story of the aged Marshal Lyautey of France debating with his gardener the wisdom of planting a certain tree. 'It will not bloom,' the gardener argued, 'for decades.' 'Then,' said the marshal, 'plant it this afternoon.'"[12]

Based on the evidence provided by the scientific community, global partners wait for the United States to take appropriate action at home and offer leadership abroad. Domestic political actors must set aside their differences and emphasize a commitment to cooperate if mutual benefits are to be achieved. It is time to break the gridlock created by partisanship, ideology, and economic interests, for the good of the country and the global community. But achieving this end will be difficult.

As we have discussed in this book, US domestic political actors have been successful in setting aside their differences in a variety of circumstances. For instance, differences were set aside in an effort to resolve two major problems, one regional and one global—the US acid rain conflict with Canada, and stratospheric ozone depletion. The climate change problem awaits this same kind of bipartisanship. As former vice president Al Gore has argued:

> The scientific consensus [on global climate change] is even stronger [than the consensus on cigarettes causing lung cancer]. It has been endorsed by every National Academy of science of every major country on the planet, every major professional scientific society related to the study of global warming and 98 percent of climate scientists throughout the world. In the latest and most authoritative study by 3000 of the very best scientific experts in the world, the evidence was judged "unequivocal."[13]

But despite the importance of regional and global partners working together to solve the acid rain and ozone depletion problems, climate change is much more complex and involves farther-reaching and more costly solutions.

Evaluation of Key Players and Prospects for the Future

How helpful have policy agendas been in confronting climate change? Have the actions of key institutional players been positive, mixed (cautious or symbolic), or negative? As we see in Table 8.1, most of the key institutional players generally have not acted in ways that encourage cooperation rather than conflict, problem-solving rather than controversy. Among these key players, only the scientific community has provided a near consensus on the problem, noting the specific environmental and public health threats that will result from a warming planet and climate change. In contrast, the US Congress has exhibited divisiveness and acrimony rather than putting the national interest above the differences of its members. The legislative process has in effect succumbed to ideological dissension and partisan bickering. While the scientific community has been increasingly consistent in providing a body of knowledge that documents the evolution and impact of human-induced climate change, the Congress has been just as consistent in preventing and delaying efforts to address climate change.

Table 8.1   Evaluation of Key Institutional Players' Actions on Climate Change

Positive	Mixed	Negative
Scientific community	Federalism and the states Interest groups Judiciary Presidency Public opinion	Congress

The remaining institutional players have exhibited a mixed record in their actions on climate change, with some successes but also sufficient problems that need to be overcome. For example, on the one hand, some presidents (e.g., Bill Clinton, Barack Obama) have attempted to address climate change within institutional constraints. Yet on the other hand, Congress has obstructed these efforts rather than agreeing to negotiate and compromise. On the one hand, the Supreme Court, in *Massachusetts v. Environmental Protection Agency* (2007), has provided a foundation upon which others can take action. Yet on the other hand, Congress has thwarted actions taken by Obama's EPA. On the one hand, environmental groups have encouraged federal action on climate change. Yet on the other hand, organized interests, such as the fossil fuel industry, have opposed such action. Despite variation over time, Americans have for the most part accepted the existence of climate change, yet they are divided by partisanship and ideology regarding the proposition that human activities are the primary cause of the warming of the planet. As a result, federal action on climate change has been characterized by inaction, but this has not stopped green initiatives at the subnational level among individual states, or in concert with other states regionally or nationally.

The scientific community and the bureaucracy. The community of climate scientists has made public an abundance of data demonstrating that human activities rather than natural factors are increasingly responsible for the warming of the planet and for climate change. In early 2012, NASA confirmed that greenhouse gases produced by human activities rather than by solar activity are the "primary force driving global warming."[14] The space agency's climate research is based on observations of Earth's energy imbalance—the difference between released and absorbed solar energy—despite low solar activity.

At about the same time, Climate Central released a report based on research from several sources, including the IPCC, that led to the following conclusion: "global warming has caused the great majority, if not all, of [sea-level rise]. Warming has acted in two main ways: by heating up and thus expanding the global ocean; and by attacking glaciers and polar ice sheets, pouring meltwater and icebergs into the sea. The planet has heated by more than one degree Fahrenheit over the last century, rising faster as we have burned coal, oil and gas faster, and so sent ever more heat-trapping gases into the air. Scientists overwhelmingly agree that these building gases are responsible for most of the warming observed thus far."[15]

On the issue of climate change, the US political setting tends to be dominated by politics rather than science, by partisanship rather than bipartisanship. A small but vocal group of deniers of human-caused climate change (scientists, academics, media celebrities, legislators) continue to argue either that the warming of the planet is absolutely false, or that climate changes are due to natural factors. Global partners are waiting on the United States to resolve its domestic conflict and take the international lead on climate policy.

As far as the scientific community is concerned, it is likely that the body of knowledge confirming the global climatic impact of human activities will increase. Politically, however, resistance to scientific opinion will continue among the array of contrarians and deniers of human-induced climate change. Notwithstanding national, regional, and international concerns, this small but vocal constituency of contrarians and deniers will persist in using their resources to delay and prevent actions to fundamentally address the threat posed by climate change. Contrarians and deniers can be found in government, academia, business and industry, and the news media. As a result, the larger body of climate scientists and political actors will continue to be forced to deal with "climate politics" as much as they are involved in climate science and problem-solving.

Congress and the legislative process. The US Congress has exhibited a diverse response to climate change, characterized by partisan and ideological differences that have framed the debate and influenced votes on climate legislation. Although the Senate ratified the 1992 Earth Summit's Convention on Global Climate Change, this international agreement incorporated voluntary rather than mandatory goals and guidelines. When the Senate had the opportunity to commit the

United States to binding requirements in the 1997 Kyoto Protocol, it failed to do so. Positive action on climate change policy was derailed by the Byrd-Hagel Resolution and the Senate's clear intimation that any climate change legislation would be considered dead on arrival.

During his first two years in office, President Barack Obama had Democratic majorities in the House of Representatives and the Senate. However, even though the House passed climate change legislation, the bill died in the Senate. In a brief, two-month period in 2011, congressional Republicans opposed several efforts to improve climate science policy. In late 2011, the Republican majority in the House blocked a reorganization plan by NOAA that would have provided better climate forecasts.[16] During a standing room–only talk to the Conservative Political Action Conference in February 2012, Oklahoma Republican senator James Inhofe attacked climate science, cap and trade, and EPA regulation of greenhouse gases. A few days later, the outgoing assistant administrator and science adviser in President Obama's EPA advocated an emphasis on the "role played by research in the agency [in order] to counter attacks by Congressional Republicans and industry," a position taken recently by two former Republican EPA administrators, William Ruckelshaus and William Reilly, who have raised questions about Republican attacks on the EPA.[17]

It seems likely that problematic political relations on climate change policy, between the House and the Senate and between Democrats and Republicans, will continue. There must be improved and continued communication between scientists and members of Congress in order to succeed in passing viable climate change legislation. Progress will depend on the ability of legislators to cooperate with each other and employ science rather than politics in the climate change policymaking process. However, as this study has shown, on the issue of climate change the legislative process is more about politics and entrenched interests than about science. In order to transcend the politics, strong presidential leadership is required along with a supportive Congress and a mobilized citizenry in favor of substantive climate legislation. Based on the record so far, it seems that state legislators and governors rather than congressional lawmakers are the more likely to succeed in changing climate politics in the United States.

Presidential leadership. The presidential administration of Jimmy Carter set a foundation upon which future presidents could pursue action on climate change. He commissioned the *Global 2000 Report to the President,* which raised the issue of climate change as an important environmental concern among other global environmental problems. In contrast, Ronald Reagan refused to take action on clean air legislation or the emerging climate change issue. George H. W. Bush, although he contributed to weakening the requirements of the 1992 United Nations Framework Convention on Climate Change, did sign this international environment agreement, which provided a sense of legitimacy to the issue of global climate change.

Bill Clinton attempted to address climate change policymaking with the assistance of his vice president, Al Gore. However, he was confronted with senators who were unwilling to work with him on this issue. George W. Bush, unlike his father, who had given some credence to the issue of climate change, renounced the Kyoto Protocol only two months into his first term as president. His subsequent actions on air pollution and climate change were efforts to weaken rather than strengthen initiatives to address these two important environmental issues.

Barack Obama, during his presidential campaign in 2008, made a commitment to deal with the global climate issue. However, as president, Obama, despite having Democratic majorities in both the House and the Senate during his first two years in office as mentioned, was unable to put his commitment into action. Though the House passed "cap and trade" climate change legislation, the Senate refused to pass the bill. During the last two years of his first term, Obama was challenged by a Republican-controlled House of Representatives that successfully stopped any progress on climate change legislation.

When focusing on global climate change as an important policy issue, presidential leadership and presidential-congressional relations are linked together in the US system of government. When both are attuned to each other's goals, then progress, both nationally and globally, is more likely to occur on this transnational environmental problem. Even so, strong, committed presidential leadership will be required to successfully pass climate legislation, regardless of the partisan composition of Congress. During the 2012 presidential campaign, it was understandable that the candidates and the voters expressed primary concern about the economy, job growth, and healthcare. However, the issue of climate change was the conspicuous "elephant in the room" during the campaign, which included three debates during which none of the debate moderators nor either presidential candidate raised the issue for discussion. Obama's reelection to a second term indicated that we will see increased efforts by the White House to pursue a climate change agenda. In contrast, had Mitt Romney won the presidency, it is likely he would have supported energy deregulation, a weakening of the EPA, and continued reliance on fossil fuels.

Judicial action. The courts have been forced to address climate change due to the failure of Congress and the presidency to cooperate in passing and implementing climate change legislation. Courts at different levels of the judicial system have provided guidelines and decisions that have the potential to influence the future of climate change policy in the United States. Two primary Supreme Court cases, *Massachusetts v. Environmental Protection Agency* (2007) and *American Electric Power v. Connecticut* (2011), have provided a foundation upon which greenhouse gases can be regulated by the EPA under the authority of the Clean Air Act. These cases also have the potential to encourage the president and Congress to join together in producing climate change legislation.

Recent court cases have set a precedent for a future judicial role in climate change policymaking should Congress and the president fail to move forward, but this will depend on the Court's membership. It is doubtful that the conservative majority on the John Roberts Court will be sympathetic to remedies to rectify global climate change. We expect that both Court and environmental activist observers will watch closely if President Obama has the opportunity to appoint one or two new members to the Supreme Court.

Interest groups and public opinion. The role of organized interests in climate change policy has been characterized by the actions of two key stakeholder groups—constituencies who favor government action on climate change and constituencies who oppose government action due to their concern about increased federal regulatory power imposed on business and industry. Stakeholder groups that support government action on climate change have been bolstered in their position by increasing evidence provided by the scientific community that human activities have a major impact on the production of greenhouse gases and therefore on global warming and climate change.

Public opinion also plays a role in climate change policy. Although most Americans believe that the Earth is warming, many are unsure about the source of this climatic phenomenon. Democrats and Independents are more likely than Republicans and Tea Party adherents to believe that climate change is the result of human activities. Moreover, Americans differ in their views compared to their neighbors to the north, as Canadians are more likely to view climate change as a serious issue.

Because the issue of global climate change has been politicized and has become increasingly divisive, politics rather than science tends to dominate the discussion as organized interests attempt to shape climate change policy. Continued concerns will remain about increasing government intervention and regulatory measures and their potential negative impact on financial interests. Given the profound impact that global warming may have on the planet, it is not surprising that environmental groups have been active in supporting government efforts to address climate change. At the same time, government-mandated actions to reduce greenhouse gas emissions have forced various vested interests that benefit from the status quo to change the way they do business. Consequently, the governmental and nongovernmental actors that are pushing for climate change legislation have been met by countervailing efforts on the part of these vested interests and the deniers of human-caused climate change.

Given the ambivalence of American opinion on climate change, the scientific community needs to do a better job of communicating its research and findings to the American public. The instability of American public opinion on climate change is due to confusion resulting from conflicting positions advocated by organized interests, a lack of education about the science and politics involved in the issue, and the intrusion of disinformation campaigns. The news media also need to do a better job of educating Americans about climate change, and of debunking the disinformation campaigns mounted by the deniers of global warming.

US federalism and the states. State innovation in climate change policymaking has taken several forms, including climate action plans, regional alliances, renewable energy and energy efficiency standards, reduction of automobile emissions and adoption of fuel efficiency standards, and green job growth. However, this innovation by some states has been countered with obstruction by others, which is not surprising given the large number of states in the country. A possible reason for this is that some efforts at the state level have been met with resistance by federal officials. For example, the administrator of the EPA during the George W. Bush administration opposed California's move to improve vehicle emission standards beyond those set by the federal government.

As states seek to fill the vacuum created by federal inaction on climate change, there is considerable potential for innovation either individually or in concert with other states. Though states will of course differ in their approaches to climate change policymaking, successful states can serve as models for others, even as still others continue to regress or oppose innovative models. The impact of Obama's reelection is also important. He has attempted to continue the climate change issue as part of his larger agenda. However, since the Republican Party retained its majority in the House of Representatives, we expect continued conflict between the president and lawmakers in the House over this issue. We expect, therefore, continued actions by the states. For example, will California again step forward and offer leadership? Will the country experience the emergence of different coalitions of states such as the new North America 2050 group, or one that is based on their common dependence on certain types of energy sources (e.g., oil, coal, hydroelectric power)? In short, the states have an important role to play in general and with respect to the climate change issue. However, while different scenarios may occur, it is our contention that the United States would be better served if the federal government were primarily responsible for a nationwide climate change policy.

Conclusion

In August 2012 the US Energy Information Administration (EIA) released a technical report that provided updated information regarding greenhouse gas emissions for the period 1992–2012.[18] The EIA reported that carbon dioxide emissions were at the lowest level in twenty years. The report noted three reasons for the decline: mild temperatures during the previous winter, reduced gasoline demand due to economic constraints, and increased use of less expensive but cleaner-burning natural gas by some power plants that had formerly burned coal to produce electricity. As the EIA explained, "Natural gas is the least-carbon-intensive fossil-fuel, producing the lowest CO_2 emissions. Power plants that burn natural gas are also usually more efficient at converting fuel into electricity . . . than coal-fired power plants."[19]

As reported in the *Washington Post* later that same month, two well-known members of the scientific community offered the following observations in light of the EIA report. Michael Mann, director of the Earth System Science Center at Pennsylvania State University, stated that "ultimately people follow their wallets," while Roger Pielke Jr., a climate scientist at the University of Colorado, argued that "there's a very clear lesson here. What it shows is that if you make a cleaner energy source cheaper, you will displace dirtier sources," although he added that "while natural gas burns cleaner than coal, it still emits some CO_2. And drilling has its own environmental consequences, which are not yet fully understood."[20]

It is not surprising that the fossil fuel industry and environmentalists were on opposite sides of the issue. Referring to the use of natural gas, a representative of the Sierra Club stated that "without sufficient oversight and protections, we have no way of knowing how much dangerous pollution is being released into Americans' air and water by the gas industry. For those reasons, our ultimate goal is to replace coal with clean energy and energy efficiency and as little natural gas as possible."[21] In response to this, a spokesperson for the American Coal Council argued that "cheap gas won't last" as long as the coal industry enjoys a stable monopoly in the US economy: "[coal] is going to be here for a long time. Our export markets are growing. Demand is going up around the world" and the coal industry will "meet the challenge" of government regulations concerning greenhouse gas emissions.[22] In the end, continued reliance on fossil fuels—coal, oil, natural gas—does not solve the problem of human-induced climate change. Greenhouse gas emissions will remain an issue in the United States as domestic actors confront the challenge of transitioning to a clean energy future. Moreover, greenhouse gas emissions will assume increased importance as continuing inaction on the part of the United States results in negative environmental effects on countries and peoples around the globe.

While there is potential for progress on climate change policy in the decades ahead, there are also new and ongoing impediments. But we can take some comfort in the findings of the National Research Council in its study of strategies to deal with the impact of climate change: "Actions taken now can reduce the risk of major disruptions to human and natural systems; inaction could serve to increase these risks, especially if the range of magnitude of climate change is particularly large. Mobilizing now to increase the nation's adaptive capacity can be viewed as an insurance policy against an uncertain future."[23]

We end where we began. The structure of the US political system—with its separation of powers and federalism—has had a profound impact on climate change policymaking. The scientific community and

Congress sit at opposite ends of the policy debate over global warming. The scientific community has indicated that the debate is over, that human activities are a major contributor to a warming planet and alterations in climate patterns, and that it is time to take action. In contrast, Congress is polarized by partisanship and ideology and pressured by entrenched economic interests. In between the scientific community and Congress are the remaining key climate policy actors, some of which have succeeded and some of which have failed. In the presidency, for instance, whereas Bill Clinton and Barack Obama attempted to reduce greenhouse gas emissions, George H. W. Bush supported voluntary rather than mandatory regulations and George W. Bush rejected the Kyoto Protocol. In the judicial system, although the Supreme Court ruled in *Massachusetts v. Environmental Protection Agency* in 2007 that greenhouse gases could be regulated by the EPA, opponents continue to question or challenge the EPA's regulatory power. And at the state level, important efforts are being made to address climate change, in part due to inaction by the federal government. However, although some states have supported a green energy agenda, others have obstructed such efforts or have withdrawn from commitments made. Alexis de Tocqueville long ago informed us of the role and importance of organized interests in US politics; accordingly, the climate change issue has been a focal point for countervailing pressures from a variety of interests in support of and in opposition to government action. Americans as a whole remain somewhat confused about global warming and climate change; while they generally accept the existence of climate change, they remain unsure about its cause, whether human-induced or natural. Furthermore, while Democrats and Republicans are divided on the issue, a not so subtle difference also divides Independents, Republicans, and Tea Party factions within the Republican Party.

The climate change issue demonstrates what happens when entrenched economic interests or strongly held belief systems are challenged by science. And the climate change issue is but one of many examples of this problem. When science challenged the enormously profitable US tobacco industry, as Stephen Schneider informs us, the industry engaged in a "three-decade record of distortion that helped stall policy actions . . . despite the horrendous health consequences" imposed on the public.[24] Moreover, as of 2012, as reported by *New York Times* columnist Nicholas Kristof, the US chemical industry is still railing against the regulation of asbestos, three decades after scientists determined that asbestos is a carcinogen, and is also lobbying

Congress to dismiss a scientific report indicating that formaldehyde is a carcinogen and needs to be regulated.[25]

Modern American environmental history is replete with examples of key players engaging in productive discourse and positive initiatives that have culminated in legislative and policymaking success. Nonetheless, we remain cautious about the prospects for success regarding the issue of climate change due to strong opposition from entrenched economic interests and their political allies in Congress and the state legislatures. The future seems problematic unless effective measures can be brought to fruition. This will require a strong (rather than measured) response, including presidential leadership, the willingness of Congress to work with the president, environmental federalism, and putting science above partisanship and ideological rigidity in response to climate change.

Notes

1. Al Gore, "Climate of Denial," *Rolling Stone,* July 7–21, 2011.

2. DeSombre, *Domestic Sources of International Environmental Policy,* 17.

3. David Brown, "As Temperatures Rise, Health Could Decline," *Washington Post,* December 17, 2007, www.washingtonpost.com.

4. Meg Sullivan, "Global Warming's Silver Lining: Northern Countries Will Thrive, Grow," *UCLA News,* September 3, 2010.

5. Marianne Lavelle, "The 'Clean Coal' Lobbying Blitz," Center for Public Integrity, April 20, 2009, www.publicintegrity.org/investigations/climate_change/articles/entry/1280.

6. Lavelle, "Tally of Interests on Climate Bill Tops a Thousand."

7. Glen Sussman, "Global Climate Change: A Very Serious Environmental Threat That Developed Countries and Major Emerging Industrialized Countries Should Share the Burden in Addressing," in *Issues: Understanding Controversy and Society* (Santa Barbara: ABC-CLIO, 2012), http://issues2.abc-clio.com.

8. Ibid.

9. Daniel Sarewitz, "Liberating Science from Politics," *American Scientist* 94 (2006): 104.

10. William Foege, "CDC's 60th Anniversary: Director's Perspective—William Foege, MN.D., M.P.H., 1977–1983," *Morbidity and Mortality Weekly Report,* October 2006, www.cdc.gov/mmwr/preview/mmwrhtml/mm5539a4.htm.

11. Elizabeth Rosenthal and Andrew C. Revkin, "Science Panel Calls Global Warming 'Unequivocal,'" *New York Times,* February 3, 2007.

12. James Gustave Speth, *Red Sky at Morning* (New Haven: Yale University Press, 2004), 201.

13. Al Gore, "Climate of Denial," 78.

14. ClickGreen Staff, "NASA Confirms Man's Role in Global Warming," *Environmental News Network*, January 31, 2012, www.enn.com/pollution /article/43927/print.

15. Ben Strauss, Claudia Tebaldi, and Remik Ziemlinski, "Surging Seas: Sea Level Rise, Storms, and Global Warming's Threat to the US Coast," *Climate Central*, March 14, 2012, www.climatecentral.org.

16. Justin Gillis, "Politics Slows Climate Study," *New York Times,* December 24, 2011.

17. "Former EPA Chiefs Defend Agency Against Political Attacks," *Fuelfix,* January 24, 2012, www.fuelfix.com/blog/2012/01/24/former-epa-chiefs-defend-agency-against-political-attacks.

18. US Department of Energy, Energy Information Administration, "US Energy-Related CO_2 Emissions in Early 2012 Lowest Since 1992," August 1, 2012, www.eiz.gov/todayinenergy/detail.cfm?id=7350.

19. Ibid.

20. "AP Impact: CO_2 Emissions in US Drop to 20-Year Low; Some Experts Optimistic on Global Warming," *Washington Post,* August 16, 2012, www.washingtonpost.com/national/energy-environment/ap-impact-co2-emissions.

21. Ibid.

22. Ibid.

23. National Research Council, *Adapting to the Impacts of Climate Change* (Washington, DC: National Academies Press, 2010), 4.

24. Stephen Schneider, *Science as a Contact Sport: Inside the Battle to Save Earth's Climate* (Washington, DC: National Geographic, 2009), 259.

25. Nicholas Kristof, "An Insult to Science and Democracy," *Virginian-Pilot,* October 11, 2012.

Bibliography

Abbott, Charles. "House Bill Would Prevent EPA Regulating Carbon." Reuters, February 3, 2010. www.reuters.com.

Agrawala, Shardul, and Steinar Andresen. "Indispensability and Indefensibility? The United States in the Climate Treaty Negotiations." *Global Governance* 5 (1999): 457–482.

Aldy, Joseph E., and Robert N. Stavins, eds. *Post-Kyoto International Climate Policy: Summary for Policymakers.* New York: Cambridge University Press, 2009.

Allianz and World Wildlife Fund. "G8 Climate Scorecards 2009." Berlin and Munich, July 2009. www.worldwildlifefund.org/climate/Publications/WWFBinaryitem12911.pdf.

Amantegui, Javier. "Is Renewable Energy Still a Green Investment?" June 15, 2012. www.corporatelivewire.com/top-story.html?id=is-renewable-energy-still-a-green-investment.

American Council for an Energy-Efficient Economy. "2010 State Energy Efficiency Scorecard." October 13, 2010. www.aceee.org.

Antilla, L. "Climate of Skepticism: US Newspaper Coverage of the Science of Climate Change." *Global Environmental Change* 15 (2005): 338–352.

"AP Impact: CO_2 Emissions in US Drop to 20-Year Low; Some Experts Optimistic on Global Warming." *Washington Post,* August 16, 2012. www.washingtonpost.com/national/energy-environment/ap-impact-co2-emissions.

Arctic Council. "Arctic Climate Impact Assessment: Policy Document." November 24, 2004. www.acia.uaf.edu/PDFs/ACIA_Policy_Document.pdf.

———. "Arctic Resilience Report." 2012. www.arctic-council.org/arr.

Aristotle. *Meteorology.* Translated by E. W. Webster. http://classics.mit.edu/Aristotle/meteorology.1.i.html.

Begley, Sharen. "Leaders of the Pack." *Newsweek,* November 30, 2009.

Bender, Morris A., Thomas R. Knutson, Robert E. Tuleya, Joseph J. Sirutis, Gabriel A. Vecchi, Stephen T. Garner, and Isaac M. Held. "Modeled Impact of Anthropogenic Warming on the Frequency of Intense Atlantic Hurricanes." *Science* 327 (January 2010): 454–458.

BeSpacific. "Waxman Introduces the Safe Climate Act of 2007." *GAO Report on Fiscal Year 2006,* March 20, 2007. www.bespacific.com/mt/archives/014322.html.

Best, Joseph L. "Michael Crichton Is Right!" Heartland Institute, January 11, 2005. www.heartland.org/policybot/results/16260/Michael_Crichton.

"Beyond Copenhagen." *New York Times,* December 7, 2009. www.nytimes.com/2009/12/07/opinion.

Black, Richard. "'No Sun Link' to Climate Change." *BBC News,* July 10, 2007. http://news.bbc.co.uk/2/hi/6290228.stm.

Blair, Tony. "A Year of Huge Challenges." *The Economist,* December 29, 2004. www.economist.com/node/3518491/print.

Bloch, Michael. "What Is the Kyoto Protocol?" Carbonify.com, February 12, 2013. www.carbonify.com/articles/Kyoto-protocol.htm.

Boden, Tom, and T. J. Blasing. "Record High 2010 Global Carbon Dioxide Emissions from Fossil-Fuel Combustion and Cement Manufacture Posted on DCIAC Site." Oak Ridge, TN: Carbon Dioxide Information Analysis Center, Oak Ridge National Laboratory, US Department of Energy, 2010. http://cdiac.ornl.gov/ftp/trends/co2_emis/Preliminary_CO2_emissions_2010.xlxs.

Boden, T. A., G. Marland, and R. J. Andres. "Global, Regional, and National Fossil-Fuel CO_2 Emissions." Oak Ridge, TN: Carbon Dioxide Information Analysis Center, Oak Ridge National Laboratory, US Department of Energy, 2010.

Borick, Christopher. "American Public Opinion and Climate Change." In *Greenhouse Governance,* edited by Barry G. Rabe. Washington, DC: Brookings Institution, 2010.

Borick, Christopher, Erick Lachapelle, and Barry Rabe. "Climate Compared: Public Opinion on Climate Change in the United States and Canada." Ann Arbor: Center for Local, State, and Urban Policy, University of Michigan, 2011. www.sustainableprosperity.ca/article911.

Boykoff, M., and J. Boykoff. "Balance as Bias: Global Warming and the US Prestige Press." *Global Environmental Change* 14 (2004): 125–136.

Brechin, Steven R. "Review of *Global Commons, Domestic Decisions: The Comparative Politics of Climate Change,* by Kathryn Harrison and Lisa McIntoch Sundstrom." *Perspectives on Politics* (March 2011): 132–133.

Brick, Philip, and R. McGreggor Cawley. "Producing Political Climate Change: The Hidden Life of US Environmentalism." *Environmental Politics* 17 (April 2008): 200–218.

Broder, John M. "'Cap and Trade' Loses Its Standing as Energy Policy of Choice." *New York Times,* March 26, 2010.

———. "Climate Deal Likely to Bear Big Price Tag." *New York Times,* December 9, 2009. www.nytimes.com/2009/12/09/science/earth.

———. "A Novel Tactic in Climate Fight Gains Some Traction." *New York Times,* November 9, 2010.

———. "Obama Administration Abandons Stricter Air-Quality Rules." *New York Times,* September 2, 2011. www.nytimes.com/2011/09/03/science /earth.

———. "Past Decade Warmest on Record, NASA Data Shows." *New York Times,* January 22, 2010. www.nytimes.com/2010/01/22/science/earth.

———. "Poor and Emerging States Stall Climate Negotiations." *New York Times,* December 17, 2009. www.nytimes.com/2009/12/17/science/earth /17climate.html.

———. "Qatar, a Greenhouse Gas Titan, to Host U.N. Climate Meeting." *New York Times,* November 29, 2011. http://green.blogs.nytimes.com.

———. "Senate Poses Obstacles to Obama's Climate Pledge." *New York Times,* December 12, 2009. www.nytimes.com/2009/12/13/weekin review.

———. "Senators Offer New Climate Proposals." *New York Times,* December 10, 2009. http://green.blogs.nytimes.com/2009/12/10.

———. "US Pushes to Cut Emissions of Some Pollutants That Hasten Climate Change." *New York Times,* February 15, 2012. www.nytimes.com /2012/02/16/science/earth.

———. "US to Set Emissions Target Before Climate Talks." *New York Times,* November 24, 2009. www.nytimes.com/2009/11/24/science /earth.

Broder, John M., and Clifford Krauss. "Advocates of Climate Bill Scale Down Their Goals." *New York Times,* January 27, 2010. www.nytimes .com/2010/01/27/science/earth.

Brown, David. "As Temperatures Rise, Health Could Decline." *Washington Post,* December 17, 2007. www.washingtonpost.com.

Bruce, J. P., Yi Hoe-song, and Erik F. Haites. *Climate Change 1995.* New York: Cambridge University Press, 1996.

Brunner, Ronald D., and Amanda H. Lynch. *Adaptive Governance and Climate Change.* Boston: American Meteorological Society, 2010.

Bryner, Gary. "Failure and Opportunity: Environmental Groups in US Climate Change Policy." *Environmental Politics* 17 (April 2008): 319–336.

———. "The Rapid Evolution of Climate Change Law." *Utah Bar Journal,* April 30, 2007. http://webster.utahbar.org/barjournal/2007/04/the_rapid _evolution_of_climate.html.

Burghart, Tara. "Survey Finds Widespread Agreement Across Globe That Climate Change Is a Pressing Problem." March 14, 2007. www.world publicopinion.org.

Bush, George H. W. "Letter to Congressional Leaders on Legislation to Amend Clean Air Act." September 26, 1990. Online by John Woolley and Gerhard Peters, *The American Presidency Project.* www.presidency.ucsb .edu/ws/index.php?pid=18867.

———. "Message to the Senate Transmitting the United Nations Framework Convention on Climate Change." September 8, 1992. Online by John Woolley and Gerhard Peters, *The American Presidency Project.* www.presidency.ucsb.edu/ws/index.php?pid= 21432.

―――. "Paris Economic Summit: Economic Declaration." July 16, 1989. In *Public Papers of the Presidents: George H. W. Bush, 1989.* Washington, DC: Government Printing Office, 1990.

―――. "Remarks to Residents of Leiden, the Netherlands." July 17, 1989. Online by John Woolley and Gerhard Peters, *The American Presidency Project.* www.presidency.ucsb.edu/ws/index.php?pid=17302.

―――. "Remarks to the Intergovernmental Panel on Climate Change." February 5, 1990. Online by John Woolley and Gerhard Peters, *The American Presidency Project.* www.presidency.ucsb.edu/ws/index.php?pid=18117.

Bush, George W. "Address Before a Joint Session of the Congress on the State of the Union." January 23, 2007. Online by John Woolley and Gerhard Peters, *The American Presidency Project.* www.presidency.ucsb.edu/ws/index.php?pid=24446.

―――. "Address Before a Joint Session of the Congress on the State of the Union." January 28, 2008. Online by John Woolley and Gerhard Peters, *The American Presidency Project.* www.presidency.ucsb.edu/ws/index.php?pid=76301.

―――. "Joint Statement: U.S.-German Joint Actions on Cleaner and More Efficient Energy, Development, and Climate Change." February 23, 2005. Online by John Woolley and Gerhard Peters, *The American Presidency Project.* www.presidency.ucsb.edu/ws/?pid=63265.

―――. "Joint Statement by the United States of America and Japan on Energy Security, Clean Development, and Climate Change." April 27, 2007. Online by John Woolley and Gerhard Peters, *The American Presidency Project.* www.presidency.ucsb.edu/ws/?pid=25226.

―――. "President Calls for Conservation and Stewardship on Earth Day." White House, Office of the Press Secretary, April 22, 2002. www.georgew-bush-whitehouse.archives.gov/news/releases/2002 /04/20020422-I.html.

―――. "Remarks During a Meeting on Energy Security and Climate Change." September 28, 2007. Online by John Woolley and Gerhard Peters, *The American Presidency Project.* www.presidency.ucsb.edu /ws/index.php?pid=75839.

Bush, George W., Felipe Calderón, and Stephen Harper. "Joint Statement by President George W. Bush, President Felipe de Jesus Calderón Hinojosa of Mexico, and Prime Minister Stephen Harper of Canada." April 28, 2008. Online by John Woolley and Gerhard Peters, *The American Presidency Project.* www.presidency.ucsb.edu/ws/?pid=77160.

Bush, George W., and John Howard. "Joint Statement by President George W. Bush and Prime Minister John Howard of Australia on Climate Change and Energy." September 5, 2007. Online by John Woolley and Gerhard Peters, *The American Presidency Project.* www.presidency.ucsb.edu/ws/?pid=75735.

"Bush and Gore Air Opposite Policies on Earth Day." Environmental News Service, April 23, 2002. www.ens-newswire.com/ens/apr2002/2002-04 -23-01.html.

Byrnes, Michael. "Scientist Says Sea Level Rise Could Accelerate." Environmental News Network, March 13, 2007. www.enn.com.

Caldwell, Lynton Keith. *Between Two Worlds: Science, the Environmental Movement, and Policy Choice.* New York: Cambridge University Press, 1990.

———. "Binational Responsibilities for a Shared Environment." In *Canada and the United States,* edited by Charles F. Dornan and John H. Siglar. Englewood Cliffs, NJ: Prentice Hall, 1985.

———. *International Environmental Policy: From the Twentieth Century to the Twenty-First Century.* 3rd ed. Durham, NC: Duke University Press, 1996.

California Climate Change Portal. "History of California's Involvement in Air Pollution and Global Climate Change." State of California, 2012. www.climatechange.ca.gov/background/history.html.

California Department of Justice, Office of the Attorney General. "Attorney General Lockyer Files Lawsuit Against 'Big Six' Automakers for Global Warming Damages in California." *In the News,* September 20, 2006. http://oag.ca.gov/news/press_release?id=1338.

"Canada to Withdraw from Kyoto Protocol." *BBC News,* December 13, 2012. www.bbc.co.uk/news.

"The Carbon Ruling." *New York Times,* June 21, 2011. www.nytimes.com /2011/06/22/opinion/22wed2.html.

Carroll, John E. "Environmental Issues and Future Canadian Policy." In *Canada and the United States in the 1990s,* edited by William Winegard et al. Washington, DC: Brassey's, 1991.

Carter, Jimmy. "National Energy Plan: Address Delivered Before a Joint Session of the Congress." April 20, 1977. Online by John Woolley and Gerhard Peters, *The American Presidency Project.* www.presidency .ucsb.edu/ws/print.php?pid=7372.

———. "Science and Technology Message to Congress." March 27, 1979. Online by John Woolley and Gerhard Peters, *The American Presidency Project.* www.presidency.ucsb.edu/ws/print.php?pid=32109.

Center for Climate and Energy Solutions. "Hurricanes and Global Warming: Q&A." 2007. www.pewclimate.org/hurricanes.cfm.

———. "Legislation in the 109th Congress Related to Global Climate Change." www.c2es.org/federal/congress/109.

———. "Legislation in the 110th Congress Related to Global Climate Change." www.c2es.org/federal/congress/110.

———. "111th Congress Climate Change Legislation." www.c2es.org/federal /congress/111.

———. "Regional Initiatives." May 13, 2011. www.pewclimate.org/sites /default/modules/USmap.

Center for New American Security. "Climate Change." April 2010. www.cnas .org/naturalsecurity/consequences/climate-change.

Chang, Kenneth. "Charles D. Keeling, 77, Who Raised Global Warming Issue, Dies." *New York Times,* June 23, 2005. www.nytimes.com/2005 /06/23/science.

Civic Impulse. "Bill Overview of H.R. 1: Full-Year Continuing Appropriations Act, 2011." www.govtrack.us/congress.

ClickGreen Staff. "NASA Confirms Man's Role in Global Warming." Environmental News Network, January 31, 2012. www.enn.com/pollution /article/43927/print.

"Climate Change for 1993 to 2001." Online by John Woolley and Gerhard Peters, *The American Presidency Project,* www.presidency.ucsb.edu.

Clinton, Bill. "Address Before a Joint Session of the Congress on the State of the Union." January 27, 2000. Online by John Woolley and Gerhard Peters, *The American Presidency Project.* www.presidency.ucsb.edu /ws/index.php?pid=58708.

———. "Memorandum on Carbon Dioxide Emissions." *Weekly Compilation of Presidential Documents* (April 15, 1999): 654–655.

———. "Remarks to the 52d Session of the United Nations General Assembly in New York City." September 22, 1997. In *Public Papers of the Presidents: William J. Clinton, 1997.* Washington, DC: Government Printing Office, 1999.

———. "Russia–United States Joint Statement on Cooperation to Combat Global Warming." June 4, 2000. In *Public Papers of the Presidents: William J. Clinton, 2000–2001.* Washington, DC: Government Printing Office, 2001.

———. "Speech at City of Montreal Event Coinciding with the United Nations Climate Change Conference." 2005. www.clintonfoundation.org /120905-sp-cf-gn-env-can-sp-remarks-at-montreal-event-coinciding -with-un-climate-change-conference.htm.

Clinton, Hillary R. "Remarks at the Climate and Clean Air Coalition to Reduce Short-Lived Climate Pollutants Initiative." US Department of State, February 16, 2012. www.state.gov/secretary/rm/2012/02/184061.htm.

Committee on Energy and Commerce Democrats. "The Anti-Environment Record of the 112th House of Representatives." http://democrats .energy.house.gov/index.php?q=legislative-database-anti-environment &legislation=All&stop=All&statute=All&agency=All.

Conway, Erik. *Atmospheric Science at NASA.* Baltimore: Johns Hopkins University Press, 2008.

Council of State Governments. "Climate Change: States with Measures to Combat Climate Change." 2009. www.csg.org/knowledgecenter/docs /TIA_FF_ClimateControl.pdf.

———. "Trends in America: Climate Change Mitigation." November 2007. www.csg.org/knowledgecenter/docs/TIA_ClimateChangeMitigation.pdf.

———. Eastern Regional Conference. "US State and Regional Efforts to Address Climate Change." *Green Matters,* February 2010. http://green matters.csgeast.org/climate-change.

Council on Environmental Quality and US State Department. *The Global 2000 Report to the President.* New York: Penguin, 1982.

———. *The Global 2000 Report to the President: Documentation on the Government's Global Sectorial Models.* Vol. 3, chapter 4, "The Climate Section." 174-207. www.geralbarney.com/Global_2000_Report/G2000 -Eng-GPO/G2000-GPO-Vol3.pdf.

Crichton, Michael. *State of Fear.* New York: HarperCollins, 2004.

Cromwell, David, and Mark Levene, eds. *Surviving Climate Change.* Ann Arbor: Pluto, 2007.

Curtis, Kenneth M., and John E. Carroll. *Canadian-American Relations.* Lexington, MA: Lexington Books, 1983.

Darling, Brian. "Want Stimulus? Reduce Regulations." Heritage Network, August 26, 2011. http://blog.heritage.org/2011/08/26/want-stimulus -reduce-regulation.

Davis, G. Gordon. "Essay Review: The Making of Environmental Law." *Perspectives in Biology and Medicine* 49, no. 2 (Spring 2006): 286–293.

Daynes, Byron W., and Glen Sussman. "Comparing the Environmental Policies of Presidents George H. W. Bush and George W. Bush." *White House Studies* 7 (2007): 163–179.

———. "Global Warming: Environmental Crisis or Scientific Hoax?" In *Moral Controversies in American Politics,* 4th ed., edited by Raymond Tatalovich and Byron W. Daynes. Armonk, NY: Sharpe, 2011.

———. "The 'Greenless' Response to Global Warming." *Current History* 104 (December 2005): 438–443.

———. *White House Politics and the Environment: Franklin D. Roosevelt to George W. Bush.* College Station: Texas A&M University Press, 2010.

"Democratic Party Platform of 1992." Online by John Woolley and Gerhard Peters, *The American Presidency Project.* www.presidency.ucsb.edu/ws /index.php?pid=29610.

"Democratic Party Platform of 1996." Online by John Woolley and Gerhard Peters, *The American Presidency Project.* www.presidency.ucsb.edu /ws/index.php?pid=29611.

DeSombre, Elizabeth R. *Domestic Sources of International Environmental Policy.* Cambridge: Massachusetts Institute of Technology Press, 2000.

Dessler, Andrew L., and Edward A. Parson. *The Science and Politics of Global Climate Change.* Cambridge: Cambridge University Press, 2006.

———. *The Science and Politics of Global Climate Change.* 2nd ed. Cambridge: Cambridge University Press, 2010.

Diaz, Henry F., and Richard J. Murnane, eds. *Climate Extremes and Society.* New York: Cambridge University Press, 2008.

Dickerson, John. "What in the Hell Do They Think Is Causing It?" *Slate,* December 8, 2009. www.slate.com.

Digges, Charles. "Putin Signals Russia Will Sign Kyoto Protocol for WTO Membership." Bellona, May 23, 2004. www.bellona.org/English_import _area/energy/34179.

Dimitrov, Radoslav S. "Inside UN Climate Change Negotiations: The Copenhagen Conference." *Review of Policy Research* 27, no. 6 (2010): 795–821.

Dispensa, J. M., and R. J. Bruille. "Media's Social Construction of Environmental Issues: Focus on Global Warming—A Comparative Study." *International Journal of Sociology and Social Policy* 23 (2003): 74–105.

Dockery, D. W., and C. A. Pope. "Acute Respiratory Effects of Particulate Air Pollution." *Annual Review of Public Health* 15 (May 1994): 107–132.

Doyle, Alister. "Carbon Dioxide at Record High, Stoking Warming: WMO." Environmental News Network, November 23, 2007. www.enn.com.

"Dreamliner Makes Its Debut in Chile." *New York Times,* September 16, 2012.

Duffy, Robert J. *The Green Agenda in American Politics.* Lawrence: University of Kansas Press, 2003.

Dunlap, R. E., C. Xiao, and A. M. McCright. "Politics and Environment in America: Partisan and Ideological Cleavages in Public Support for Environmentalism." *Environmental Politics* 10, no. 4 (2001): 23–48.

Dutton, John. "The Challenges of Global Change." In *Science, Technology, and the Environment,* edited by James Roger Fleming and Henry A. Gemery. Akron, OH: University of Akron Press, 1994.

Dutzik, Tony, Rob Kerth, Kari Wohlschlegel, Rob Sargent, and Dan Jacobson. "America on the Move: State Leadership in the Fight Against Global Warming and What It Means for the World." Boston: Environment America Research and Policy Center, December 2009.

Earman, Sam. "The Intersection of Science and the Law: Who Has the Right-of-Way?" In *At the Nexus: Science Policy,* edited by Dennis L. Soden. Commack, NJ: Nova Science, 1996.

Eilperin, Juliet. "Fighting Global Warming Block by Block." *Washington Post,* May 4, 2008. www.washingtonpost.com.

———. "Obama Pulls Back Proposed Smog Standards in Victory for Business." *Washington Post,* September 2, 2011. www.washingtonpost.com /national/health-science.

———. "Protesters Demand 'Climate Justice.'" *Washington Post,* December 13, 2009. www.washingtonpost.com/wp-dyn/content/article/2009/12/12 /AR2009121200641.html.

———. "Scientists Report Further Shrinking of Arctic Ice." *Washington Post,* August 27, 2008. www.washingtonpost.com/wp-dyn/content/article /2008/08/26.

Eilperin, Juliet, and Steven Mufson. "Senators to Propose Abandoning Cap-and-Trade." *Washington Post,* February 27, 2010. www.washington post.com.

Eisenhower, Dwight D. "Annual Message to the Congress on the State of the Union." January 6, 1955. Online by John Woolley and Gerhard Peters, *The American Presidency Project.* www.presidency.ucsb.edu/ws/?pid=10416.

———. "Special Message to the Congress Recommending a Health Program." January 31, 1955. Online by John Woolley and Gerhard Peters, *The American Presidency Project.* www.presidency.ucsb.edu/ws/?pid=10399.

Elsner, James B., and Thomas H. Jagger. *Hurricanes and Climate Change.* New York: Springer, 2009.

Emanuel, Kerry. *What We Know About Climate Change.* Cambridge: Massachusetts Institute of Technology Press, 2007.

Environmental Law Institute. "California v. General Motors Corp." In *Endangered Environmental Laws,* 2010. www.endangeredlaws.org/case _california.htm.

Environmental Protection Agency. "Basic Information: Climate Change." December 14, 2006. www.epa.gov/climatechange/basicinfo.html.

———. "California Greenhouse Gas Waiver Request." 2009. www.epa.gov /otaq/climate/ca-waiver.htm.

————. "Climate Change: State of Knowledge." 2006. www.epa.gov /climatechange/stateofknowledge.html.

————. "The 40th Anniversary of the Clean Air Act: Public Health Improvements, Technology Advancements, and Remaining Air Quality Challenges." September 14, 2010. www.epa.gov/oar/caa/40th.html.

————. "State and Local Climate and Energy Program: Climate Change Action Plans." August 23, 2010. www.epa.gov/statelocalclimate/state/state -examples/action-plans.html.

————. "State of Knowledge: Climate Change Science." October 19, 2006. www.epa.gov/climatechange/science/stateofknowledge.html.

"EPA Issues Greenhouse Gas Warning Despite Concerns over Leaked E-Mails." *Fox News,* December 7, 2009. www.foxnews.com/politics/2009 /12/07/republicans-slam-epa-decision-declare-public-health-danger.

Erickson, Robert S., and Kent L. Tedin. *American Public Opinion.* 7th ed. New York: Longman, 2007.

Fahrenthold, David A. "Environmental Groups at Odds over New Tack in Climate Fight." *Washington Post,* November 6, 2009. www.washington post.com.

Falkner, Robert. "Business Conflict and US International Environmental Policy: Ozone, Climate, and Biodiversity." In *The Environment, International Relations, and US Foreign Policy,* edited by Paul G. Harris. Washington, DC: Georgetown University Press, 2001.

Fisher, Dana. *National Governance and the Global Climate Change Regime.* Lanham: Rowman and Littlefield, 2004.

Fisher, Dana, Philip Leifeld, and Yoko Iwaki. "Mapping the Ideological Networks of American Climate Politics." White Paper no. 2. College Park: Center for Society and Environment, University of Maryland, 2012. http://cse.umd.edu/pdf/csewhitepaper2_MappingIdeologicalNetworks.pdf.

Foege, William. "CDC's 60th Anniversary: Director's Perspective—William Foege, MN.D., M.P.H., 1977–1983." *Morbidity and Mortality Weekly Report,* October 2006. www.cdc.gov/mmwr/preview/mmwrhtml/mm5539a4.htm.

Ford, Gerald. "Remarks and a Question-and-Answer Session at a Forum in Houston." April 28, 1976. Online by John Woolley and Gerhard Peters, *The American Presidency Project.* www.presidency.ucsb.edu/ws/index.php?pid=5892.

————. "Special Message to the Congress Urging Enactment of Proposed Energy Legislation." February 26, 1976. Online by John Woolley and Gerhard Peters, *The American Presidency Project.* www.presidency .ucsb.edu/ws/?pid=5623.

"Former EPA Chiefs Defend Agency Against Political Attacks," Fuelfix, January 24, 2012. www.fuelfix.com/blog/2012/01/24/former-epa-chiefs -defend-agency-against-political-attacks.

Friedman, Lisa. "A Near-Consensus Decision Keeps U.N. Climate Process Alive and Moving Ahead." *New York Times,* December 13, 2010. www.nytimes.com/cwire/2010/12/13.

Friedman, Thomas L. *Hot, Flat, and Crowded.* New York: Farrar, Straus, and Giroux, 2008.

Gabel, David A. "How Rising Sea Levels Will Affect the US Coastline." *Environmental News Network,* February 18, 2011. www.enn.com.

Garraeau, J. "Batten Down the Hatches: Climate Change Already Has a Chilling Effect on Coastal Homeowners." *Washington Post National Weekly* 24 (2006).

Gelber, Ben. "Ben Franklin on Global Warming." *New York Times,* November 18, 2009. www.nytimes.com/2009/11/18/opinion.

Gelbspan, Ross. *Boiling Point.* New York: Basic, 2004.

————. *The Heat Is On.* Reading, MA: Addison-Wesley, 1997.

Gillis, Justin. "Politics Slows Climate Study." *New York Times,* December 24, 2011.

Gillis, Justin, and Leslie Kaufman. "In Documents, a Plan to Discredit Climate Teaching." *New York Times,* February 16, 2012.

Global Climate Coalition. "Statement of the Global Climate Coalition Before the Senate Committee on Environment and Public Works Hearing on S.556, the Clean Power Act." November 1, 2001. US Senate Committee on Environment and Public Works. http://eps.senate.gov/107th /Global_Climate_Coalition.htm.

"A Global Warming." *CBS News,* August 6, 2006. www.cbsnews.com.

Glantz, Michael H. *Climate Affairs.* Washington, DC: Island, 2003.

"Going Green: 10 Green Giants." CNN Money, July 3, 2007. http://money.cnn .com/galleries/2007/fortune/0703/gallery.green_giants.fortune/index.html.

Goldenberg, Susan. "US Climate Change Legislation Q&A: What Will Happen in 2010?" *The Guardian,* January 7, 2010. www.guardian.co.uk /environment/2010/jan/07.

Goodal, Jeff. *Big Coal.* Boston: Houghton Mifflin, 2006.

Gore, Al. "Climate of Denial." *Rolling Stone,* July 7–21, 2011.

Govtrack.us. "S. 1462 (111th): The American Clean Energy Leadership Act." www.govtrack.us/congress/bills/111/s1733#overview.

Gray, Louise. "Cancun Climate Change Conference Agrees Plan to Cut Carbon Emissions." *The Telegraph,* December 11, 2010. www.telegraph.co .uk/earth/environment/climatechange.

————. "Durban Climate Change: Last Minute Talks Produce 'Historic Deal to Save the Planet.'" *The Telegraph,* December 11, 2011. www.telegraph.co.uk/earth/environment/climatechange.

Guber, Deborah Lynn, and Christopher J. Bosso. "Past the Tipping Point? Public Discourse and the Role of the Environmental Movement in a Post-Bush Era." In *Environmental Policy: New Directions for the Twenty-First Century,* 7th ed., edited by Norman J. Vig and Michael E. Kraft. Washington, DC: Congressional Quarterly, 2010.

Gunther, Marc. "Green Is Good." CNN Money, March 22, 2007. http://money.cnn.com/magazines/fortune/fortune_archives/2007/04/02 /8403418.

Guterl, Fred. "Iceberg Ahead." *Newsweek,* March 1, 2010.

Hance, Jeremy. "NASA: 2009 Second Warmest Year on Record." Environmental News Network, January 25, 2010. www.enn.com.

Hansen, James. "Cap and Fade." *New York Times,* December 7, 2009. www.nytimes.com/2009/12/07/opinion.

————. "Global Climate Change: NASA's Eyes on the Earth." June 24, 1988. http://climate.nasa.gov/NasaRole/index.cfm?Print=Yes.

———. "The Greenhouse Effect: Impacts on Current Global Temperature and Regional Heat Waves." Testimony to the US Senate, Committee on Energy and Natural Resources, June 23, 1988. Washington, DC.

———. "Power Failure: Politicians Are Fiddling While the Planet Burns—What's a Voter to Do?" *Newsweek,* December 14, 2009.

———. "The Temperature of Science." December 16, 2009. www.columbia.edu/~jehl/mailings/2009/20091216_TemperatureOfScience.pdf.

Harris, Richard. "Stolen E-Mails Raise Questions on Climate Research." Environmental News Network, November 16, 2009. www.enn.com/top_stories/article/40759.

Harrison, Kathryn, and Lisa McIntosh Sundstrom. *Global Commons, Domestic Decisions: The Comparative Politics of Climate Change.* Cambridge: Massachusetts Institute of Technology Press, 2010.

Harrison, Neil, and Gary Bryner. "Toward Theory." In *Science and Politics in the International Environment,* edited by Neil Harrison and Gary Bryner. Lanham: Rowman and Littlefield, 2004.

Hart, David M., and David G. Victor. "Scientific Elites and the Making of US Policy for Climate Change Research, 1957–74." *Social Studies of Science* 23 (November 1993): 643–680.

Hayden, Thomas. "Super Storms: No End in Sight." *National Geographic,* August 2006..

Heilprin, John. "Earth Hottest It's Been in 2000 Years." Environmental News Network, June 23, 2006. www.enn.com.

Henry, Laura A., and Lisa McIntosh Sundstrom. "Russia and the Protocol: From Hot Air to Implementation?" In *Global Commons, Domestic Decisions,* edited by Kathryn Harrison and Lisa McIntosh Sundstrom. Cambridge: Massachusetts Institute of Technology Press, 2010.

Horner, Christopher C. *Red Hot Lies.* Washington, DC: Regnery, 2008.

Horsley, Scott, and Robert Siegel. "In Canada, Obama Pledges Stronger Ties." National Public Radio, February 19, 2009. www.npr.org.

Hsu, Tiffany. "Job Growth in California Is Going Green." *Los Angeles Times,* December 9, 2009. http://articles.latimes.com/print/2009/dec/09/business/la-fi-green-jobs9-2009dec09.

Hudson, Paul. "What Happened to Global Warming?" *BBC News,* October 9, 2009. http://newsvote.bbc.co.uk.

"Humans Affect Sea Warming in Hurricane Zones." Environmental News Network, 2007. www.enn.com.

Hunter, David B. "The Implications of Climate Change Litigation: Litigation for International Environmental Law-Making." In *Adjudicating Climate Change: State, National, and International Approaches,* edited by William C. G. Burns and Hari M. Osofsky. Cambridge: Cambridge University Press, 2009.

International Council for Science and World Meteorological Organization. "The State of Polar Research." 2009. www.wmo.int.

International Energy Agency. "Prospect of Limiting the Global Increase in Temperature to 2° Is Getting Bleaker." May 30, 2011. www.iea.org.

International Monetary Fund. *World Economic Outlook Database.* October 19, 2009. http://222.imf.org/external/pubs/ft/weo/2009/02/wepdata/index.aspx.

Jacobs, Jeremy P. "Inhofe Blasts Climate Science, EPA Regs to Rally Republican Base." *Greenwire,* February 10, 2012.

———. "Play Up Science to Counter GOP and Industry: Outgoing Assistant Administer." *Greenwire,* February 16, 2012.

Jacques, Peter J., Riley E. Dunlap, and Mark Freeman. "The Organisation of Denial: Conservative Think Tanks and Environmental Skepticism." *Environmental Politics* 17 (June 2008): 349–385.

Jagers, Sverker C., Matthew Paterson, and Johannes Stripple. "Privatizing Governance, Practicing Triage: Securitization of Insurance Risks and the Politics of Global Warming." In *The Business of Global Environmental Governance,* edited by David L. Levy and Peter J. Newell. Cambridge: Massachusetts Institute of Technology Press, 2005.

Janofsky, Michael. "Bush's Chat with Novelist Alarms Environmentalists." *New York Times,* February 19, 2006. www.nytimes.com/2006/02/19 /national.

Jasanoff, Sheila. *The Fifth Branch: Science Advisors as Policymakers.* Cambridge: Harvard University Press, 1990.

Jehl, Douglas. "On Environmental Rules, Bush Sees a Balance, Critics a Threat." *New York Times,* February 23, 2003.

Johnson, Lyndon B. "Annual Message to the Congress on the State of the Union." January 10, 1967. In *Public Papers of the Presidents: Lyndon B. Johnson, 1967.* Washington, DC: Government Printing Office, 1968.

———. "Special Message to the Congress: Protecting Our Natural Heritage." January 30, 1967. In *Public Papers of the Presidents: Lyndon B. Johnson, 1967.* Washington, DC: Government Printing Office, 1968.

———. "Statement by the President in Response to Science Advisory Committee Report on Pollution of Air, Soil, and Waters." November 6, 1965. In *Public Papers of the Presidents: Lyndon B. Johnson, 1965.* Washington, DC: Government Printing Office, 1966.

Jolusha, John. "Bush Pledges Aid for Environment." *New York Times,* September 1, 1988.

Jones, Charles O. *Separate but Equal Branches: Congress and the Presidency.* 2nd ed. New York: Chatham, 1999.

Jones, Jeffrey M. "In US, Concerns About Global Warming at Lower Levels." *Gallup World.* March 14, 2011. www.gallup.com/poll/146606 /Concerns-Global-Warming-Stable-Lower-Levels.aspx?version=print.

Kanter, James, and Andrew C. Revkin. "Europe Pledges Billions in Climate Aid for Poor Nations." *New York Times,* December 12, 2009. www.ny times.com/2009/12/12/science/earth.

Kaufman, Leslie. "Republicans Seek Big Cuts in Environmental Rules." *New York Times,* July 27, 2011. www.nytimes.com/2011/07/28/science/earth.

Kennedy, John F. "Annual Message to the Congress on the State of the Union." January 11, 1962. Online by John Woolley and Gerhard Peters, *The American Presidency Project.* www.presidency.ucsb.edu/ws/print .php?pid=9082.

———. "Special Message to the Congress on Improving the Nation's Health." February 7, 1963. Online by John Woolley and Gerhard Peters, *The American Presidency Project.* www.presidency.ucsb.edu/ws/?pid=9549.

———. "Special Message to the Congress on Protecting the Consumer Interest." March 15, 1962. Online by John Woolley and Gerhard Peters, *The American Presidency Project.* www.presidency.ucsb.edu/ws/print .php?pid=9108.

Keohane, Robert O., and David G. Victor. "The Regime Complex for Climate Change." *Perspectives on Politics* (March 2011): 7–23.

Key, V. O., Jr. *Public Opinion and American Democracy.* New York: Knopf, 1964.

Kingdon, John. *Agendas, Alternatives, and Public Policies.* New York: Longman, 2003.

Klyza, Christopher McGrory, and David Sousa. *American Environmental Policy, 1990–2006: Beyond Gridlock.* Cambridge: Massachusetts Institute of Technology Press, 2008.

Koch, Wendy. "States Take Lead in Efforts to Fight Climate Change." *USA Today,* January 23, 2011. http://content.usatoday.com/communities/greenhouse.

———. "Which US States Are Most Energy Efficient?" *USA Today,* October 13, 2010. http://content.usatoday.com/communities/greenhouse.

Kolbert, Elizabeth. "Comment: Leading Causes." *New Yorker,* October 5, 2009. www.newyorker.com/talk/comment/2009/10/05.

Kollipara, Puneet. "Former EPA Chiefs Defend Agency Against Political Attacks." Fuelfix, January 24, 2012. http://fuelfix.com/blog/2012/01/24 /former-epa-chiefs-defend-agency-against-political-attacks.

Kolmes, Steven. "Climate Change: A Disinformation Campaign." *Environment* 53 (July–August 2011): 33–37.

Koss, Geof. "'Green' Funds Withering in Current Climate." *CQ Weekly—In Focus,* December 12, 2011. http://public.cq.com/docs/weeklyreport /weeklyreport-000003997655.html.

Kraft, Michael. *Environmental Policy and Politics.* 2nd ed. New York: Longman, 2001.

Kristof, Nicholas. "An Insult to Science and Democracy." *Virginian-Pilot,* October 11, 2012.

Larsen, J. "Hurricane Dangers Soar to New Levels." 2007. Environmental News Network. www.enn.com/archive.html?id=1629&cat=net/.

Lavelle, Marianne. "The 'Clean Coal' Lobbying Blitz." Center for Public Integrity, April 20, 2009. www.publicintegrity.org/investigations/climate _change/articles/entry/1280.

———. "The Climate Change Lobby Explosion." Center for Public Integrity, February 25, 2009. www.publicintegrity.org/investigations /climate_change/articles/entry/1171.

———. "Tally of Interests on Climate Bill Tops a Thousand." Center for Public Integrity, August 10, 2009. www.publicintegrity.org/investigations /climate_change/articles/entry/1608.

League of Conservation Voters. "Scorecard: 1999 National Environmental Scorecard." www.lcv.org/scorecard.

———. "Scorecard: 2011 National Environmental Scorecard, 112th Congress, First Session." www.lcv.org/scorecard.

Lee, Henry, ed. *Shaping National Responses to Climate Change.* Washington, DC: Island, 1995.

Leggett, Jane A. "Climate Change: Science and Policy Implications." Report for Congress. Washington, DC: Congressional Research Service, 2007.

———. "A US-Centric Chronology of the International Climate Change Negotiations." Report for Congress. Washington, DC: Congressional Research Service, February 8, 2011.

Lehmann, Evan. "Claiming That It Is a Hoax Victim, Skeptic Group Insists Climate Change Will Be Only a 'Bad Memory.'" *ClimateWire,* February 16, 2012.

———. "Huntsman Warns That GOP Can't Win the White House by Denying Climate Science." *New York Times,* September 8, 2011. www.ny times.com/cwire/2011/09/08.

Lehmann, Evan, Lisa Friedman, Lauren Morello, and Saqib Rahim. "House Republicans Fire White House Advisers As Frenzied Budget Debate Continues." *New York Times,* February 18, 2011. www.nytimes.com /cwire.

Leiserowitz, A., E. Maibach, C. Roser-Renouf, and J. D. Hmielowski. *Politics and Global Warming: Democrats, Republicans, Independents, and the Tea Party.* New Haven: Yale Project on Climate Change Communication, 2011. http://environment.yale.edu/climate/files/PoliticsGlobal Warming2011.pdf.

Lemonick, Michael D. "High Above the Earth, Satellites Track Melting Ice." Environmental News Network, July 8, 2010. www.enn.com.

Leonard, Wendy. "University of Utah Professor Tim Garrett Says Conservation Is Futile." *Deseret News,* November 23, 2009. www.deseretnews .com/article/print/705346695/University-of-Utah-professor-Tim.

Lerer, Lisa. "New Climate Coalition Launches." *Politico,* September 8, 2009. http://dyn.politico.com/news/stories/0909/26873.html.

Lester, James. "Federalism and State Environmental Policy." In *Environmental Politics and Policy,* 2nd ed., edited by James Lester. Durham, NC: Duke University Press, 1995.

Levy, David L. "Business and the Evolution of the Climate Regime: The Dynamics of Corporate Strategies." In *The Business of Global Environmental Governance,* edited by David L. Levy and Peter J. Newell. Cambridge: Massachusetts Institute of Technology Press, 2005.

———. "Mobilizing the Private Sector on Climate Change." Climate Inc., June 14, 2011. http://climateinc.org/2011/06/ti_bus_models.

Lieberman, Ben, and Nicolas D. Loris. "Five Reasons the EPA Should Not Attempt to Deal with Global Warming." Heritage Foundation, April 23, 2009. www.heritage.org/Research/EnergyandEnvironment/wm2407.cfm.

Limbaugh, Rush. "From the Climate Hoax to Health Care to 'Hope,' Liberalism Is Lies." *Rush Limbaugh Show,* November 23, 2009. www.rush limbaugh.com.

———. *See, I Told You So.* New York: Pocket, 1993.

Lindzen, Richard S. "Global Warming: The Origin and Nature of the Alleged Scientific Consensus." CATO Institute, 1992. www.cato.org/pubs /regulation/regv15n2/reg15n2.html.

Ljunggren, David, and Randall Palmer. "Canada First Nation to Pull Out of Kyoto Protocol." Environmental News Network, December 13, 2011. www.enn.com/top_stories/article/43704.

Loven, Jennifer. "Obama's First 100 Days in Office Putting Up the Numbers." *Virginian-Pilot,* April 30, 2009.

MacDonald, Gordon. "Scientific Basis for the Greenhouse Effect." In *The Challenge of Global Warming,* edited by Dean Edwin Abrahamson. Washington, DC: Island, 1989.

Manza, Jeff, and Fay Lomax Cook. "A Democratic Polity: Three Views of Policy Responsiveness to Public Opinion in the United States." *American Politics Research* 30 (2002): 630–667.

Marquart-Pyatt, Sandra T., Rachael L. Shwom, Thomas Dietz, Riley E. Dunlap, Stan A. Kaplowitz, Aaron M. McCright, and Sammy Zahran. "Understanding Public Opinion on Climate Change: A Call for Research." *Environment* 53 (July–August 2011): 38–42.

Marquis, Christopher. "Bush Energy Proposal Seeks to 'Clear Skies' by 2018." *New York Times,* July 30, 2002.

Maslin, Mark. *Global Warming.* Oxford: Oxford University Press, 2009.

Mastrandrea, Michael D., and Stephen H. Schneider. "Global Warming." In *World Book Online,* 2005. www.worldbookonline.com/wb/Article?id =ar226310.

Matthias, William. "China and India Endorse Copenhagen Climate Accord." Environmental News Network, March 10, 2010. www.enn.com.

McCain, John. "McCain's Speech on Climate Change." *New York Times,* May 12, 2008. www.nytimes.com/2008/05/12/us/politics.

McCarthy, James J. "Presidential Address: Reflections on Our Planet and Its Life, Origins, and Futures." *Science* 326 (December 2009): 1646–1655.

McCrea, Hanna. "Why the Second Circuit 'Nuisance' Case Brings Good News, and Bad (Part II)," Grist: A Beacon in the Smog, September 25, 2009. http://grist.org/article/2009-09-24-why-second-circuit-nuisance -case-brings-good-news-and-bad-part-2.

McCright, Aaron M., and Riley E. Dunlap. "Defeating Kyoto: The Conservative Movement's Impact on US Climate Change Policy." *Social Problems* 50 (2003): 348–373.

————. "The Politicalization of Climate Change and Polarization in the American Public's Views of Global Warming, 2001–2010." *Sociological Quarterly* 52, no. 2 (Spring 2011): 155–194.

Miller, Norman. *Environmental Politics.* 2nd ed. New York: Routledge, 2009.

Mills, E., et al., "Insurance in a Climate of Change: Availability and Affordability." 2013. http://insurance.ibl.gov/availability-affordability.html.

Mitchell, Robert B., William C. Clark, David W. Cash, and Nancy M. Dickson, eds. *Global Environmental Assessments.* Cambridge: Massachusetts Institute of Technology Press, 2006.

Montzka, S. A., E. J. Dlugokencky, and J. H. Butler. "Non-CO_2 Greenhouse Gases and Climate Change." *Nature* 476 (August 2011): 43–50.

Mooney, Chris. *The Republican War on Science.* New York: Basic, 2005.

Morano, Marc. "UN Blowback: More Than 650 International Scientists Dissent over Man-Made Global Warming Claims." *Inhofe EPW Press Blog,* December 10, 2008. http://epw.senate.gov.

Morgan, Claude. "Sea-Level Rise: Does a Rising Tide Lift All Boats?" Environmental News Network, September 21, 2000. www.enn.com.

Moser, Susanne C. "In the Long Shadows of Inaction: The Quiet Building of a Climate Protection Movement in the United States." *Global Environmental Politics* 7 (May 2007): 124–144.

Moss, Walter G. "Obama, Copenhagen, and the Global Warming Skeptics." History News Network, November 8, 2009. http://hnn.us/articles /121037.html.

"Mr. Gore's Mission in Kyoto." *New York Times,* December 4, 1997.

Mufson, Steven. "Vehicle Emission Rules to Tighten." *Washington Post,* May 19, 2009. www.washingtonpost.com.

"Multi-State Climate Initiatives." Center for Climate and Energy Solutions, 2012. www.c2es.org/print/us-states-regions/regional-climate-initiatives.

Murphy, Jarrett. "White House Guts Warming Study: Strong Language on Climate Change Deleted from EPA Report." *CBS News,* June 19, 2003.

Myers, Doug. "Overview of State Renewable Portfolio Standards." Council of State Governments, December 1, 2008. http://knowledgecenter.csg.org.

———. "Take Your State's Transportation to the Next Level." Council of State Governments, July 27, 2010. http://knowledgecenter.csg.org/drupal /content/take-your-state%E2%80%99s-transportation.

Myers, Doug, and Sean Slone. "Green Transportation." Council of State Governments, July 27, 2010. http://knowledgecenter.csg.org/drupal /content/green-transportation.

National Oceanic and Atmospheric Administration. "Arctic Report Card: Region Continues to Warm at Unprecedented Rate." October 21, 2010. www.noaanews.noaa.gov/stories2010/20101021_arcticreportcard.html.

———. "Arctic Report Card: Update for 2011." www.arctic.noaa.gov/report card/exec_summary.html.

———. "Global Warming: Frequently Asked Questions." National Climate Data Center, August 20, 2012. www.ncdc.noaa.gov/oa/climate/global warming.html.

———. "NOAA Study: Slowing Climate Change by Targeting Gases Other Than Carbon Dioxide." August 3, 2011. www.noaanews.noaa.gov/stories 2011/20110803_nonco2.html.

———. "State of the Arctic Report 2006." www.arctic.noaa.gov/soa2006.

National Research Council. *Adapting to the Impacts of Climate Change.* Washington, DC: National Academies Press, 2010.

Nelson, Gabriel. "It's Red States vs. Blue in Legal War over EPA Rules." *Greenwire,* October 12, 2010.

Nemery, Benoit, Peter H. M. Hoet, and Abderrahim Nemmar. "The Meuse Valley Fog of 1930: An Air Pollution Disaster." *Lancet* 357 (March 3, 2001): 704–708.

Neubecker, Robert. "Hot Seat." *New Republic,* February 4, 2010.

Newport, Frank. "Americans' Global Warming Concerns Continue to Drop." *Gallup World,* March 11, 2010. www.gallup.com/poll/126560/Americans -Global-Warming-Concerns-Continue-Drop.aspx.

Newton, Paula. "Obama: Leaders Will Work Together on Climate." July 9, 2009. www.cnn.com/2009/WORLD/europe/07/09/g8.summit/index.html.

Nilsson, Annika E. "Arctic Climate Change: North American Actors in Circumpolar Knowledge in Production and Policymaking." In *Changing*

Climates in North American Politics, Institutions, Policymaking, and Multilevel Governance, edited by Henrik Selin and Stacy D. VanDeveer. Cambridge: Massachusetts Institute of Technology Press, 2009.

Nisbet, Matthew C., and Teresa Myers. "The Polls: Trends—Twenty Years of Public Opinion About Global Warming." *Public Opinion Quarterly* 71 (Fall 2007): 444–470.

Nixon, Richard. "Annual Message to the Congress on the State of the Union." January 22, 1970. In *Public Papers of the Presidents of the United States: Richard Nixon, 1970.* Washington, DC: Government Printing Office, 1971.

————. "Remarks on Signing the Clean Air Amendments of 1970." December 31, 1970. Online by John Woolley and Gerhard Peters, *The American Presidency Project.* www.presidency.ucsb.edu/ws/index.php?pid=2874.

Nordhaus, Ted, and Michael Shellenberger. "Apocalypse Fatigue: Losing the Public on Climate Change." *Environment* 360 (November 16, 2009). http://e360.yale.edu/content/feature.msp?id=2210.

"NY Sues EPA over Global Warming Regulations." *North Country Gazette,* April 2, 2008. www.northcountrygazette.org/2008/04/02/global_warming _suit.

Obama, Barack. "Address Before a Joint Session of Congress on the State of the Union." January 24, 2012. Online by John Woolley and Gerhard Peters, *The American Presidency Project.* www.presidency.ucsb.edu/ws /index.php?pid=99000.

————. "Address to the United Nations General Assembly in New York City." September 23, 2009. Online by John Woolley and Gerhard Peters, *The American Presidency Project.* www.presidency.ucsb.edu/ws /index.php?pid=86659.

————. "Joint Statement by the United States and the European Union." November 28, 2011. Online by John Woolley and Gerhard Peters, *The American Presidency Project.* www.presidency.ucsb.edu/ws/index.php ?pid=97341.

————. "Remarks at a Plenary Session of the United Nations Climate Change Conference in Copenhagen, Denmark." December 18, 2009. Online by John Woolley and Gerhard Peters, *The American Presidency Project.* www.presidency.ucsb.edu/ws/index.php?pid=87011.

————. "Remarks at the United Nations Climate Change Summit in New York City." September 22, 2009. Online by John Woolley and Gerhard Peters, *The American Presidency Project.* www.presidency.ucsb.edu/ws /index.php?pid=86657.

————. "Remarks on Energy at Andrews Air Force Base, Maryland." March 31, 2010. Online by John Woolley and Gerhard Peters, *The American Presidency Project.* www.presidency.ucsb.edu/ws/index.php?pid=87685.

————. "Remarks on Health Care Reform and Climate Change." December 19, 2009. Online by John Woolley and Gerhard Peters, *The American Presidency Project.* www.presidency.ucsb.edu/ws/index.php?pid=87007.

————. "Remarks on Signing a Memorandum Improving Energy Security, American Competitiveness and Job Creation, and Environmental Protection Through a Transformation of Our Nation's Fleet of Cars and

Trucks." May 21, 2010. Online by John Woolley and Gerhard Peters, *The American Presidency Project*. www.presidency.ucsb.edu/ws/index .php?pid=87932.

———. "State of the Union 2012: Obama Speech Full Text." *Washington Post*, January 25, 2012. http://washingtonpost.com/politics.

———. "Text: Obama's State of the Union Address." *New York Times*, January 28, 2010. www.nytimes.com/2010/01/28/us/politics.

———. "Videotaped Remarks to the Bi-Partisan Governors Global Climate Summit." November 18, 2008. Online by John Woolley and Gerhard Peters, *The American Presidency Project*. www.presidency.ucsb.edu /ws/index.php?pid=84875.

Pachauri, R. K. "The IPCC: Establishing the Evidence." In *Global Warming: Looking Beyond Kyoto*, edited by Ernesto Zedillo. Washington, DC: Brookings Institution, 2008.

"Participating in Multilateral Treaties." September 18, 2012. http://untreaty .un.org/ola-internet/Assistance/handbook_eng/chapter3.htm.

Pew Center on the States and Pew Center on Global Climate Change. "Climate Change 101: State Action." January 2009. www.c2es.org.

Pew Charitable Trusts. "The Clean Energy Economy." June 2009. www.pew environment.org/uploadedFiles/PEG/publications/Report/clean%20 Energy%20Economy.pdf.

Pew Research Center for the People and the Press. "Modest Rise in Number Saying There Is 'Solid Evidence' of Global Warming." December 1, 2011. http://pewresearch.org/pubs/2137/global-warming-environment -partisan-divide-?src=prc-headline.

———. "Public Praises Science; Scientists Fault Public, Media." July 9, 2009. http://peoplepress.org/report/?pageid=1550.

Pielke, Roger, Jr., and Daniel Sarewitz. "Wanted: Scientific Leadership on Climate." *Issues in Science and Technology* (Winter 2002–2003). www.issues.org/19.2/p_pielke.htm.

Pilkey, Orrin H., and Rob Young. *The Rising Sea*. Washington, DC: Island, 2009.

Plato. *Myth of Atlantis*. http://library.flawlesslogic.com/atlantis.htm.

Plummer, Brad. "Will the EPA's New Climate Rules Get Killed in Court?" *Washington Post*, February 27, 2012. www.washingtonpost.com/blogs.

Pomerance, Rafe. "The Dangers from Climate Warming: A Public Awakening." In *The Challenge of Global Warming*, edited by Dean Edwin Abrahamson. Washington, DC: Island, 1989.

Posner, Eric A., and David Weisbach. *Climate Change Justice*. Princeton: Princeton University Press, 2010.

Povilitis, Tony, and Kieran Suckling. "Addressing Climate Change Threats to Endangered Species in U.S. Recovery Plans." *Conservation Biology* 24 (April 2010): 372–379.

Price, J. H. "A Lukewarm Theory? Scientists Roast Global Warming's 'Uncertainties.'" *Washington Times*, November 30, 1997.

Pugliese, Anita, and Julie Ray. "Fewer Americans, Europeans View Global Warming As a Threat." *Gallup World*, April 20, 2011. www.gallup.com /poll/147203/Fewer-Americans-Europeans-View-Global-Warming -Threat.asp.

Rabe, Barry G. "Can Congress Govern the Climate?" Research Brief no. 1. New York: John Brademas Center for the Study of Congress, New York University, April 2007.

———. "Contested Federalism and American Climate Policy." *Publius: Journal of Federalism* 41, no. 3 (2011): 494–521.

———. *Greenhouse Governance: Addressing Climate Change in America.* Washington, DC: Brookings Institution, 2010.

———. "Second Generation Climate Policies in the States: Proliferation, Diffusion, and Regionalization." In *Changing Climates in North American Politics,* edited by Henrik Selin and Stacy D. VanDeveer. Cambridge: Massachusetts Institute of Technology Press, 2009.

———. *Statehouse and Greenhouse: The Emerging Politics of American Climate Policy.* Washington, DC: Brookings Institution, 2004.

Rahmstorf, Stefen. "Anthropogenic Climate Change: Revisiting the Facts." In *Global Warming: Looking Beyond Kyoto,* edited by Ernesto Zedillo. Washington, DC: Brookings Institution, 2008.

Ranlet, Philip. "What Does Weird Weather Really Tell Us?" History News Network, September 3, 2007. http://hnn.us/articles/42243.html.

Ray, Julie, and Anita Pugliese. "World's Top-Emitters No More Aware of Climate Change in 2010." *Gallup World,* August 26, 2011. www.gallup.com/poll/149207/World-Top-Emitters-No-Aware-Climate-Changes-2010.

Reagan, Ronald. "Statement on Signing the Montreal Protocol on Ozone-Depleting Substances." April 5, 1988. Online by John Woolley and Gerhard Peters, *The American Presidency Project.* www.presidency.ucsb.edu/ws/index.php?pid=35639.

"Report Warns Great Barrier Reef Could Die in 20 Years." Environmental News Network, February 14, 2005. www.enn.com.

"Republican Contract with America." www.c2es.org/federal/congress/111.

Revkin, Andrew C. "Bush Aide Edited Climate Reports." *New York Times,* June 8, 2005.

———. "Climate Changing, US Says in Report." *New York Times,* June 3, 2002.

———. "Industry Ignored Its Scientists on Climate." *New York Times,* April 24, 2009.

Revkin, Andrew C., and James Kanter. "Global Warming Is Not Slowing, New Analysis Says." *New York Times,* December 9, 2009. www.nytimes.com/2009/12/09/science/earth.

Revkin, Andrew C., and Katherine Q. Seelye. "Report by the E.P.A. Leaves Out Data on Climate Change." *New York Times,* June 19, 2003.

Richter, Burton. *Beyond Smoke and Mirrors: Climate Change and Energy in the 21st Century.* New York: Cambridge University Press, 2010.

Ringquist, Evan. *Environmental Protection at the State Level.* Armonk, NY: Sharpe, 1993.

Roberts, J. Timmons, and Bradley C. Parks. *A Climate of Injustice: Global Inequality, North-South Politics, and Climate Policy.* Cambridge: Massachusetts Institute of Technology Press, 2007.

Rosenbaum, Walter A. *Environmental Politics and Policy.* 8th ed. Washington, DC: Congressional Quarterly, 2011.

————. "Science, Politics, and Policy at the EPA." In *Environmental Policy,* edited by Norman J. Vig and Michael E. Kraft. 7th ed. Washington, DC: Congressional Quarterly, 2010.

Rosenstone, Steven J., and John Mark Hansen. *Mobilization, Participation, and Democracy in America.* New York: Macmillan, 1993.

Rosenthal, Elizabeth. "Obama's Backing Raises Hopes for Climate Pact." *New York Times,* March 1, 2009.

Rosenthal, Elizabeth, and Andrew C. Revkin. "Science Panel Calls Global Warming 'Unequivocal.'" *New York Times,* February 3, 2007.

Sabine, Christopher L., Richard A. Feely, Nicolas Gruber, Robert M. Key, Kitack Lee, John L. Bullister, Rik Wanninkhof et al. "The Ocean Sink for Anthropogenic CO_2." *Science* 305 (July 2004): 367–371.

Samuelsohn, Darren. "Both Sides Gird for Bruising Senate Debate over EPA Amendment." *New York Times,* January 8, 2010. www.nytimes.com.

Sarewitz, Daniel. "Liberating Science from Politics." *American Scientist* 94 (2006): 104–106.

Savage, David G. "Supreme Court Kills Global Warming Suit." *Los Angeles Times,* June 21, 2011. http://latimes.com/news/nationworld/nation.

Scherer, Ron. "Report: 'Green' Jobs Outpacing Traditional Ones." *Christian Science Monitor,* June 10, 2009. www.csmonitor.com/Business.

Schlosberg, David, and Elizabeth Bomberg. "Perspectives on American Environmentalism." *Environmental Politics* 17 (April 2008): 187–199.

Schneider, Stephen. *Science as a Contact Sport: Inside the Battle to Save Earth's Climate.* Washington, DC: National Geographic, 2009.

Schreurs, Miranda. "Climate Change Politics in the United States: Melting of the Ice." *Analyse & Kritik* 32, no. 1 (2010): 177–189.

————. "20th Anniversary of the Rio Summit: Taking a Look Back and at the Road Ahead." 2012. http://creativecommons.org/licenses/by/3.0.

Schreurs, Miranda, and Yves Tiberghin. "European Leadership in Climate Change: Mitigation Through Multilevel Reinforcement." In *Global Commons, Domestic Decisions,* edited by Katherine Harrison and Lisa McIntosh Sundstrom. Cambridge: Massachusetts Institute of Technology Press, 2010.

Schwartz, John. "Courts as Battlefields in Climate Fights." *New York Times,* January 27, 2010. www.nytimes.com/2010/01/27/business/energy-environment.

Schwarzenegger, Arnold. "Schwarzenegger: Beyond Copenhagen, Global Warming Requires Grassroots Action." *Christian Science Monitor,* December 14, 2009. www.csmonitor.com.

Scott, John A. "Fog and Deaths in London, December 1952." *Public Health Reports* 68, no. 5 (May 1953): 474–479.

Scripps Institution of Oceanography. "Research Overview: Global Change and the Greenhouse Effect." 2000. www.sio.ucsd.edu/about_scripps /research_overview/global_change.htm.

Selin, Henrik, and Stacy D. VanDeveer. "Climate Leadership in Northeast North America." In *Changing Climates in North American Politics,* edited by Henrik Selin and Stacy D. VanDeveer. Cambridge: Massachusetts Institute of Technology Press, 2009.

————. "US Climate Change Politics and Policymaking." *Wiley Interdisciplinary Reviews: Climate Change* 2, no. 1 (2011). http://people.bu.edu /selin/publications/SelinVanDeveerWileyReview2011.pdf.

Senate Committee on Energy and Commerce. "Anti-Environmental Votes in the 112th Congress, 1st Session." http://democrats.energycommerce .house.gov/sites/default/files/image_uploads/Anti-Environment Votes.pdf.

Shabecoff, Philip. "E.P.A. Report Says Earth Will Heat Up Beginning in 1990s." *New York Times,* October 18, 1983.

———. "Washington Talk: State Department: The Environment as a Diplomatic Issue." *New York Times,* December 25, 1987.

Shackleton, Robert. *Potential Impacts of Climate Change in the United States.* Washington, DC: Congressional Budget Office, May 2009.

Sharp, Elaine. *The Sometime Connection: Public Opinion and Social Policy.* Albany: State University of New York Press, 1999.

Shearman, David, and Joseph Wayne Smith. *The Climate Change Challenge and the Failure of Democracy.* Westport: Praeger, 2007.

Slone, Sean, and Doug Myers. "Climate Change and Transportation." Council of State Governments, February 22, 2010. http://knowledgecenter .csg.org/drupal/content/climatechange-and-transportation.

Smart Growth America and Natural Resources Defense Council. "Getting Back on Track: Aligning State Transportation Policy with Climate Change Goals." December 14, 2010. www.nrdc.org/smartgrowth/files /GettingBackonTrack_4pgr.pdf.

Smith, Zachary. *The Environmental Policy Paradox.* 5th ed. Upper Saddle River, NJ: Prentice Hall, 2009.

Soden, Dennis L. "At the Nexus: Science Policy." In *At the Nexus: Science Policy,* edited by Dennis L. Soden. Commack, NY: Nova Science, 1996.

Soroka, Stuart, and Christopher Wlezien. "Public Opinion and Public Policy." In *Oxford Handbook of Canadian Politics,* edited by John Courtney and David Smith. Oxford: Oxford University Press, 2010.

Soroos, Marvin S. "From Stockholm to Rio: The Evaluation of Global Environmental Governance." In *Environmental Policy in the 1990s,* edited by Norman J. Vig and Michael E. Kraft. 2nd ed. Washington, DC: Congressional Quarterly, 1994.

———. "Negotiating Our Climate." In *Global Climate Change,* edited by Sharon L. Spray and Karen L. McGlothlin. Lanham: Rowman and Littlefield, 2002.

Sourcewatch. "Global Climate Coalition." www.sourcewatch.org/index.php ?title=Global_Climate_Coalition.

Speth, James Gustave. *Red Sky at Morning.* New Haven: Yale University Press, 2004.

Spotts, Peter. "Climate Change Talks: What to Look for at Copenhagen." *Christian Science Monitor,* December 7, 2009. www.csmonitor.com /2009/1207.

State of Virginia, Governor's Commission on Climate Change. "Final Report: A Climate Change Action Plan." December 15, 2008.

"States Sue EPA to Move on Global Warming." April 2008. www.nbcnews.com.

Steel, Brent, Richard Clinton, and Nicholas Lovrich Jr. *Environmental Politics and Policy.* Boston: McGraw Hill, 2003.

Strauss, Ben, Claudia Tebaldi, and Remik Ziemlinski. "Surging Seas: Sea Level Rise, Storms, and Global Warming's Threat to the US Coast." Climate Central, March 14, 2012. www.climatecentral.org.

"Study: Warming Tied to Hurricanes." June 22, 2006. www.msnbc.msn.com.
Sullivan, Meg. "Global Warming's Silver Lining: Northern Countries Will Thrive, Grow." *UCLA News,* September 3, 2010.
Sunstein, Cass R. "Of Montreal and Kyoto: A Tale of Two Protocols." *Harvard Environmental Law Review* 31, no. 1 (2007): 3–4, 25.
"Supreme Court: Arguments on Climate Change." *Environmental Policy and Law* 37, no. 1 (2007): 53–54.
Susskind, Lawrence. *Environmental Diplomacy: Negotiating More Effective Global Agreements.* Oxford: Oxford University Press, 1994.
Sussman, Glen. "Global Climate Change: A Very Serious Environmental Threat That Developed Countries and Major Emerging Industrialized Countries Should Share in the Burden in Addressing." In *Issues: Understanding Controversy and Society.* Santa Barbara: ABC-CLIO, 2012. http://issues2.abc-clio.com.
———. "The Science and Politics Problem: Policymaking, Climate Change, and Hurricanes." In *Hurricanes and Climate Change,* edited by James B. Elsner and Thomas H. Jagger. New York: Springer, 2009.
———. "The USA and Global Environmental Policy: Domestic Constraints on Effective Leadership." *International Political Science Review* 25 (October 2004): 349–369.
Sussman, Glen, Byron W. Daynes, and Jonathan West. *American Politics and the Environment.* New York: Longman, 2002.
Tankersley, Jim, and Alexander C. Hart. "Bush-Era EPA Document on Climate Change Released." *Los Angeles Times,* October 14, 2009.
Tatalovich, Raymond, and Byron W. Daynes, eds. *Moral Controversies in American Politics.* 4th ed. Armonk, NY: Sharpe, 2011.
"Texas Loses Third Try at Blocking EPA Greenhouse Gas Controls." Environmental News Service, January 12, 2011. www.ens-newswire.com/ens/jan2011/2011-01-12-091.html.
Tierney, John. "Findings: Corporate Backing for Research? Get Over It." *New York Times,* January 26, 2010. www.nytimes.com/2010/01/26/science.
Times Topics. "Copenhagen Climate Talks (UNFCCC)." *New York Times,* January 15, 2010. http://topics.nytimes.com/top/reference/timestopics.
Tribal Climate Change Project. "Climate Change: Realities of Relocation for Alaska Native Villages." University of Oregon, 2010. http://tribalclimate.uoregon.edu/files/2010/11/AlaskaRelocation_04-1-11.pdf.
Truman, Harry. "Message to the United States Technical Conference on Air Pollution." May 3, 1950. In *Public Papers of the Presidents: Harry S. Truman, 1950.* Washington, DC: Government Printing Office, 1965.
Underdal, Arild. "Science and Politics: The Anatomy of an Uneasy Partnership." In *Science in International Environmental Regimes,* edited by S. Andresen et al. New York: Manchester University Press, 2000.
Union of Concerned Scientists. "Global Warming Deniers Are Full of Hot Air." N.d. www.ucsusa.org/cation/GotScience.
United Nations Environment Programme. "Doha Climate Conference Opens Gateway to Greater Ambition and Action on Climate Change." UNEP News Centre. www.unep.org/newscentre/default.aspx?DocumentID=2700& ArticleID=9353.

Walker, Julian, and Scott Harper. "State Vehicles Set for a Conversion." *Virginian-Pilot,* October 3, 2012.

Walker, Ruth. "Will Words Fail Us in Copenhagen?" *Christian Science Monitor,* November 29, 2009.

Walsh, Bryan. "EPA's CO_2 Finding: Putting a Gun to Congress's Head." *Time,* April 18, 2009. www.time.com.

Walsh, Bryan, et al. "Global Warming: The Causes, the Perils, the Solutions." *Time,* special edition, 2012.

Weart, Spencer. "The Public and Climate Change." American Institute of Physics, February 2013. www.aip.org/history/climate/public2.htm.

Weisskopf, Michael. "The Evidence on the Greenhouse Effect." *Washington Post National Weekly,* August 29–September 4, 1988.

"Where the Action Is on Climate." *New York Times,* January 4, 2010. www.nytimes.com/2010/01/02/opinion.

White House. "US–Mexico Announce Bilateral Framework on Clean Energy and Climate Change." April 16, 2009. www.whitehouse.gov/the-press -office.

Wigley, Tom M. L., V. Ramaswamy, J. R. Christy, J. R. Lanzante, C. A. Mears, B. D. Santer, and C. K. Folland. "Temperature Trends in the Lower Atmosphere: Understanding and Reconciling Differences." Executive summary. National Climatic Data Center, April 2006. http://climatescience .gov/Library/sap/sap1-1/finalreport/sap1-1-final-execsum.pdf.

Witter, W. "Gore Offers Flexibility on Emission Cuts; Attempts to Break Deadlock in Kyoto." *Washington Times,* December 8, 1997.

Wolkomir, Richard. "The Greenhouse Revolution." *Oceans* (April 1988): 17–20, 59.

Woolley, John, and Gerhard Peters. *The American Presidency Project.* www.presidency.ucsb.edu.

World Bank. "Public Attitudes Toward Climate Change: Findings from a Multi-Country Poll." In *World Development Report 2010.* Washington, DC, 2010.

World Resources Institute. "WRI Report Says Human Activities Threaten Bulk of Caribbean Coral Reefs." Environmental News Network, September 30, 2004. www.enn.com.

Wynn, Gerard, and Pete Harrison. "US Backs $100 Bln Climate Fund, World Leaders Meet." Reuters, December 17, 2009. www.reuters.com.

Yarnold, David. "Why Do Climate Deniers Hate America?" Environmental Defense Action Fund e-mail, February 12, 2010. Cited in Byron W. Daynes and Glen Sussman, "Global Warming: Environmental Crisis or Scientific Hoax?" In *Moral Controversies in American Politics,* 4th ed., edited by Raymond Tatalovich and Byron W. Daynes. Armonk, NY: M. E. Sharpe, 2011.

Young, Oran R., Leslie A. King, and Heike Schroeder. *Institutions and Environmental Change: Principal Findings, Applications, and Research Frontiers.* Cambridge: Massachusetts Institute of Technology Press, 2008.

Zabarenko, Deborah. "NASA Says That 2005 Was Warmest Year on Record." Environmental News Network, January 25, 2006. www.enn.com.

Zedillo, Ernesto, ed. *Global Warming: Looking Beyond Kyoto.* Washington, DC: Brookings Institution, 2008.

Zeller, Tom, Jr. "Thousands March in Copenhagen, Calling for Action." *New York Times,* December 13, 2009. www.nytimes.com/2009/12/13/science /earth/13climate.html.

Index

Alabama, 169
Alaska, 117, 178, 182
Albright, Madeleine, 37–38
Aldy, Joseph, 5
Alley, Richard, 198
American Chemistry Council v. EPA and Lisa Jackson (2011), 118, 126
American Clean Energy and Security Act, 61, 63
American Coalition for Clean Coal Electricity, 196
American Electric Power v. Connecticut (2011), 110, 113–115, 123, 125, 204
American Petroleum Institute, 61
America's Natural Gas Alliance, 197
Arctic Council, 33, 35
Aristotle, 2
Arizona: emissions, 170, 179; and Kyoto, 169; regional alliances, 175, 176; renewable energy, 177
Australia, 89, 90

Babbitt, Bruce, 84
Bachmann, Michelle (R-MN), 54
Baja California, 175

Beck, Glenn, 26, 137
Blair, Tony, 31, 167
Boehner, John (R-OH), 54
Border Power Plant v. Department of Energy (2003), 121
Boston, 187
Brazil, 96
Brennan, William, 122
Britain. *See* United Kingdom
British Columbia, 175, 176
Brown, Jerry, 123
Browner, Carol, 67, 84, 94
Burford, Anne, 81
Bush, George H. W.: international agreements, 42–43, 82–83, 84, 203; organizing support, 93, 153
Bush, George W.: Clear Skies initiative, 89–90; on climate change, 13, 90–91, 110; and deniers, 12, 138; and EPA, 30, 111–112, 115, 123; and Kyoto Protocol, 13, 89, 164, 197, 203; and regulation, 31; and scientists, 91–92, 135
Byrd-Hagel Resolution, 66, 85, 202

Calderón, Felipe, 94–95
Caldwell, Lynton, 7

California: court cases, 114, 123; energy efficiency, 178, 188; green jobs, 181–182; innovation, 165, 166–168, 173, 186, 205, 206; reducing emissions, 91, 100, 166–168, 180, 185; regional alliances, 167, 175, 176; renewable energy, 176, 187; vehicle emission standards, 119, 120, 123, 179, 186

California v. General Motors (2007), 123, 126

Canada: greenhouse gases, 22; international agreements, 90, 94, 151, 156, 167; public opinion, 149–151, 157; regional alliances, 175, 176

Cancun Accord, 96–97, 98

cap and trade, 44, 59–60, 93, 175, 203

carbon dioxide: emissions increase, 21, 38–39, 40, 44; producers, 87, 88; regulation, 111–112, 114, 116, 124; by state, 170, 171, 172, 179, 180. *See also* greenhouse gases

Carter, Jimmy, 42, 80–81, 82, 202–203

CATO Institute, 139–140, 196

Center for Biodiversity v. National Highway Traffic Safety Administration (2008), 119–12

Center for Biological Diversity v. Brennan (2007), 121–122

Central Valley v. Goldstene (2007), 120, 126

Chihuahua, 175

China: greenhouse gases, 6, 87; Kyoto Protocol, 66, 85, 86, 89; other international agreements, 96, 97, 167; public opinion, 151–152, 157–158; and United States, 91, 92

Clear Skies Initiative, 89–90

Clean Air Act, 78–80, 82, 153; and California emission standards, 119, 120, 167; and enforcement, 111–113; and EPA, 31, 94, 111–113, 114, 119; opposition, 53, 54, 84, 89; regulation, 116, 123, 140

Clean Energy Jobs and American Power Act, 52, 61

Clean Energy Works, 135

Clean Power Act (2001), 138

climate action plans, 170, 172–174

Climate and Clean Air Coalition, 98

climate change: deniers, 10–11, 26, 31, 137, 154; global, 3, 5–6, 7; politicization of, 25, 197; and presidency, 98–99, 202–204; and private sector, 136, 137–139, 140–141; public interest, 194–195; results of, 30–31, 33–40, 194–195; and Supreme Court, 111–115

Climate Change Summit (2011), 5–6, 57, 97–98, 151

Climategate, 142–143, 156

Clinton, Bill: and climate change, 87, 89, 203; and Congress, 62, 65–66; and Kyoto Protocol, 60, 84–87, 197; and regulation, 110

Clinton, Hillary, 98

Clinton, Richard, 9

Coahuila, 175

Coalition for Responsible Regulation v. EPA (2011), 115–116, 120–121, 126

Coalition for Responsible Regulation v. EPA (2012), 116–117, 126

Coke Oven Environmental Task Force v. EPA (2006), 122–123

Colorado, 169, 170, 179

Comer v. Murphy Oil (2009), 117–118, 126

Conference of New England Governors, 174–175

Congress. *See* US Congress

Connecticut: court case, 114; energy efficiency, 178, 188; green jobs, 182; reducing emissions, 179, 180, 185; regional alliances, 175, 176; renewable energy, 165

Contract with America, 52

Convention on Global Climate Change, 42–43, 201

Cooney, Philip, 91–92
Copenhagen Accord, 8, 9, 57, 65, 95–96, 142
Crichton, Michael, 11–12, 31, 137
Crombie, George, 120

Delaware, 175, 176, 177, 182, 187
DeMint, Jim (R-SC), 58
Dimitrov, Radoslav, 95–96
Durban Summit. *See* Climate Change Summit (2011)

Earth Summit (1992), 42, 82–83, 84, 197
Eisenhower, Dwight, 78
emissions trading, 6
endangerment finding, 115–116, 121, 126, 168, 186
Engler, John, 169
Environmental Defense Fund, 135
Environmental Defense v. Duke Energy (2007), 122, 125, 126
Environmental Protection Agency (EPA): and Bush, 30, 111–112, 115; and California, 167–168, 186; and Clean Air Act, 31, 94, 111–113, 114, 116, 119, 126; and Congress, 44, 53, 55, 58–59, 61–62; deterioration rule, 118; endangerment finding, 115–116, 121, 126, 168, 186; and greenhouse gases, 3, 31–32, 204; and Obama, 53, 94, 167; regulation, 61, 126, 140, 185; and states, 168, 169, 172; tailoring, 116–117, 126; Tailpipe Rule, 120–121; timing, 116, 126; US Climate Action Report, 30
EPA. *See* Environmental Protection Agency
European Union, 44, 86, 97, 165
Evangelical Climate Initiative, 135
Exxon Mobil, 117

fee and dividend, 60
Fisher, Dana, 5
Florida, 182
Ford, Gerald, 79–80

France, 22
Friedman, Thomas, 137, 153

Garrett, Tim, 10
Gelbspan, Ross, 9
Georgia, 169, 182
Germany, 22–23, 90
Gersh Korsinsky v. US EPA (2005), 124, 126
Gingrich, Newt (R-GA), 52, 62
Ginsburg, Ruth Bader, 114, 115
Global 2000 Report to the President, 42, 80, 81, 202
Global Change Research Act, 121
Global Climate Coalition (GCC), 137–138, 196
global warming. *See* climate change
Global Warming Solutions Act, 167, 173
Goldstene, James, 120
Gore, Al, 9–10, 13, 60, 66, 84, 90, 203; on climate change, 153
Graham, Lindsey (R-SC), 64, 65
Granholm, Jennifer, 169
Green (Climate) Fund, 57–58, 97
greenhouse gases: and human activity, 13–14, 21, 22; and Kyoto Protocol, 3, 85; non-carbon gases, 39–40, 98; and private sector, 141, 206–207; reduction in states, 164–165, 166; and transportation, 179. *See also* carbon dioxide
green jobs, 181–182, 183–184, 188
Green Mountain v. Crombie (2007), 120, 126
Greenpeace, 135

Hannity, Sean, 11
Hansen, James, 26, 42, 134–135, 142–143
Harper, Stephen, 94, 151
Harrison, Kathryn, 13
Hart, Alexander, 31–32
Hawaii, 170, 177, 185, 187
Heartland Institute, 143
Heritage Foundation, 139–140, 196
Holdren, John, 134–135

Horner, Christopher, 12
hurricanes, 36–37, 41, 195

Idaho, 169, 172, 177, 182
Illinois, 169, 175, 176, 179, 182
India: greenhouse gases, 6; Kyoto
    Protocol, 66, 85, 86, 89; other
    international agreements, 96, 97;
    public opinion, 151–152,
    157–158; and United States, 91
Indiana, 169, 182
Industrial Revolution, 2
Inhofe, James (R-OK), 11, 26, 65,
    137, 154, 202
insurance industry, 141–142
interest groups: deniers, 10–12, 26,
    31, 137–142, 154, 196, 201; di-
    visions between, 132–134,
    195–196; lobbying, 133–134;
    and public policy, 131, 154–155,
    204; supporting government ac-
    tion, 134–137, 195, 200–201
Intergovernmental Panel on Climate
    Change (IPCC), 1, 21, 32–33,
    41, 43
International Council for Science,
    34
Iowa, 114, 165, 170, 175
IPCC. *See* Intergovernmental Panel
    on Climate Change
Italy, 22

Jackson, Lisa, 31, 94, 167–168, 186
Japan, 22, 90, 151–152, 157–158
Johnson, Lyndon, 78–79
Johnson, Stephen, 31, 167, 185, 186
joint implementation, 6

Kaine, Tim, 173
Kansas, 175, 178, 182
Keeling, Charles, 28–29
Keeling Curve, 28–29
Kennedy, John F., 78
Kent, Peter, 151
Kentucky, 169
Kerry, John (D-MA), 64, 65
King, Leslie, 15
Klyza, Christopher, 4

Kraft, Michael, 7–8
Kyoto Protocol: and Bush, 13, 89,
    164, 197, 203; and Canada, 151,
    156; and Clinton, 60, 164; and
    Congress, 43, 65–66, 164, 197,
    202; greenhouse gas, 3; opposi-
    tion, 85–86, 87, 138; and Russia,
    23–24, 86; second commitment,
    6, 97; and subnational efforts, 5,
    91, 186–187; support, 9, 84,
    86–87

Lee, Henry, 5
Lester, James, 165–166
Lieberman, Ben, 140
Lieberman, Joseph (I-CT), 64, 65
Limbaugh, Rush, 11, 26, 137, 154
Loris, Nicolas, 140
Louisiana, 178
Lovrich, Nicholas, 9

Mabus, Ray, 93
Maine, 165, 175, 176, 179, 188
Manitoba, 175, 176
Martinez, Susana, 169, 178
Maryland, 175, 176, 178, 179, 180
Massachusetts: court cases, 112,
    113, 119; energy efficiency, 178;
    green jobs, 182; reducing emis-
    sions, 165, 170, 179, 185; re-
    gional alliances, 175, 176
Massachusetts v. EPA (2007), 110,
    111–113, 114, 123, 125; result-
    ing action, 185, 200, 204
*Mayo Foundation v. Surface Trans-
    portation Board* (2006), 124
McCain, John, 92
McDonald, Gordon, 29
Merkel, Angela, 23
Mexico, 90, 94–95, 167, 175
Midwestern Greenhouse Gas Ac-
    cord, 175
Midwestern Initiative, 174, 175, 187
Michigan, 169, 175, 182
Minnesota, 166, 175, 176, 178
Mississippi, 169, 178
Missouri, 178
Montana, 175, 176, 177, 182

Montreal Protocol, 81, 133, 153
Mullan, James, 26
Murkowski, Lisa (R-AK), 53

*Native Village of Kivalina v. Exxon
Mobil* (2009), 117, 126
NASA. *See* National Aeronautics
and Space Administration
National Aeronautics and Space Ad-
ministration (NASA), 9, 29, 30
National Automobile Dealers Asso-
ciation (NADA), 119
National Climate Act (1978), 29
National Climatic Data Center, 9
National Environmental Policy Act
(NEPA), 119, 163
National Highway Traffic Safety
Administration (NTSA),
119–120
National Oceanic and Atmospheric
Administration (NOAA), 29, 30,
32, 33–34, 35
national security, 37–38, 173, 195
Natural Resources Defense Council,
135
Nebraska, 170, 176, 178, 182, 187
NEPA. *See* National Environmental
Policy Act
Nevada, 165
Newell, Brent, 109–110
New Hampshire, 175, 182
New Jersey: court cases: 114, 119;
green jobs, 182; reducing emis-
sions, 179, 180, 185; regional al-
liances, 175, 176; renewable en-
ergy, 165, 176, 187
New Mexico, 169, 175, 176,
178–179
New York: court cases, 114, 119,
124; energy efficiency, 178, 188;
green jobs, 182; reducing emis-
sions, 170, 172, 179, 185; re-
gional alliances, 175; renewable
energy, 176, 187
New York City, 114, 124, 187
Nixon, Richard, 79
NOAA. *See* National Oceanic and
Atmospheric Administration

North America 2050, 175–176, 206
North Carolina, 169
North Dakota, 169, 178
*Northwest Environmental Defense
Center v. Owens Corning* (2006),
125, 126
Nuevo Leon, 175

Obama, Barack: approaches to climate change, 59–60, 70, 93,
98–99; and Congress, 64–65,
66–67, 70, 92–94, 153, 156; and
EPA, 53, 94, 113, 186; and international cooperation, 94–98; legislation, 13, 63; priorities, 57,
125, 206; and standards, 123,
179
Ohio, 169, 182
Ontario, 175, 176
Oregon: energy efficiency, 178,
188; reducing emissions, 166,
179; regional alliances, 175; renewable energy, 176, 187; transportation, 179, 180

Paris Economic Summit (1990), 82
Parks, Bradley, 6–7
partisanship, 198; in Congress, 52,
53, 153; in public opinion,
146–148, 155; in the states, 173
party opposition, 52–54
Pennsylvania, 119, 169, 179, 182
Posner, Eric, 4
public health, 173, 195
public opinion: American, 143–148,
151–154, 157; causes of global
warming, 145–148; divisions,
144, 146–148; global, 149–152,
156; and public policy, 131–132,
155, 204–205
Putin, Vladimir, 86

Quebec, 175, 176

Rabe, Barry, 4
Rahmstorf, Stefen, 40
Reagan, Ronald, 81–82, 153, 165,
203

regional alliances, 174–176, 187
Regional Greenhouse Gas Initiative,
174, 175–176, 187
Reid, Harry (D-NV), 53
Reilly, William, 202
renewable energy, 176–177, 187
Revelle, Roger, 27–28, 134
Rhode Island: court case, 114; en-
ergy efficiency, 178, 188; reduc-
ing emissions, 179; regional al-
liances, 175, 176; renewable
energy, 177, 187
Richter, Burton, 4–5
Roberts, John, 113
Roberts, J. Timmons, 6–7
Rockefeller, Jay (D-WV), 59
Rohrabacher, Dana (R-CA), 57
Romney, Mitt, 156, 204
Ruckelshaus, William, 202
Rudd, Kevin, 96
Russia, 22, 23–24, 86, 151–152,
157–158

Salt Lake City, 187
Santorum, Rick (R-PA), 154
Scalia, Antonin, 113
Schreurs, Miranda, 12
Schroeder, Heike, 15
Schwarzenegger, Arnold, 91, 166,
167, 168, 186
science: and politics, 24–27,
134–135, 197–199, 200–201;
and public opinion, 143,
144–145, 205
Scripps Institute of Oceanography,
27–28, 30
sea ice, 30, 33–36, 195
sea level, 35–36, 41, 112, 195
Selin, Henrik, 5
Shearman, David, 7
Sierra Club, 135
Smith, Joseph, 7
Sonora, 175
Sotomayor, Sonia, 114
Sousa, David, 4
Souter, David, 122
South Carolina, 169, 170
South Dakota, 178, 182

Speth, James Gustave, 198
states: climate action plans, 170,
172–174; energy efficiency,
177–179; and EPA, 168, 169,
172; and greenhouse gas reduction, 164–165, 166, 170, 171,
172, 185; and green jobs,
181–182, 183–184, 188; innovation, 165, 166–168, 205–206;
obstruction, 168–169; regional
alliances, 174–176; renewable
energy, 176–177, 185–186; and
transportation sector, 179–180,
181, 185
Stavins, Robert, 5
Steel, Brent, 9
Stern, Todd, 67
Stevens, John Paul, 112–113
Suess, Hans, 27–28
Sullivan, John (R-OK), 59
Sundstrom, Lisa, 13
Supreme Court, 111–115, 122, 125

Tamaulipas, 175
Tankersley, Jim, 31–32
Tennessee, 169
Texas, 176, 178–179, 181, 182, 187
transportation sector, 179–180, 181
Truman, Harry, 78

Underdal, Arild, 24–25
United Kingdom, 22, 90
*US Chamber of Commerce and Na-
tional Automobile Dealers Association v. EPA* (2011), 118–119,
126
US Climate Change Science Program, 121–122
US Congress: bicameralism, 54–55;
committees, 55–56; and EPA, 44,
53, 55, 58–59, 61–62; and funding, 56–58; and international
agreements, 42–43, 65–66, 164,
197, 202; legislation, 61, 62,
63–64, 125, 201–202; and
Obama, 64–65, 66–67, 70,
92–93, 94, 153, 156; partisanship, 51–54, 153, 199; and the

presidency, 64–66, 68–69, 84, 153, 200
US Global Change Research Program, 42
US Navy, 38, 93
Utah, 168, 172, 175, 182, 186

VanDeveer, Stacy, 5
Vermont: court cases, 114, 120; energy efficiency, 178, 188; reducing emissions, 179; regional alliances, 175, 176
Virginia, 169, 173–174, 180

Washington: energy efficiency, 178, 188; green jobs, 182; reducing emissions, 179, 180, 185; regional alliances, 175; renewable energy, 176, 187

Watt, James, 81
Waxman, Henry (D-CA), 57, 59, 61
Weisbach, David, 4
Western Climate Initiative, 174, 175–176, 187
Western Fuels Association, 139, 196
West Virginia, 169, 178
Whitman, Christine, 30
Wisconsin, 114, 165, 175, 182
World Climate Conference (1990), 82
World Meteorological Organization, 9, 34, 41
World Trade Organization, 86
Wyoming, 169, 172, 178

Young, Oran, 15

Zedillo, Ernesto, 5

About the Book

Why is climate change the subject of such vehement political rhetoric in the United States? What explains the policy deadlock that has existed for nearly two decades—and that has resulted in the failure of US leadership in the international arena? Addressing these questions, Glen Sussman and Byron Daynes trace the evolution of US climate change policy, assess how key players—the scientific community, Congress, the president, the judiciary, interest groups, the states, and the public—have responded to climate change, and explore the prospects for effective policymaking in the future.

Glen Sussman is University Professor of Political Science at Old Dominion University. **Byron W. Daynes** is professor of political science at Brigham Young University. The two are coauthors, most recently, of *White House Politics and the Environment: Franklin D. Roosevelt to George W. Bush.*